Teaching
Reading
Comprehension

Teaching Reading Comprehension

P. David Pearson
University of Minnesota

Dale D. Johnson
University of Wisconsin

HOLT, RINEHART AND WINSTON
New York   Chicago   San Francisco   Dallas
Montreal   Toronto   London   Sydney

Library of Congress Cataloging in Publication Data

Pearson, P. David.
    Teaching reading comprehension.

    Companion vol. to Teaching reading vocabulary
by D. D. Johnson and P. D. Pearson.
    Includes bibliographies.
    1. Reading comprehension.   I. Johnson, Dale D.,
joint author.   II. Title.
LB1050.45.P43   372.4′1   77-19132
ISBN 0-03-020281-7

Pages 148–151 reprinted with permission. Copyright © 1972 by Rand McNally & Company,
1974 printing. All rights reserved.

Excerpts from Thomas C. Barrett's "A Taxonomy of Reading Comprehension" on pp.
168–175 are reprinted with permission of Ginn and Company.

To
Mary Alyce,
Matthew,
and
Susan

Preface

This book, and its complement, *Teaching Reading Vocabulary* by Johnson and Pearson (Holt, Rinehart and Winston, 1978), are intended for use as supplements in undergraduate and graduate courses in reading methods. Used together, the two books cover much of the content of most survey courses on the teaching of reading since they cover the vitally important areas of reading comprehension development and reading vocabulary development.

In addition, *Teaching Reading Comprehension* will be useful as a supplementary text for a course in secondary reading. Save for the particular words, sentences, or passages that children are asked to process, we see little in the realm of reading comprehension that is unique to a particular grade level. Therefore, we have tried to use examples of instructional activities that cut across the primary-intermediate-secondary continuum. The book could also serve as the primary text for a course in intermediate or middle school reading because such courses usually place a great emphasis on comprehension.

Our interest in comprehension led us to read as much as we could find in the current research and theoretical literature in psycholinguistics and cognitive psychology. In addition, we observed the materials and practices of successful teachers. We found an amazing degree of consistency between what the psychologists had to say and what good teachers were doing, which confirmed a suspicion we have long held—that good teachers have good (and sound) intuition.

In this volume, we have attempted to integrate theory and practice. We wanted to be theoretical because we want to offer teachers broad principles that will transfer to a variety of specific circumstances. We wanted to be practical because we sympathize with the common complaint, held by many inside as well as outside the educational community, that teacher education is "practically irrelevant." We wrote the book for teachers, and we hope they find it useful and informative.

The book falls naturally into three parts (although there is no such *formal* organization). Chapters 1, 2, and 3 provide the background and rationale on which the heart of the book (Chapters 4–9) is based. Chapter 1 introduces basic issues and conflicts in comprehension instruction. Chapter 2 focusses on those factors—psychological and environmental—that influence comprehension. Chapter 3 presents the model of the comprehension process on which the book is based.

Chapters 4–9 have an instructional focus. In Chapters 4–7 we deal with those comprehension tasks related to words, sentences, and larger units of discourse. Each chapter is organized into several of these "tasks." For each task, we present a description and rationale, followed by instructional guidelines for teaching it and/or specific materials and activities for student practice. Chapters 8 and 9 relate to questioning and discussion strategies for promoting the reading program.

Chapters 10 and 11 provide conclusions. Chapter 10 deals with the issue of assessing reading comprehension. In addition to suggestions for general assessment, the chapter covers methods of assessing tasks dealt with in earlier chapters. Chapter 11 summarizes what we hope the book has done for the reader and what we hope it has not done.

Philosophically we owe many debts. We have been influenced by the thinking of people like Frank Smith and Ken Goodman, authorities whose psycholinguistic views have earned them a "liberal" label in the reading field. Just as surely, we have been influenced by the more "conservative" skills-oriented views of colleagues like Wayne Otto, Robert Calfee, Richard Venezky, and S. Jay Samuels. Outside the reading field, the work of Lindsay and Norman, Rumelhart, Schank, and Thorndyke has provided us with new models and fresh perspectives. In trying to place our views along a philosophical continuum of reading instruction, we find ourselves in what Jules Fieffer once called (in describing Eisenhower's politics) "the radical middle."

We owe many practical debts. Students (mainly teachers) in all our graduate reading courses provided germs for many of the teaching activities included in the text. Several students—especially Allan Neilsen, Beth Marr, Ellen Sylvester, and Tom Nicholson—offered valuable suggestions for revisions of the earlier versions of the manuscript. More importantly, in informal discussions, they helped us form many of the concepts we have described in the book. Jill Almendinger and Stephanie Koklas typed and retyped several versions of the manuscript along the way. Diana Pinkston traced references and made sure that all the pages and copies got into the right place at the right time.

Finally, there is our editor, Richard Owen. We thank him for his editorial and managerial expertise, but, most of all, for his faith in a book like this.

Minneapolis, Minnesota   P.D.P.
Madison, Wisconsin   D.D.J.
December 1977

Contents

1

THE CONFUSED WORLD OF READING COMPREHENSION

WE HOPE the title of this chapter is not a bad omen. Indeed, we have written this book precisely because we hope to bring some structure and some depth to a topic that has received inadequate emphasis both in the professional literature and in the education of teachers.

By the end of this book, we hope you will become as committed as we are to the following statement of faith: *A teacher can serve no greater end than to help a student comprehend, interpret, evaluate, and appreciate the written word.* For if you have done that, you have given the student a gift that will last a lifetime and make that lifetime more worth living.

But let us save our optimism for later. First we must dwell a while on the pessimistic aspects of reading comprehension. To set the stage, let us try to convince you that there is a need for what we have to say.

SOURCES OF CONFUSION

Old Wine in New Bottles

Pick up any two reading methods texts. Turn to the comprehension chapter of each. Now compare them. Add a third or a fourth text to your experiment. Does it appear that one writer's oranges are another writer's apples? You will find some overlap. But you will also find conflicting terminology and conflicting scope and sequence charts. Now replicate the experiment with two or three developmental reading series. Again conflict arises. One series will start right off in first grade suggesting that teachers ask a range of comprehension questions from literal recall of factual details to critical thinking questions. A second will use only literal recall questions in grade one, reserving higher-order questions for later years. A third will direct the teacher not to worry about comprehension at all until second or third grade.

How can this state of affairs exist? Is the topic so elusive that it defies accurate description? Do we know so little about the comprehension process that one writer's opinion will serve as well as any other writer's opinion? Are we all using different words to describe the same underlying process?

We suspect the latter explanation is most accurate. We know there is a natural human (and especially professional) tendency to inject uniqueness into our own creations. If someone else has a skill called, "grasping the main idea," we may choose to call it, "identifying the central thought." Faced with seventeen other texts which list a skill called "drawing conclusions," the label, "drawing inferences," may seem attractive to us. So the first source of confusion in reading comprehension stems from the fact that a given skill may exist under a variety of labels from one source to another.

Redundancy

A second source of confusion can be found within a single account of comprehension skills rather than between one account and another. Quite often a given taxonomy will exhibit internal redundancy. For example, McCanne (1963) lists each of these skills as separate entities:

1. Classifying things
2. Classifying things and ideas
3. Recognizing wholes and parts
4. Finding details to support main ideas
5. Recalling information for objectives
6. Suggesting a title for a story
7. Deciding on subtitles
8. Finding the main idea of a story
9. Finding the main idea of a paragraph
10. Finding major thought units

Granted, there are *some* differences among these tasks. Yet a common thread runs through all of them: relating more general ideas to more specific ideas. Furthermore, skills 6–10 differ only in the size of the linguistic unit; the same process is used to complete the task. There is an inherent problem with lists: Because each skill is listed separately, a list leaves the impression that each skill has a separate and equal identity when, in fact, they are either highly interrelated or different names for the same thing. As long as we persist in making long lists of comprehension skills, that separate but equal illusion will persist in confusing us.

Fuzzy Distinctions

Additional confusion arises because some skills that get classified as a comprehension skill in one system are labeled as word identification skills in another. Ironically, this mismatch pleases us because it serves to support our underlying conviction that any attempt to separate the reading process into little compartments is, at best, an arbitrary convenience allowing us to talk about one thing at a time.

For example, where should one include structural analysis—the study of root words, prefixes, suffixes, and inflectional endings? Are they part of word identification or comprehension? Clearly, readers can use knowledge of morphemes (parts of words that carry meaning) to aid them in achieving the correct pronunciation of a word. But those same readers can use that same morphemic knowledge to help them decide upon the meaning of a word. Consider contextual analysis. Even the most avid phonic-oriented writers concede that—at some point—readers use knowledge of context to aid in the word identification process. But should we consider the ability to utilize contextual information a comprehension or a word identification skill? We are not certain that we could ever eliminate all the fuzziness that exists in our terminology. We are not even sure we want to. Nevertheless, a recognition of how comprehension interfaces with word identification processes may help us keep things straight.

Whether Comprehension Is Teachable

A fourth source of confusion results from the controversy concerning whether reading comprehension is teachable. At the one extreme, there is a position that contends that in teaching reading, we can only *teach* word identification processes. After that it is up to native intelligence and experience to aid children in understanding what we have taught them to read. A middle position argues that while we may not be able to teach comprehension per se, we can arrange instructional and practice conditions in such a way as to increase the likelihood that children will understand what they read. Then there are those, ourselves included, who contend that comprehension can be taught directly—that we can model comprehension processes for students, provide cues to help them understand what they are reading, guide discussions to help children know what they know, ask pointed, penetrating, or directional questions, offer feedback (both informational and reinforcing) at the appropriate time, and generate useful independent practice activities. In a less direct fashion, we can help to expand and clarify children's meaning vocabularies (for listening and reading), we can teach children how to handle various types of visual formats (charts, graphs, and so on), and we can offer guidance (often falling under the rubric of study skills) regarding how a reader should organize his reading and study of a body of text. We hope to persuade you not only that comprehension is teachable but also that it is best learned through the guidance of a well-informed and sensitive teacher.

Process versus Product

A fifth source of confusion in the comprehension literature centers on the rather loose distinction often offered between comprehension as a *product* and comprehension as a *process*.

Comprehension as a *process* is an elusive entity. It is what happens to readers as they read. It is what keeps them going when they read. It involves the intuitive comment, "Oh, sure! That makes sense to me." It is what has broken down when we say to ourselves, "It's all Greek to me," or "I can't take it any longer"; or when we find that we have just skimmed our eyes over two pages and realize that we have not understood one iota of those two pages.

Comprehension as a *product* is not so elusive. On the other hand, we wonder about its importance. Comprehension as a *product* involves measuring, in some more or less objective way, the net result of the process. Typically it involves evaluating responses to specific questions we may have asked our readers. Comprehension as a product is what we assess by means of the dazzling array of tests we give to children. It is what we assess when we ask our readers, "Tell me what you remember about (got out of, thought about, learned in) that story." It is what we get when we ask for an outline or a summary of a passage. Now, most of us would like to think that we can draw references about the *processes* children must have used on the basis of the *products* they provide us with. Whether or not such inferences are legitimate is an unsettled issue. However, when we get down to the bottom line, most of us would probably agree that processes are either totally or mostly inaccessible. Hence we are stuck with products as our usual means of evaluating the quality and quantity of students' comprehension processes.

The first chapter is not the place to resolve these conflicts and confusions. Hopefully, that is what the book will do. This, among other reasons, is why we decided to write it. We hope to shed some light on each of these important issues. In fact, we hope to convince you that our resolution of each of these issues is reasonable and helpful to anyone responsible for guiding children's growth in comprehension.

AN OVERVIEW OF THE BOOK

The Organization

This book has three basic parts, represented schematically in the following list. Chapters 1, 2, and 3 provide the framework, the rationale, and background that will enable you to understand better our later sections. Chapters 4, 5, 6, 7, 8, 9 and 10 form the instructional component. Therein we deal with issues of materials, lesson presentation, questions, and discussion strategies for promoting better reading comprehension. Chapter 11 is a set of reflections on where we have been and what we hope you have learned.

Background	*Instruction*	*Reflections*
1. The Confused World of Reading Comprehension	4. Understanding Concepts	11. Reflections on Reading Comprehension
2. Factors Influencing Reading Comprehension	5. Understanding Longer Discourse: Part I	
3. The Nature of Reading Comprehension	6. Understanding Longer Discourse: Part II	
	7. Making Judgments About the Written Word	
	8. Questions	
	9. Interaction Strategies for Promoting Reading Comprehension	
	10. Assessing Reading Comprehension	

In trying to convince you that our approach to comprehension is both reasonable and helpful, we plan to take you on a journey *through* your own mind *into* the minds of children, *onto* the printed page of textbooks and fiction, and *over* the surface of the notorious workbook and ditto master. We will not withhold theory (even though there is an apparent movement afoot to remove theory from the lives of teachers). Neither will we avoid specific matters of practice (including step-by-step procedures as well as games, worksheets, kits, and so on). What we really want to do is to integrate theory and practice as well as we can. We want to persuade you that nothing is more practical than a good theory. We plan to carry out this friendly persuasion by showing you how a theory generates instructional principles that can be translated into methods and materials that a classroom teacher can readily put to use.

REFERENCES

McCanne, R. *Use of a Checklist of Reading Skills with Migratory Children.* Office of Instructional Services, Colorado State Department of Education, June, 1963.

2

FACTORS
INFLUENCING
READING
COMPREHENSION

READING IS often referred to as a complex cognitive process. In fact, Edmund Burke Huey, in 1908, believed that if we could understand reading we would understand the mysteries of the human mind. Edward Thorndike (1917) wrote an article entitled, "Reading as Reasoning. . . ." David Russell, in 1961, considered reading to be an application of basic cognitive processes. The most recent influence on understanding reading comes from the academic disciplines of cognitive psychology and artificial intelligence (computer simulation of mental processes). In these works (for example, Anderson, 1977), reading comprehension is viewed as a process subject to the same constraints as human memory and problem solving.

It is not difficult to see why so many scholars and lay persons have thought of reading—especially reading comprehension—as a reflection of the inner workings of the human mind. Reading comprehension seems to involve language, motivation, perception, concept development, the whole of experience itself. It seems to be subject to the same constraints as thinking, reasoning, and problem solving. The only distinction one might want to make is in the source of input for the cognitive processing. When we perceive an event and react to it, the source of stimulation for our perception and our reaction is direct and immediate. If we see the house is on fire, we get out as fast as we can. If we do not perceive the fire but hear someone tell us the house is on fire, we are forced to react to a symbolic stimulus (that is, the sentences we hear) whose meaning is familiar to us; but our actions are likely to be similar. And when we read a story about a house being on fire, we react to another symbolic stimulus (that is, the words on the page). And we are able to understand the scenario and to anticipate the occurrence of certain actions (for example, escape attempts by the character) because of our accumulated experience about fires and what people do when they encounter fires.

In short, it should not surprise you to learn that many experts think of reading comprehension as similar to other kinds of human behavior. In fact, most of us would reject the argument that we have separate mental entities for processing and comprehending information received by reading (as opposed to listening or experiencing). Intuitively, we believe that the human mind is built as economically as possible (religious or not, we believe that God [or nature] operates on a principle of economy of effort). Hence, we might be convinced that the mind has special "perceptors" or processes for recognizing print, but we would be skeptical of any "comprehendors" specifically suited to information gathered by reading the printed page. It just does not make good sense!

If our argument is convincing thus far, then you will probably accept this assertion: *Whatever influences general thinking or problem-solving ability also influences reading comprehension.* In fact, the purpose of this chapter is, in part, to describe those aspects of human experience that have the greatest effect on thinking, problem solving, and reading comprehension. We would add a second assertion: *There are a few factors that influence reading comprehension but do not influence thinking or problem solving.*

The purpose of this chapter is to delineate those factors which affect reading comprehension and to discuss how and why they have an effect. As such, this chapter is not practical in the sense that the ideas expressed can be put into practice in your classroom tomorrow. But the chapter is practical in a broader sense. We believe that knowledge about the reading process can make a difference in how you teach. We believe that it helps to have a framework for making day-to-day instructional decisions. For example, if you know that changing a student's motivation changes his or her comprehension of a story or an article, then you are in a better position to change what you do prior to or subsequent to asking a student to read a particular selection. If you know that prior experience with a topic improves a student's comprehension, then you might offer experience with the topic prior to reading. If you know that abstract words are more difficult to understand than concrete words, you may make judicious selection of reading material for particular students.

INSIDE AND OUTSIDE [1]

We can conveniently separate the factors which influence comprehension into two categories—*inside the head* and *outside the head*. The inside factors will be things like linguistic competence (what the reader knows about the language), interest (how much the reader "cares" about various topics that might be encountered), motivation (how much the reader "cares" about the task at hand as well as his or her general mood about reading and schooling), and accumulated reading ability (how well the reader can read). The outside factors fall into two categories—the elements *on the page* and the qualities of *the reading environment*. The elements on the page—textual characteristics—include factors like text readability (how hard the material is) and text organiza-

---

[1] Those familiar with Frank Smith's work will recognize the source of this distinction. Smith (1970) talked about "What the Eye Tells the Brain and What the Brain Tells the Eye."

tion (what kind of help is provided by headings, visual arrays, and so on). The qualities of the reading environment include factors like the things the teacher does before, during, or after reading to help students understand what is in the text; the ways peers react to the task; and the general atmosphere in which the task is to be completed (distractions, and so on).

The problem with these categories is that they are not mutually exclusive and separate. For example, interest is an aspect of motivation, and reading ability is correlated with linguistic ability (better readers probably know more about their language). Nor is there independence between *inside the head* and *outside the head* factors. Text readability really boils down to linguistic factors like word difficulty (how familiar are the words) and sentence complexity (how difficult is it to wade through coordinated and subordinated text segments?). Hence, one cannot know how difficult a text will be until and unless one knows something about the linguistic and conceptual sophistication of the reader: one person's *Scientific American* is another person's daily newspaper. In short, all of these factors interact with one another. We discuss them separately only because of the limitations of the human mind—we can only take one step at a time. In so doing, we sometimes give the impression that each factor has a separate existence. If we were to portray their interactive, interdependent nature, we would have to print passage on top of passage—a messy way to communicate.

In the rest of the chapter, we will treat each set of factors in turn, trying to establish a generalization (a rule of thumb) about the way in which each factor will affect comprehension of written discourse.

INSIDE THE HEAD

Linguistic Competence

Children learn language. They do it on their own (as long as they can hear others talk) sometimes, it seems, almost in spite of our efforts to perpetuate "charming" baby talk. When they learn language, they learn three systems: phonological, semantic, and syntactic.

PHONOLOGICAL KNOWLEDGE. The phonological system includes knowledge of the different phonemes (individual sounds) in the language, knowledge of how they are blended together to create words, as well as knowledge of things like stress, juncture, and pitch. Stress is exemplified by the difference between I FOUND a red bandana (I did not buy it) and I found a RED bandana (not a blue one). Juncture is characterized by the difference between I SCREAM and ICE CREAM, in short, word boundaries. Pitch enters the picture in terms of the intonation pattern differences between, You went downtown. You went downtown! You went downtown?

Since the focus of this book is comprehension, we will not dwell on the phonological system. While phonological knowledge is prerequisite to comprehension (if you do not have it, you cannot understand auditory messages), once developed, it seems not to play so major a role in comprehension as do the syntactic and semantic systems. Nevertheless, it is clear that factors like juncture, stress, and pitch are important in comprehending written and spoken messages.

SYNTACTIC KNOWLEDGE.   The syntactic system refers to the orderly arrangement among words in sentences. A child's knowledge of syntax is remarkably sophisticated by the time he or she enters school. A six-year-old has probably spoken and/or understood some 80 to 90 percent of the basic sentence patterns he or she will encounter or use as an adult.[2]

Syntactic knowledge is what is at work when we recognize that (1) and (2) but not (3) and (4) are grammatically acceptable English sentences. It is also syntax that accounts for our ability to recognize that (1) and (2) are equivalent in meaning.

(1) The boy thanked the girl.
(2) The girl was thanked by the boy.
(3) Girl was the by thanked boy the.
(4) Thanked girl boy was by the the.

It is syntax that is at work when we are able to read (5) and answer questions (6), (7), and (8).

(5) The argle zoolked the bordiddy in the ershent because the bordiddy larped the argle.
(6) Who zoolked the bordiddy?
(7) Why did the argle zoolk the bordiddy in the ershent?
(8) What did the bordiddy do to the argle?

Notice that there is not real meaning in (5). Yet we are able to answer (6), (7), and (8) because of our syntactic knowledge and our ability to recognize the syntactic similarities between (5) and the questions (6), (7), and (8). It is not clear that our ability to answer questions (6) to (8) is evidence that we have actually understood (5).

Think about what you did when you answered (6), (7), and (8). Then compare it to what you did when you were a student and you were

[2] Even so, as C. Chomsky (1968) and Olds (1968) have pointed out, there are some syntactic structures that develop after entry into school.

asked that infamous question in your geography classes: What are the major products of X? (Where X is the name of some country). If you were clever, you probably searched the text for a sentence beginning with: The major products of X are. . . . But did you really understand what you read? Did the fact that you could answer the question prove anything except that you could visually match a question with a similar segment of text? For example, close your eyes and try to paraphrase (5). Chances are that you cannot do it. The reason you cannot paraphrase (5) is that there is no way you can integrate those meaningless nonsense words with anything that you already know about—anything that is already "in your head."

SEMANTIC KNOWLEDGE.   Your inability to paraphrase (5) leads to a discussion of the importance of the semantic system. Semantic knowledge refers to our knowledge of word meanings (the concepts that underly the labels we call words). But it is more than that. It also includes our knowlege of the relationships among words. Dogs *are* mammals; dogs *have* ears; dogs *do* bark; dogs *are* loyal; dogs and cats *are both* pets.

It is semantic knowledge that accounts for our surprise when we encounter the word *whale* in the same context as the words *horse, farm,* and *plow,* as well as our smugness when we encounter it in the same context as shark, dolphin, or harpoon. It is semantic knowledge that accounts for the fact that most of you will order the random array of words in (9) as they are ordered in (10). You cannot order (9) like (10) by using syntactic knowledge alone.

(9) Cows dog barn into the the the chased.
(10) The dog chased the cows into the barn.
(11) The cows chased the dog into the barn.
(12) The barn chased the cows into the dog.

If you used just syntactic knowledge, both (11) and (12) would be acceptable. But knowledge about the world tells you that (10) is the most probable order.

This section has highlighted some of the aspects of linguistic competence that affect comprehension. Of the three aspects, we believe that the semantic system is most important. Later, in Chapter 3, we will detail how the semantic system works in comprehension. The basic generalization to be gleaned from this discussion is that the closer the match between the syntactic and semantic information on a page of print and syntactic and semantic information in our heads, the greater the likelihood we will understand the text.

Interest

Most of us would agree with the assertion that we are likely to understand something better if we are interested in the topic presented in a text. Indeed, the research on interest suggests that students comprehend better when they read passages that discuss topics of high interest to them (Estes and Vaughn, 1973). Unfortunately the research on interest has not properly sorted out the influence of prior experience. That is, do students better comprehend passages of high interest because of the motivational value of a personally interesting topic or because they know more about topics for which they indicate high interest?

One of the best examples illustrating the influence of interest came from a colleague's junior high school civics class. The students were all so-called low-track achievers. And when it came to reading the text on government, they proved that they deserved that label. But during the unit on drivers' education (that unit continues to remain an integral part of social science), a transformation occurred! Suddenly students who could not cope with words and concepts like *congress* and *government* were very adept at understanding words and concepts like *semaphore* and *right-of-way*. The irony (as any of you who have flunked a written drivers' test will verify) is that, in all likelihood, the state drivers' manual was more difficult than the civics text.

In spite of our earlier disclaimer, we are inclined to believe that interest plays an important part in comprehension. And we suggest that one way to improve comprehension of a given topic is to generate student interest in that topic through a variety of means—filmstrips, movies, field trips, other books, community resource persons. Another way to capitalize on interest is to allow students to read selections of high interest. Although we must point out that while such a practice promotes student enjoyment, it does not necessarily help students to understand topics for which they do not possess intrinsic interest. If your goal is to get students to understand seemingly uninteresting material, you are better off to pursue the former strategy, that is, promoting interest prior to reading.

Motivation

The topic of interest leads quite naturally into the more general issue of motivation. We chose to list interest separately only to highlight its importance. Earlier in this chapter, we indicated that sometimes our distinctions among factors would be fuzzy. Nowhere is this more evident than with the topic of motivation. Is it inside the head or outside the head? As teachers we try to *motivate* students so that they will be more *motivated*. We talk about increasing a student's *motivational* level. We have reached the following closure on the issue. Motivation is in the reader; as teachers we offer incentives, reinforcers, feedback, and other stimuli to try to alter a student's level of motivation.

At least in the reading field, we have been emphasizing the cognitive aspects of learning to read at the expense of the affective. And we believe any good instructional model of reading must include motivational factors. As a somewhat negative example, fear and anxiety can improve comprehension test scores quite dramatically: when people know they are going to be tested, they appear to gain more from their reading (Thompson, 1976). Only slightly less positively, we know we can improve performance on comprehension worksheets simply by giving students time off from completing comprehension worksheets (Hopkins et al, 1971). In a more positive vein, we know that regular feedback about one's progress can alter performance beneficially. Suffice to say for now: other things being equal, changing a student's motivational state will alter comprehension.

Reading Ability

It is almost tautological to say that the more reading ability one possesses, the better one will comprehend. If we talk about decoding ability, the generalization becomes more sensible. It is difficult to comprehend if you cannot read the words on the page.

If we turn to the increasingly popular notion of "automaticity," the generalization is even more sensible. LaBerge and Samuels (1973) have coined the term *automaticity* to describe the fact that some readers are able to achieve word identification automatically while others seem to struggle with words as they read. Their contention is that since a reader can attend to only one task at a given time, the reader who devotes considerable attention to word identification has little or no attention left over to direct toward processing the meaning of the message. Hence, comprehension is minimal. On the other hand, the readers who have honed their word identification skills to the point where they proceed automatically (that is, require little attention) can devote most of their attention to processing the meaning of the message.

If LaBerge and Samuels are right, there are important consequences for reading instruction. First, it is unreasonable to expect novice readers to understand much of what they read; their attention is directed toward word identification. Second, less able older readers will suffer from the same attention problem as novice readers. Third, with novice or poorer readers, we probably should spend most of our time promoting accuracy and automaticity of the word identification processes, reserving concern for comprehension for a later point in those students' development.

Though we agree with the first two of these consequences, we disagree with the third for two reasons: (1) Comprehension helps word identification as much as word identification helps comprehension. That is, having understood part of the message helps you to decode another part. In short, context can help to short circuit the amount of attention you have to pay to print (Pearson and Studt, 1975; Tulving and Gold, 1963). (2) We think there is an inherent danger in deflecting attention away from comprehension *at any point in a reader's development*. Reading is comprehending. We should never give a student any reason to believe that it is anything else.

Perhaps the most appropriate generalization for this section is: comprehension is easier if you can read the words accurately and automatically, but reading the words is easier when you can understand the message.

OUTSIDE THE HEAD

The Written Message

There is probably no aspect of reading instruction that has been studied more than the effects of altering the characteristics of the text. Yet it continues to be one of the most widely researched topics in reading. In short, while we know a great deal about what makes writing hard to read, we still have much to learn. We are convinced that one of the reasons reading educators and psychologists are so intrigued by the characteristics of the written message is that they are so amenable to alteration. For example, if we could determine that particular types of sentence structures facilitated comprehension more than others, then we could improve comprehension simply by changing the language in textbooks and storybooks. Unfortunately, the problem is not that simple.

WORDS.   It is painfully obvious that some words are harder to understand than others. But what dimensions characterize difficult versus easy words?

1. Frequency. Words differ in terms of how commongy they are used in the language. *The* is the most common word in the language; *ubiquitous* is not ubiquitous (you rarely hear or see it). There is good evidence to suggest that people at all levels of development have more difficulty understanding passages composed of infrequently used rather than frequently used words. And it is intuitively obvious why

this is true. Readers may not even know some of the infrequently used words. Or if they have heard or read them occasionally, they remain only faint traces in the mind.

2. Abstractness. Some words have concrete referents in the world: *dog, cat, platypus, divan.* Others have quite abstract referents: *love, pity, psychiatry, parsimonious.*[3] There is evidence that readers have more difficulty selecting the meanings of abstract words (Greiling, 1973) and that they have more difficulty understanding text that is riddled with abstract words (Thorndyke, 1977). Again, such evidence fits our intuitions about language and experience. It is not too difficult to get a group of people to agree on whether or not the animal they are examining is a dog. It is much harder to get that same group to agree on whether or not a particular government is a democracy.

Frequency and abstractness seem to have more or less additive effects. High-frequency concrete words are easiest to understand. Low-frequency abstract words are hardest. The other two categories fall somewhere in between.

SENTENCES.   There is an impressive body of evidence to suggest that longer sentences and more complex sentences tend to appear in passages that people have difficulty understanding. Conversely, shorter and simpler sentences tend to be associated with passages that are easy to understand (see Bormuth, 1966).

The solution seems obvious: write everything in short, simple sentences. There is a problem in jumping to that conclusion. When you rewrite longer and more complex sentences in simple, less complex forms, it is not clear that you still have the same message. Also, there is some counterevidence indicating that in certain conditions, longer more complex sentences communicate a given message more effectively. For example, if you want students to answer question (13), you may help them more by presenting (14) than (15).

(13) Why did the peasant revolt?
(14) The peasants revolted because the king raised taxes.
(15) The king raised taxes. The peasants revolted.

There seems to be a trade-off between simplicity and explicitness (Pearson, 1974–1975). When you write in short simple sentences, you run the risk of destroying the explicitness of a relation between two sen-

---

[3] The term *abstractness,* as it is used here, refers to the difference between abstract and concrete words—words you can visualize and those you cannot. Other writers use the term to refer to a general-specific dimension: animal is more abstract than dog or collie.

tence parts, as, for example, the cause-effect relation in (14). If you decide to make that relation clear and explicit, then you are forced to use longer more complex sentences. All the evidence is not in on the sentence length and complexity issue. But a good piece of advice might be to beware of textbook representatives who tell you that they have a particular kind of text that has been "written down" to a lower readability level. Even though it has a lower readability score, it may be masking some relations between ideas that could be stated more clearly at a higher readability level.

There is one other problem with writing down to a lower readability level. If you alter a piece of writing too much, you may no longer be communicating the same idea. It may be easier to "read, " but that alleged ease may stem from the fact that the ideas in the rewritten version are simpler. Simple sentences may be good vehicles for simple ideas. Complex sentences may be necessary to communicate complex ideas. The appropriate question to ask is: I have a certain idea I want to get across; what is the best way to communicate that idea? Short sentences and simple sentences will not always be the answer.

BEYOND THE SENTENCE.   There is a new branch of linguistic and psychological investigation broadly labeled discourse analysis. Discourse analysis goes beyond the sentence to consider characteristics of paragraphs and passages as well as relations between sentences.

STORY STRUCTURE.   Several theoreticians (Rumelhart, 1975; Stein and Glenn, 1976) have developed story grammars that are analogous to sentence grammars. There appear to be some particular story structures that create more difficulty than others. For example, passages that proceed in a more-or-less cause-effect-to-cause-effect fashion appear to be more comprehensible than those which are characterized by detail after detail without such neat causal links between the ideas in the stories (Thorndyke, 1977). Thorndyke interprets these differences as an indication that the structure of a story influences its comprehensibility. Thorndyke leans toward an environmentalist explanation of these differences, suggesting that certain structures become more familiar to us with experience. Our intuitions support Thorndyke's interpretation. For example, there is something very predictable about the structure of events in a fairy tale, folktale, or fable, even when we have not heard or read the particular story in question.

THEMATIC INFORMATION.   Several recent studies have verified what English teachers have been recommending to composition students for decades: providing a statement of theme at the outset of a passage increases comprehension and memory for the passage (Bransford and

Johnson, 1972; Dooling and Mullett, 1973; Thorndyke, 1977), especially when the passage presents otherwise difficult material.

Such findings provide support for a point of view that Ausabel has been espousing for several years. Ausabel has conducted a series of studies to verify his construct of "advance organizer."

An advance organizer is usually a summary statement of the more general set of concepts that the following text tries to explicate in more specific detail. For example, a text dealing with how to put wheels on a bicycle might be preceded by general principles about putting bolts and nuts together or material on how to [true wheels] of any type. The rationale is that the advance organizer helps a reader to tap appropriate information in his or her head—information that will facilitate comprehension of the new data in the passage.

Ausubel (for example, 1960, 1961, 1963) has marshaled an impressive body of evidence to prove that advance organizers facilitate comprehension. As is often the case in educational research, there is another body of counterevidence (for example Schultz, 1966; Capponecchi, 1970; Feller, 1973) suggesting that they do not help at all. As we will show in the next chapter, we strongly believe in the concept of advance organizers.

Visual displays—tables, graphs, charts, pictures—are also intended to facilitate comprehension. Writers who use these devices rely on the adage that a picture is worth a thousand words. Indeed we believe that they do make certain kinds of relations clearer. We are always more depressed about our tax money expenditures when we see them illustrated on a circle graph than when we read those same percentages in a paragraph, implying, perhaps, that we understand the graph better than the text. Bransford and Johnson (1972) have provided a clever demonstration of how a picture can make an otherwise nonsensical passage completely reasonable and comprehensible.

Factors in the Reading Environment

HOME ENVIRONMENT.   We will stipulate the fact that home environmental factors influence reading comprehension. Study after study unravels the depressing tale about the effect of income and socioeconomic status on academic achievement. We say depressing because there is so little we as teachers can do to alter the home environment. We think that the greatest influence of the home environment related to reading comprehension derives from the base of language and concepts that children bring to school. As will become obvious in Chapter 3, we regard comprehension as a direct function of prior knowledge. Hence the language and conceptual base that students bring to the printed page are critical to comprehension. Parents who help their children understand and interact with their world are preparing them to become good readers when they get to school.

SCHOOL ENVIRONMENT. Teachers, peers, and the "classroom ecology," all influence the reading comprehension of students. Since we devote the better part of seven entire chapters to direct teacher influences, we will only preview the ways teachers can affect comprehension.

1. The way they prepare students for reading
2. The kind of materials they select for instruction
3. The kind of questions they ask
4. The kind of modeling behavior they provide
5. The kind of feedback they give
6. The kind of incentives and reinforcers they use
7. The kind of atmosphere they establish for taking risks

Peer influence can be positive or negative. A certain amount of friendly competition can stimulate attention to a task and to achievement; too much can be devastating. Cooperative ventures—group problem solving—can provide models for students who are not quite sure how they should proceed. But one's peers can be mean. They can belittle scholarship to the point where a student learns that it is best not to try very hard to do well.

By classroom ecology we mean both the physical and the emotional environment. Physically, we advocate classrooms which promote curiosity by having a host of resources available. Emotionally, we advocate an environment where curiosity is valued, where students know that it is acceptable to take risks (the penalties for failure are minimized), and where the teacher models the behaviors expected of students.

If you get the impression that there is little in this section that is specific to reading comprehension, you have accurately perceived our intentions. We believe that the factors mentioned herein have a generalized effect on learning and achievement and, hence, on reading comprehension. But to exclude them from a book on reading comprehension would, in our own view, be inappropriate.

A FINAL WORD

We have divided our discussion into two parts; factors that are inside the head and those that are outside the head.

We have asserted that linguistic competence is an absolute prerequisite for reading comprehension. Such an assertion is almost tautological, since language is the medium of comprehension. In

Chapter 3, we will take our stand firmly on the side of semantics rather than syntax as the more potent of these linguistic variables in explaining comprehension.

Interest and motivation also influence comprehension. In general, students understand more when they are interested in a topic (although it is not clear whether interest or prior knowledge is the cause). By altering a student's state of motivation, positively or negatively, we can alter his or her degree of comprehension.

While the ability to identify words accurately and automatically has a direct effect on comprehension, it must be remembered that comprehension affects word identification.

Factors in the written message affect comprehension. Word frequency, word abstractness, sentence complexity, story structure, thematic information, and visual displays can all be manipulated to increase or decrease comprehension.

Finally, factors in the reading environment affect comprehension. The home environment prepares children for reading by helping them understand their world. The school environment—teachers, peers, and classroom setting—have their effects on comprehension, both positive and negative.

In this chapter we have tried to provide a comprehensive list of the factors that influence reading comprehension. In a sense, Chapter 2 is a preview of the remainder of the book, an advance organizer of sorts.

REFERENCES

Anderson, R. The Notion of Schemata and the Educational Enterprise. In R. Anderson, J. Spiro, and W. E. Montague (eds.), *Schooling and the Acquisition of Knowledge.* Hillsdale, N.J.: Lawrence Erlbaum, Associates, 1977.

Ausubel, D. P. The Use of Advance Organizers in the Learning and Retention of Meaningful Verbal Material. *Journal of Educational Psychology,* 1960, 51, 267–272.

Ausubel, D. P. In Defense of Verbal Learning. *Educational Theory,* 1961, 2, 15–25.

Ausubel, D. P. Cognitive Structure and the Facilitation of Meaningful Verbal Learning. *Journal of Teacher Education,* 1963, 14, 217–222.

Bormuth, J. R. Readability: A New Approach. *Reading Research Quarterly,* Spring, 1966, 1, 79–131.

Bransford, J., and Johnson, M. K. Considerations of Some Problems of Comprehension. In W. G. Chase (ed.), *Visual Information Processing,* New York: Academic Press, 1973.

Capponecchi, W. P. *A Comparative Study of an Advance Organizer in Mathematics To Determine its Effectiveness on Knowledge Acquisition and Retention.* Unpublished doctoral dissertation, University of Oklahoma, 1973.

Chomsky, C. *The Acquisition of Syntax in Children from 5 to 10.* Cambridge: MIT Press, 1968.

Dooling, D. J., and Mullett, R. L. Locus of Thematic Effects in Retention of Prose. *Journal of Experimental Psychology,* 1973, *97,* 404–406.

Estes, T., and Vaughn, J. Reading Interests and Comprehension: Implications. *The Reading Teacher,* 1973, *27,* 149–153.

Feller, W. A. *The Effects of Two Types of Advance Organizers and Two Types of Spaced Questions on the Ability of a Selected Group of Tenth Grade Biology Students To Recall, Comprehend and Apply Facts from Written Science Material.* Unpublished doctoral dissertation, Temple University, 1973.

Greiling, M. G. *Recognition and Comprehension of Lexical Words Used Alone or in Context as a Function of Spelling Pattern Predictability, Word Frequency and Word Abstractions.* Unpublished Master of Arts paper. University of Minnesota, 1974.

Hopkins, D. L., Schuttle, R. C., and Garten, K. L. The Effects of Access to a Playroom on the Rate and Quality of Printing and Writing of First and Second Grade Students. *Journal of Applied Behavior Analysis,* 1971, *4,* 77–87.

Huey, E. B. *Psychology and Pedagogy of Reading.* New York: Macmillan, 1908.

LaBerge, D., and Samuels, S. J. Toward a Theory of Automatic Information Processing in Reading. In H. Singer and R. Ruddell (eds.), *Theoretical Models and Processes of Reading.* Newark: International Reading Association, 1976.

Olds, H. F. *An Experimental Study of Syntactical Factors Influencing Children's Comprehension of Certain Complex Relationships.* (Report No. 4), Cambridge, Mass.: Harvard University, Center for Research and Development on Educational Differences, 1968.

Russell, D. H. *Children Learn to Read,* Boston: Ginn and Company, 1961.

Schultz, R. W. *The Role of Cognitive Organizers in the Facilitation of Concept Learning in Elementary School of Science.* Unpublished doctoral dissertation, Purdue University, 1966.

Smith, F. *Understanding Reading: A Psycholinguistic Analysis of Reading and Learning To Read.* New York: Holt, Rinehart and Winston, 1971.

Stein, N., and Glenn, C. An Analysis of Story Comprehension in Elementary School Children. In R. Freedle (ed.), *Discourse Processing:*

Multidisciplinary Perspectives, Hillsdale, N.J.: Lawrence Erlbaum Associates, in press.

Thompson, M. *Trait, State and Academic/Test Anxiety: Their Relationship to Reading Performance.* Unpublished Ph.D. dissertation, University of Minnesota, 1976.

Thorndike, E. L. Reading as Reasoning. A Study of Mistakes in Paragraph Reading. *The Journal of Educational Psychology,* 1917, *8,* 323–332.

Thorndyke, P. Cognitive Structures in Comprehension and Memory of Narrative Discourse. *Cognitive Psychology,* 1977, *9,* 77–110.

Tulving, E., and Gold, C. Stimulus Information and Contextual Information as Determinants of Tachistoscopic Recognition of Words. *Journal of Experimental Psychology,* 1963, *66,* 319–327.

3

THE NATURE
OF
COMPREHENSION

HAD WE written this chapter ten years ago, it would have looked quite different. In recent years, research and theory about the comprehension process has expanded geometrically. Psychologists, primarily in an attempt to explain human memory, have contributed greatly to our understanding of the comprehension process. Reading research appears to have shifted away from an emphasis on decoding and methods of teaching reading toward an emphasis on understanding how readers comprehend and how we can help students comprehend better (National Institute of Education, 1976). And we suspect that this chapter would look quite different if we were to write it ten years from now. Almost weekly, a new article appears which seems to shed more light on the comprehension process.

Our major goal in this chapter is modest. We want to convince you that the essence of comprehension is captured in one simple principle: *Comprehension is building bridges between the new and the known.* Beneath this simple metaphor lies a rich and complex set of implications about the process itself and about the process of teaching comprehension. Just to cite a few as a way of foreshadowing what is to come: (1) Comprehension is active, not passive; that is, the reader cannot help but interpret and alter what he reads in accordance with prior knowledge about the topic under discussion. Comprehension is not simply a matter of recording and reporting verbatim what has been read. (2) Comprehension involves a great deal of inference making. In fact the number of inferences required to comprehend even the simplest prose passage is staggering. Later on, we will demonstrate (see Chapters 3, 5, and 8) that inferences are an inevitable part of the comprehension process. (3) Comprehension is a dialogue between writer and reader; hence, we interpret statements according to our perception of what the writer is trying to do—inform us, persuade us, or direct us (see Chapter 7).

Our plan for this chapter introduces a distinction that we shall repeat in Chapters 4, 5, and 6 when we discuss issues related to teaching comprehension. First, we will discuss how people organize their minds to relate old and new concepts (simple ideas) that arise in their worlds. Then we will jump from understanding concepts to understanding longer units of discourse (propositions, sentences, stories).

ORGANIZING CONCEPTS

Try the following experiment on yourself. Better yet, do it with a group of five to ten colleagues. For each of the following words, jot down the first one, two, or three words, if any, that come to your mind:

1. dog   4. gynecocracy
2. platypus   5. sarcophagus
3. federalism

We have tried this experiment with many groups of teachers and, using different words, many groups of children. For the words listed above, some typical associations are:

1. dog: cat, bark, pet, Fido (or any other dog's name), collie, bite, animal
2. platypus: duckbilled, Australia, mammal, eggs
3. federal: government, congress, Madison, Jefferson, states, bureaucracy
4. gynecocracy: gynecologist, democracy, women, rule
5. sarcophagus: esophagus, tomb, coffin, mummy, Egypt, crypt

The stimulus words differ drastically in the number and the distribution of associations that they elicit. Everyone usually has an association for dog, platypus, and federalism. Less than half have an associate for gynecocracy or sarcophagus. For dog, about half the responses are cat, followed by names of particular pet dogs, and then pet, bark, and animal. For federal, 80 percent of the responses are government. Responses tend to be varied for platypus. For gynecocracy and sarcophagus the few responses that are given are offered with little confidence.

What is the point of the experiment? The nature of the associative responses implies that knowledge of concepts[4] associated with the stimulus words is schematically rather than randomly organized. Each association represents a predictable type of relation to the stimulus.

Class Relations

For example, dogs are related to pets and animals in that dogs belong to the class of things called animals and are likely to belong to

[4] For the sake of convenience, we will use the words *concept* and *word* interchangeably, recognizing, of course, that concepts are the meanings associated with the surface form of the word as it arises in print or speech. While linguists and philosophers would disagree with this interchangeable usage, it seems appropriate here because the whole emphasis of the book is on meaning.

the class of things called pets. Such relations are called *class relations,* implying that the stimulus concept belongs to the class of things denoted by the associative response.

Example Relations

Fido and collie are related to dog in that collie, as a category, and Fido, as a particular individual, represent examples of dogs. Such relations are designated *example relations.* Notice that class and example relations are reciprocal, at least up to a point. If a dog is a member of the *class* animal, then a dog is an *example,* or an instance, of an animal. Likewise, if a collie is an example of a dog, then any collie is a member of the class of dogs. We say at least up to a point because individual dogs probably do not have examples. Fido might be a collie, in which case Fido is a member of the class collie. But can anything be a member of the class Fido? Assuming that by Fido we mean a particular individual dog—not all dogs with that name—the answer is no.[5]

Property Relations

In addition to the reciprocal *class* and *example* relationships, there is also an important *property relation:* concepts have properties or attributes. Animals ingest food and oxygen; pets are domesticated; dogs bark, have hair, and often exhibit loyalty; collies have long shaggy hair; and Fido may have a spot of red hair under his chin. Notice that the *property* relationship interacts with the class relationship. If Fido is a member of the classes collie, dog, pet, and animal, then he inherits all the properties of collie, dog, pet, and animal by virtue of his various class memberships.

Semantic Maps

This whole set of relationships has been graphically portrayed in what is referred to as a semantic network by Collins and Quillian (1969) and Lindsay and Norman (1972), among others. Such a network consists of nodes and links between nodes (see Figure 3.1). Nodes represent concepts, and links represent relations between concepts. In Figure 3.1 the various concepts related to our discussion of dogs are presented. The network can be thought of as an incomplete semantic map for the concept *dog.*

[5] There is a sense in which there can be more than one Fido, even if we are referring to an individual dog. We can have a *manifestation* link from an individual dog like Fido to a particular manifestation of Fido, that is, my memory of the way Fido looked when he got all wet while swimming last night.

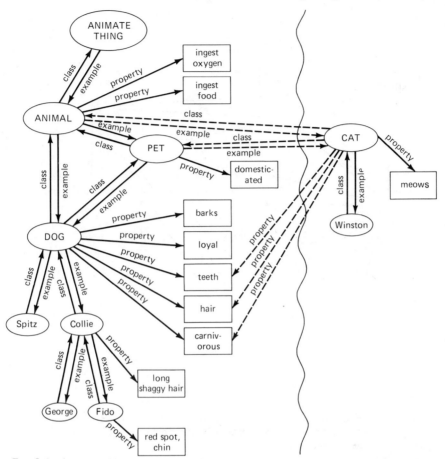

Fig. 3.1 An incomplete semantic network representation of the concept *dog* and some of its related concepts. (The network is neither complete nor totally accurate. For example, if mammals were included, as well as some of the subsets of types of mammals, then properties like teeth and hair would appear as properties of these concepts and would be inherited by dogs and cats because of their common class memberships.)

The whole scheme or semantic map will look a little more like real English, if we change a few of the link labels. For example, we can replace the *class* link with a link commonly called *isa* (a compound word built from *is* and *a*). So we can say a dog *isa* pet or *isa* animal. Also, we can replace the *property* link with *has, is,* or *does*. For example, a dog *is* loyal, *has* hair, and *does* bark. An animal *does* ingest food or oxygen. Now, the semantic map looks a little more like real English, as depicted in Figure 3.2. Notice, however, that there is no convenient single verb representation for example relations. We could say, Dog is exemplified by collie, or Dog has, as an example, collie.

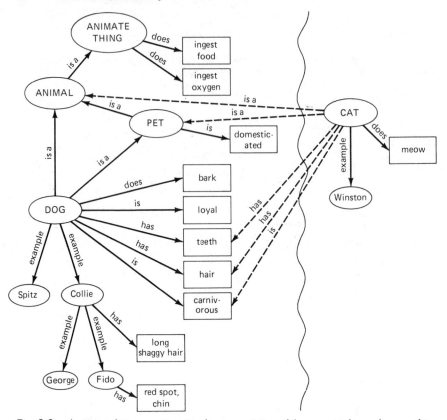

Fig. 3.2.   An incomplete semantic network representation of the concept *dog* and some of its related concepts, using substitutions for class, property, and example relationship terms.

Related Concepts

One more connection needs to be discussed. How for example, should we depict the association between dog and cat or dog and wolf? Somehow our scheme should account for the very real fact that in people's minds such words are closely associated. Do we need a new link to account for this fact? No, we do not. We can account for such connections by examining the other relations that dog and cat share with one another. These will always be class (isa) or property (has, is, or does) relationships. On the semantic map in Figure 3.2 cat and dog share the *properties* hair, teeth, and carnivorousness and the *classes* pet and animal (they also share all the properties of the classes—animal and pet—to which they both belong).

If you think back to our original experiment, this mechanism makes sense. If we were to ask you *why* you thought of cat when dog was given as a stimulus word, you would probably say, "Well, because they are both common household pets," or, "They are both animals or mammals."

The complementary question is, How does one learn to distinguish between dogs and cats? The answer again lies in our conception of classes and properties. Had we made our semantic map sufficiently complete, we would have found that while dog and cat share certain classes and properties, there are other properties that they do not share. Dogs bark but cats meow. Cats climb trees but dogs do not. Dogs learn tricks but cats do not. Cats are felines but dogs are canines. In summary, class and property links capture the character of our intuitive notions about the similarities and differences among concepts.[6]

Now, let us go back to the original experiment. Looking at the sample responses that were given, we should be able to classify each response as a class, example, property, or related concept of the stimulus. Let us see if we can.

1. Dog. From our semantic map for dog (Figure 3.1) we know that animal and pet are classes, Fido and Collie are examples, and bark is a property. Bite would also be a property.
2. Platypus. If we construct a sketchy map for platypus (Figure 3.3), we find that mammal is a class and duck billed, Australia residence, and eggs are properties.[7]
3. Federal. Figure 3.4 is a semantic map of federal. Government is a class (federal governmdnt is an example of government). Congress, states, and bureaucracy are properties of the American example of federal government. Jefferson and Madison are a bit tougher to handle. They might be classified as properties of the American example of federal government (the federal government has the property of having been shaped by Madison and Jefferson, among

[6] Were we to push this argument from a common-sense to a technical level, we would find it difficult—on the basis of easily identifiable physical features—to pinpoint the differences between dogs and cats. There are probably some dogs that meow, climb trees, and do not learn tricks and some cats that bark, cannot climb trees, and do learn tricks. Yet, clearly adults, and even five-year-olds, could unambiguously classify most examples of dogs and cats they encounter. This happens for two reasons. First, it is likely that a whole cluster of features, rather than a single feature, is utilized in concert to aid in discrimination. Second, it is likely that most of our pragmatic, everyday concepts are inaccurate from a technical point of view.

[7] These examples are oversimplified. Australian residence is not a property in the same sense as duckbilled. To do a more accurate semantic map, however, would require formal constructs more complex than are needed to illustrate the basic point. Hence, we will live with a little inaccuracy in order to avoid some unnecessary complexity.

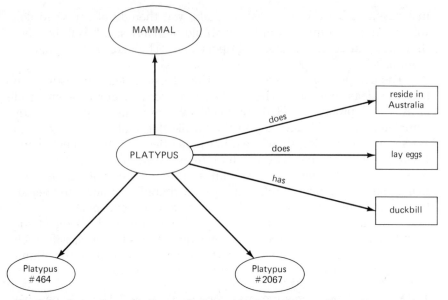

Fig. 3.3. Semantic map of platypus. (In this and in other maps we will use arbitrary numbers to indicate specific instances [examples] of concepts.)

others). They might be related because both Madison and Jefferson were executives (a property of federal government).[8]

4. Gynecocracy. Figure 3.5 is a semantic map of gynecocracy. Women must be considered an attribute. The relationship among "types of rule" is based on class. Gynecologist and democracy are both related concepts. Democracy is related to gynecocracy through the class relation they share (they are both examples of types of rule); gynecologist is related to gynecocracy through a property (having to do with women) relation that the two concepts share.

5. Sarcophagus. Coffin and sarcophagus share a class relation (a sarcophagus *isa* coffin). See Figure 3.6. Tombs and crypts are related concepts that share an even higher-order class relation with both coffin and sarcophagus (all are instruments of interment). Mummy and Egypt are properties of a particular example of sarcophagi (those in use at the point and place in history). Esophagus is also a related concept (both use the root phagus, meaning eating), but in all likelihood the association in most person's minds is acoustic or graphic (sarcophagus sounds like and looks like esophagus) rather than semantic.

[8] But, at least in our semantic maps, they are probably related acoustically (federal sounds like federalist, and Madison and Jefferson were involved in creating the *Federalist Papers*). We will not deal with such associations in this chapter.

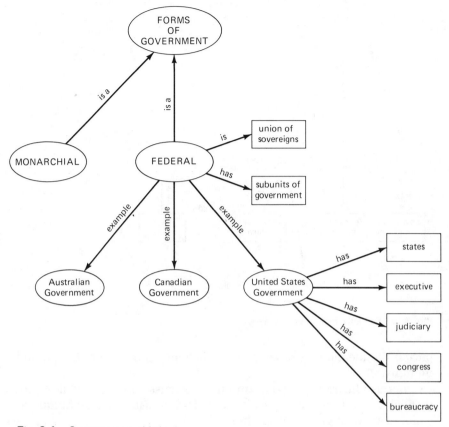

Fig. 3.4. Semantic map of federal.

SOME INSTRUCTIONAL IMPLICATIONS FOR PRESENTING CONCEPTS

Using Word Association Tasks

Our experiment has a side benefit: we can actually use it in instructional settings. It can give us a quick, informal diagnostic picture of what students *already know* and *need to know* about a set of concepts we might want to teach.

For example, take the concept of sarcophagus, for which several students in our hypothetical class had no association whatever. Obviously sarcophagus would require much more of our teaching attention than would dog (for which everyone had some association, and most had cat as an association). However, in the process of asking for associations, we did get some key anchor points through which we could ap-

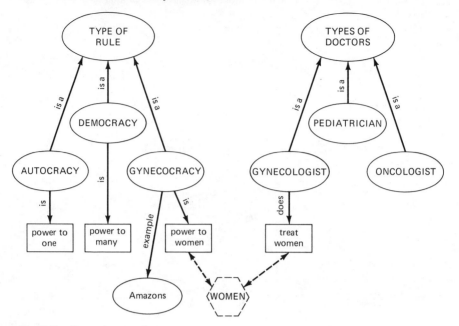

Fig. 3.5. Semantic map of gynecocracy.

proach the meaning of sarcophagus. They are coffin, tomb, Egypt, and mummy.

Let us illustrate this point through a discussion which, while hypothetical, is not unlike many we have had while using this technique in simulations with groups of teachers.

> *Instructor:* Give me some of your responses to sarcophagus.
> *Students* (composite responses): Coffin? Mummy! Tomb Egypt! Esophagus? (Instructor lists words on blackboard).
> *Instructor:* Now, how many really had no idea what sarcophagus meant when I asked you for an associate (reluctantly, some raise hands)? Okay, one of you give your idea about what you think sarcophagus means if I tell you that all those words—coffin, tomb, mummy, Egypt—have something to do with a sarcophagus.
> *Student 1:* Well, it's probably some kind of a thing to bury people in.
> *Student 2:* Well, maybe it's the case or coffin that they put mummies into in ancient Egypt. I don't know.
> *Instructor:* Let's ask one of the students who gave mummy as a response. Are they right?
> *Student 3:* More or less. I think a sarcophagus is a kind of coffin made out of stone. So those coffins they put mummies into were probably sarcophagi. But any stone, or maybe even metal, coffin could be called a sarcophagus.
> *Instructor:* I looked up sarcophagus in the dictionary, and it did say that it

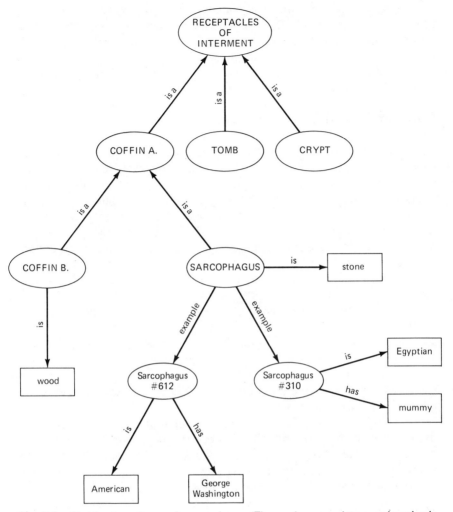

Fig. 3.6. Sketchy semantic map for sarcophagus. (The numbers are arbitrary and used only for convenience in distinguising among examples of different sarcophagi.)

was a coffin made out of stone. And in an encyclopedia it said that sarcophagi were used by Egyptians and other ancient peoples, too. It also said that George Washington was buried in a sarcophagus.

The hypothetical discussion illustrates a basic point about our experiment: as long as some of the associative responses given by the group are real associates of the key concept, the teacher has the experiential base from which to approach that concept.

We assume that the people who give associative responses like coffin, tomb, and mummy possess concepts for those words.[9] Therefore, even if all the students in the hypothetical discussion do not know what a sarcophagus is, at least some of them (and probably all of them) do know what a tomb, a coffin, a mummy, and, maybe, a crypt are. And it is precisely through the known related concepts which students do possess that we ought to approach unfamiliar concepts.

Concept Development and Experience

The discussion also serves to illustrate a more general point about concept development as it relates to comprehension. One of the axioms of instruction for concept development is that there is no substitute for direct experience. If we want children to really know about tigers, then we should take them to a zoo (or better yet to their natural jungle habitat) to observe tigers in action. We will gladly stipulate that direct experiences enhance and enrich children's concepts, but in the same breath we will argue that the realities of classroom instruction make it impossible to rely on direct experience as the major vehicle for concept development.

Our hypothetical discussion implies that there is an alternative approach. Since, in most cases, direct experiences are not possible, teachers should shift their emphasis from the question, How can I provide direct experiences to help develop this concept? to the more reasonable question, Of those concepts related to the concept I want to teach, which ones do the children already know (and maybe even have a set of direct experiences for)?

Put differently, it is like admitting that chances are pretty good that the children possess neither the concept in question nor the requisite direct experiences. So, as a teacher you say, What is it that they do know about that I can use to hang my hat on? What are the anchor points that I can use to introduce the new concept?

We like to use a catch-phrase to characterize this fact about comprehension: comprehension consists of *relating the new to the known*. You can see how readily the sarcophagus discussion illustrates this point. The notions of tomb, crypt, coffin, and mummy were *known*. They provided the anchor points. What was *new* was the label *sarcophagus* and the property *made of stone*. The instructor's task was to assist the students in assimilating the new information into their preexisting body of meaning (that is, that knowledge represented by the semantic map).

[9] Such an assumption stems from a general principle of language development: comprehension precedes production. In other words, people rarely use a word for which they have no concept (even if their concepts are not accurate according to a dictionary definition).

Similarly we could demonstrate how gynecologist and democracy could provide the anchor points for introducing gynecocracy, or how mammal, eggs, duckbilled, and Australia could provide anchor points for platypus.

To demonstrate to yourself how ubiquitous this practice is, even in our everyday experiences, think back to a situation in which you were trying to explain something to a friend. Probably you started your explanation, "Well, it's sort of like . . . , but it's different in that. . . ." Thinking back to our semantic map diagrams, what you were trying to do was to find an anchor point in your friend's preexisting store of information. First, you wanted to find a point of similarity between the new and the known. Then you were trying to identify the critical properties that distinguish the concept he or she already possessed from the one you were trying to explain.

Integrating Old and New Information

At some point in your professional education it is likely that you were required to read or read about Piaget's work in developmental psychology. You may even recall the terms *schema, assimilation,* and *accommodation.* Piaget has postulated that concepts are stored in people's minds in schemata (plural of schema). A schema is not unlike one of our semantic maps (or segments of them). For example we might have a dog schema that we use to cluster the memory representation of all the types and examples of dogs we have encountered. Likewise we might have cat, wolf, and animal schemata. Assimilation occurs when we are able to categorize a new example as belonging to a preexisting schema, Oh, there is another cat. In assimilation our schema are not substantially changed. Accommodation occurs when we have to alter our schema or schemata. For example, assume that a four-year-old has a schema for animal that includes all four-legged mammals (this, by the way, is the schema that many four-year-olds do possess). Then the child encounters a cricket. You, being the resourceful teacher that you are, say, "Oh that is a cricket. It is the kind of animal we call an insect. It has six legs and three body parts." Now the child does one of three things: (1) he can choose to ignore the information you have provided and keep his schema intact, (2) he can choose to modify his animal schema to include small six-legged creatures as well as larger four-legged creatures, (3) he can keep his original animal schema intact and postulate a second word sense (meaning) for animal: Oh, animal must mean all creatures that move around on their own *as well as* all those four-legged things I know about.

In the first situation the child has assimilated by ignoring your information. The original animal schema is intact. Accommodation has occurred in both the second and third situations. In the second, the child has altered the properties that he assigns to the concept animal. In the third instance, he has kept the original schema intact and added a new schema for the same label, animal.

The issue of accuracy is not really relevant in concept development. Granted, we want students of all ages to have accurate concepts. However, students will develop concepts whether they are accurate or not. Toddlers are famous for this. Their initial concept of cat may include squirrels, dogs, horses, and rabbits. And it is only through the process of feedback (No! that is not a cat, it is a horse) and instruction (Cats are little; they purr and climb trees) that children learn to order their world as we adults do.

FROM CONCEPTS TO EVENTS

Semantic maps proved to be a useful construct for illustrating certain basic relations among concepts. However, these relations (class, example, attribute) cannot be used to express all relations among concepts. For example, the relations between concepts in sentences (1) and (2) can be represented by a class (isa) link and an attribute (has) link respectively (see Figure 3.7).

(1) Leo is a lion.

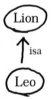

(2) Leo has a mane.

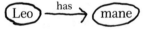

Fig. 3.7

However, as yet we have no links in our system that will capture the relations among the concepts in sentences (3) and (4).

(3) Susan went to town to buy a new bike.
(4) If Henry pitches well, he will win the game.

In short while we can express the basic semantic relations among concepts, we cannot, as yet, represent relations among events or episodes that occur. Since people understand and remember events or episodes, our system will be incomplete until we can find a way to represent relations among them. Fortunately several researchers and theorists (Fillmore, 1968; Frederiksen, 1975; Lindsay and Norman, 1972; Schank, 1973) have developed constructs that capture our intuitive perceptions about how events get related to one another.

Expanded Semantic Maps

Lindsay and Norman (1972) have utilized Fillmore's (1968) case grammar to expand the number and kind of relations that can exist in a semantic network.[10] In a case grammar analysis of an event the first step is to identify the basic *action*. Second, one identifies the actors: (1) Who is the *agent*—who caused the action to occur? (2) Who (what) is the object—who was *directly* affected or who *received* the action? Some examples may help to clarify these relations.

(5) John is gardening.
   Action: gardening
   Agent: John
   Object: none
(6) The tea is brewing.
   Action: brewing
   Agent: none
   Object: the tea
(7) Henry is cultivating the vegetables for Ms. Stuart.
   Action: cultivating
   Agent: Henry
   Object: vegetables
   Recipient: Ms. Stuart

As both Lindsay and Norman and Fillmore point out, the action becomes the focal point around which all other concepts in the event revolve. Schematically, sentence (7) can be represented as in Figure 3.8. Essentially what we have done is to add some new links to our semantic map construct to account for other relations among concepts. In order to account for normal discourse, we will have to add several

[10] In a seminal article, Fillmore revived the allegedly outdated Latin-based case grammar. It has proven to be a powerful stimulus to educators and psychologists trying to explain comprehension. Several comprehension models have case grammar underpinnings.

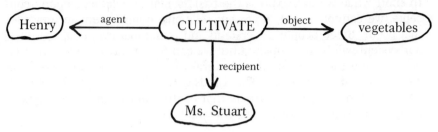

Fig. 3.8

new links, all of which represent possible relations among parts of an event. These are listed in Table 3.1 (after Fillmore, 1968; Lindsay and Norman, 1972).

Let us see how these new relations can be expressed schematically for some fairly complex sentences. Consider sentence (8).

(8) Because Samson was bewitched by Delilah, he cut his hair and lost his great strength.

In Figure 3.9 the relationships of the event are illustrated. Notice that there are three basic actions—*BEWITCH, CUT,* and *LOSE.* The three actions are linked by causal relations; that is, the bewitching caused the cutting which caused the loss of strength. Notice also that Samson is the object of one of the actions but the agent of the other two.

To foreshadow a construct we will develop more fully in Chapter 5, each of the parts of sentence (8)—BEWITCH, CUT, and LOSE—plus

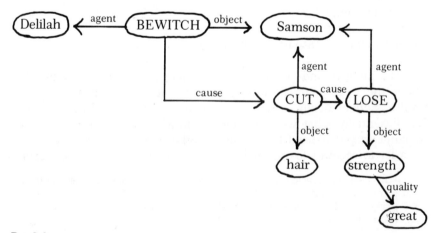

Fig. 3.9

TABLE 3.1 Possible Components of an Event

Action	The event itself. In a sentence, the action is usually described by a verb: The horse was *bitten* by a fly.
Agent	The actor who has caused the action to take place: The horse was bitten by *a fly*.
Instrument	The thing or device that caused or implemented the event: The *hail* destroyed the tomatoes. The people traveled to Madison by *boat*.
Conditional	A logical condition that exists between two events: John will win the game *if* he pitches well.
Cause	A causal condition that exists between two events: John laughed at Henry *because* Henry wore a funny mask.
Location	The place where the event takes place. Often two different locations are involved, one at the start of the event and one at the conclusion. These are identified as *from* and *to* locations. Henry went *to town*. Susan traveled *from Minneapolis to Madison*.
Object	The thing that is affected by the action: Henry thanked *Matthew*.
Purpose	Identifies the purpose of the event: Matthew went to town *to buy some candy*.
Quality	A descriptor, one that modifies a concept: The day was *humid*. There are fourteen people in our *new* class.
Recipient	The person who is the receiver of the effect of the action: John gave the drum to *Susan*.
Time	When an event takes place: I will go to town *a week from Tuesday*.
Truth	Used primarily for false statements: Henry does *not* cultivate vegetables.

the associated agents and objects and so on is a *proposition*. A *proposition* can be thought of as a unitary statement about the world. In simpler terms, a *proposition* can be thought of as what we all learned to call caluses (dependent or independent) when we took English and grammar classes in school.

Understanding relations among propositions is critical to good comprehension. In empirical studies, Kintsch (1974) and Meyer (1977) have provided evidence to support the conclusion that propositions are *basic units of thought*. Intuitively, relations among propositions seem to us to be central to comprehension. The relations among propositions (cause, purpose, condition, time, and so on in Table 3.1) carry the thread of a story or a passage in a text. Perhaps this will become clearer with a more complex example. Consider paragraph (9) and the underlying representation in Figure 3.10.

(9) Because Samson, the great biblical hero, was bewitched by Delilah, he cut his hair and lost his great strength. When he battled his enemies, he was reduced to a weakling. After they imprisoned him, Samson realized that Delilah had betrayed him.

A few points deserve note. First, the gist of the narrative is captured in the links between the actions (cause, cause, cause, time, time, object). Second, the actors are linked to at least two or more actions, sometimes as agents, sometimes as objects. Third, notice that there are a few of our old concept links (isa, for example); in the network. In fact, Lindsay and Norman (1972) have provided several examples of networks which demonstrate how the links from our old semantic maps can be included in a network along with the newer event links. Figure 3.11 is a Lindsay and Norman network for the following sentences in (10).

(10) Bob drinks beer.
Mary hit Louise hard yesterday at Luigi's.
Al owns Luigi's.
Bob likes Louise.
Al's dog, Henry, bit Sam because he yelled at Mary.
Louise drinks wine.
Mary likes Bob.

To review briefly: networks of nodes (representing concepts) and links, (representing relations) can be used to illustrate the relations among concepts in a proposition (clause) and the relations between propositions. To quote Lindsay and Norman (1972, pp. 400–401):

> We now have the basic design for the data base underlying human memory. *The memory system is an organized collection of pathways that specify possible routes through the data base.* Retrieving information from

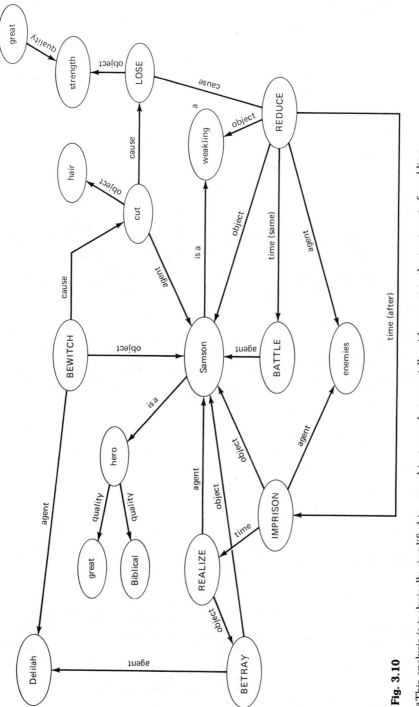

Fig. 3.10

[a]This analysis is technically simplified in several instances but especially with respect to the treatment of weakling. Even so, the interrelationship of the events in the scenario can be captured without the technical detail.

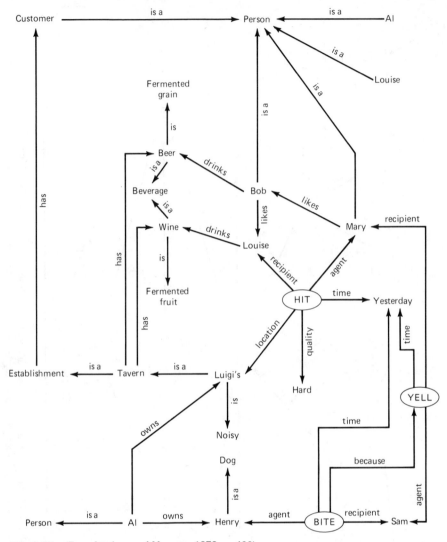

Fig. 3.11   (From Lindsay and Norman, 1972, p. 400).

such a memory is going to be like running a maze. Starting off at a given mode, there are many possible options available about the possible pathways to follow. Taking one of these paths leads to a series of crossroads, each going off to a different concept. Each new crossroads is like a brand new maze, with a new set of choice points and a new set of pathways to follow. In principle, it is possible to start at any point in the data base and, by taking the right sequence of turns through successive mazes, end up at any other point. Thus, in the memory system *all information is interconnected.*

From Passive Representation to Active Comprehension

In trying to show how longer discourse might be represented in people's heads we have invoked the semantic map construct to capture the relations within and between propositions. But we have not yet demonstrated how this representation can lead us to a realization of the "new to known" principle stated at the outset of this chapter and discussed in relation to understanding concepts. We shall now attempt such a leap. In so doing we hope to demonstrate the interactive nature of comprehension as a dialogue between writer and reader, as well as the active role of the reader in understanding written discourse. Another small experiment will serve as a departure point. Read paragraph (11) and answer questions (12) through (21).

(11) John went to Vescio's, his favorite Italian restaurant. He ordered lasagna. When the waiter brought it, John was so enraged that he left without leaving a tip. He even forgot his umbrella.
(12) Where did John go?
(13) Why did John go to Vescio's?
(14) Why did John fail to leave a tip?
(15) Why was John angry?
(16) Did John pay for the meal?
(17) Why did John forget his umbrella?
(18) Had it been raining that day?
(19) Does John like Italian food?
(20) Who seated John at his table?
(21) When did John pay for his meal?

You should recognize questions (12) and (14) as examples of what most people refer to as literal comprehension. The text states very clearly that John went to Vescio's and that he did not leave a tip because he *was so enraged*. The rest of the answers are a bit trickier; however, we would wager that you could give a plausible answer for each of them. For example:

(13) to eat (Italian food).
(15) probably something was wrong with the lasagna or else the waiter did something strange.
(16) apparently he did, otherwise the author would have mentioned it.
(17) because he was so angry.
(18) probably. Or else it looked like rain when John started out to the restaurant.

(19) he must; otherwise he would not have a *favorite* Italian restaurant.

(20) a hostess or a maître d', since Vescio's has waiters, they may have a maître d'.

(21) probably on his way out.

On what basis could you generate such responses? There is little in the text to support definitely any of the responses except (17), and even that is open to question. Most of us agree that we respond on the basis of the experience we have had, in this case with restaurants. It is almost as though each of us carries around a set of rules or generalizations about our world. They might be something like:

1. People fail to leave tips when they receive either poor food or poor service or both.
2. People go into restaurants to eat, among other things.
3. People carry umbrellas when it is raining or when they think it is going to rain.
4. Restaurants with waiters may have a maître d'.
5. If a person becomes so angry with the food or service that she fails to leave a tip, she may pay the cashier on the way out rather than deal with the waiter.

Thinking back to the questions and answers about the restaurant, we would hardly want to label literal the kind of comprehension required by these questions. Most of us would agree that they are inferences based upon experience—experience we have chosen to represent in the form of a set of generalizations.

Experience is at the heart of comprehension, especially as comprehension is assessed in today's schools. Experience is what we are referring to when we say that a person is good at reading "between the lines," or "beyond the lines."

While the details are not quite so well worked out, there are some useful frameworks that represent attempts to understand the structure readers bring to the printed page as they try to make sense out of all those little squiggles. Interestingly, the frameworks that make the most sense to us come out of a discipline totally alien to both of us—computer simulation of intelligent behavior. We have been most influenced by the work of Lehnert (1975), Minsky (1975), and Schank (1973) in constructing our own framework for comprehension of longer discourse.

Because we have found his treatment of the relationship between what is *in* the text and what the reader brings to the text so useful, we have adopted Schank's term, *script*, as a special label for experience (at least most experience).

A bit of history about attempts to get computers to act like human beings will help to clarify the usefulness of the script notion. People in a field called artificial intelligence (AI) have been trying for at least two decades to get computers to act like human beings.

In the early programs for question answering, computers could answer questions like (12) and (14) but none of the others. That is because a computer will only give back to you what you put into it. In our little story only questions (12) and (14) have explicitly stated answers. The rest require inferences. Human beings have little trouble making such inferences. AI researchers literally had to feed the computer all that extra information that humans carry around in their heads. So for a short paragraph like our example, they had to feed in about five to six times that much information so that the computer could answer questions like the ones we posed.

It became obvious that a more efficient procedure had to be devised. Several computer scientists came up with standardized, stereotyped frameworks called frames or scripts. (We will use the term script.) A script was used to represent all the mundane, take-for-granted knowledge that an information processor (be it a computer or a human) brings to a real-life situation (like going to a restaurant) or to a comprehension situation (reading or listening about going to a restaurant). Schank and his colleagues, for example, developed a restaurant script, a bus ride script, a subway script, and so on. Then whenever the computer encountered a story dealing with a particular instance of going to a restaurant or riding a bus, it called up the appropriate script. This procedure has made for much more efficient computer programs, especially those that try to answer questions.

But more important for our purposes as educators, computer scientists have provided us with a useful metaphor for conceptualizing the way in which living information processors (students) answer questions about what they read (and what they already know about what they read).

For a second, consider the wealth of knowledge that you brought to bear on that paragraph about John in Vescio's. What did you already know about going to restaurants? What was your restaurant script?

First, you know that there is a typical sequence of events involved in going to a restaurant: there is an entrance scene, a being-seated scene, an ordering scene, an eating scene, a paying-the-check scene, and a leaving scene. Furthermore, you also knew that each of those scenes has more or less predictable sub-sequences—menus arrive before the order is placed, you pay the check before you leave the tip.

Second, you brought a great deal of knowledge that could be labeled "plausible explanations." Had the text indicated that John left an extra large tip, you would have inferred that either the service or the food was extra good, or that John was trying to impress someone eating with him. These plausible explanations probably take the form of generalizations about your restaurant "world," not unlike those generalizations listed previously.

Most script knowledge is very mundane, almost taken for granted. In fact, if a writer or a speaker, in relating an instance of going to a restaurant, included all those mundane details, you would probably become bored, impatient, irritated, or concerned about his intelligence. You already knew that! What gets into a text or a speech is special or unusual. You should have seen the way Hortense ordered and tasted the wine! She was class, all the way! Or, the duck à l'orange was horrid! Overcooked and tough (you expected otherwise)!

Using the script metaphor, we believe that comprehension involves (1) processing the text information, (2) matching it against the prototypic script for such events, and (3) integrating textual and scriptal (our coined word) information, thus producing a *complete* knowledge structure for the event described in the text.

If you think about these steps in relationship to our discussion of concepts and semantic maps, you will see a remarkable similarity. Matching against a prototypic script is very much like finding a class to which a concept belongs. Integrating textual and scriptal information is akin to pinpointing those properties of a concept, say Fido, that make it like all the examples of its class, say dogs, as well as those properties which distinguish it from all other dogs. Especially with descriptions of events, it is as if we are saying to ourselves what is it that makes this event (say the Vescio's scene) like our prototype for this type of event (our restaurant script), and what is it that makes this event unique?

Since scripts are built from experience, it is painfully obvious that they are dynamic—ever changing. The relationship between our scriptal prototypes and particular instances of scriptal events is reciprocal. Surely we use our scriptal knowledge to help us interpret an event, just as we did in order to answer the questions about the Vescio's scene. However, each encounter we have with a particular instance must alter our scriptal prototype in some way. John's restaurant script will never be quite the same after the Vescio's incident. And because we have read about John's misfortune, our restaurant script is probably altered too.

Earlier, in discussing concepts we invoked Piaget's notions of assimilation and accommodation. Scripts are subject to the same set of operations. Suppose that Henry, a sheltered teen-ager from a well-to-do family in suburbia, has only been in elegant French restaurants and chic bistros. His restaurant script contains all the elements and events most of us associate with "good" restaurants. Then, at age fourteen, his parents allow him to go to McDonald's with some friends. His restaurant script is upset! You pay for the food *before* you get it! No *maître d'!* Standing in line! Food served in paper containers!

When Henry encounters this deviant information, he has three choices: (1) He can ignore the information about McDonald's altogether, perhaps claiming that McDonald's is not a restaurant at all; in this case his restaurant script remains intact. (2) He can modify his restaurant script to *accommodate* the new information; in this case, he must change some of his restaurant script rules, for example, you can pay for the food either before or after you get it. Or, (3) He can create a new script for fast-food restaurants which he keeps separate from his "good" restaurant script.

The choices are analogous to those for the four-year-old and his cricket information. But only the second and third choices are of any real use to Henry. Assuming that he will encounter other "McDonald's" in his life (an inevitability), only the modification of his old script or the creation of a new one will allow him to deal with that new information.

A FINAL WORD

The basic purpose of this chapter has been to convince you that comprehension is a complex but understandable process. Comprehension is best understood by invoking the *new to known* principle. We understand what is *new* in the context of what is already *known* to us.

To the degree that new information "fits" into preexisting schemata we have *assimilated* the new information. When that new information does not fit, we can ignore it (as we often do to preserve stereotypes), or we can modify our schemata to *accommodate* that new information.

Much of our knowledge of "words" can be thought of as being stored in *semantic maps*. These maps represent the kinds of knowledge units we store plus the linkages, or relations, between knowledge units. There are four important relations: *class*—a dog *is a* mammal; *example*—dog is exemplified by collie; *attribute*—dogs *have* ears, they *do* bark, and they *are* loyal; and *related concepts*—cats share certain attributes and class relations with dogs, but they differ in others. By thinking about the various relations of a concept, we can plan strategies for relating what is *new* to what is *known;* that is, we can find anchor points for introducing the new. Thus, our reliance on direct experiences can be lessened.

Semantic maps can be expanded to represent our knowledge about events as well as concepts. By adding new links, we can represent the relations within a proposition (agent, object, recipient, time, location, negation, and so on) as well as relations between propositions (cause, condition, purpose, time, and so on). Then if we add the notion of scripts to represent all the underlying knowledge we bring to the printed page, we see how the new to known principle works for longer discourse. The notions of scripts are similar to concepts, except that they apply to larger units of discourse and to events in the world. Otherwise, our knowledge of events acts much like our knowledge of concepts : We sometimes *assimilate* new information into existing scripts; we sometimes *accommodate* that new information by revising a script.

To foreshadow a point we will explicate in Chapter 9: awareness of prior knowledge is important because it can help students to realize what they already know about a topic before they read about it. Students do not always "know" what they "know" about what they are going to read. By underscoring the importance of prior knowledge on comprehension, we reveal our biases toward regarding reading as an active process, a dialogue between writer and reader.

REFERENCES

Collins, A., and Qullian, R. Retrieval Time From Semantic Memory. *Journal of Verbal Learning and Verbal Behavior,* 1969, *8,* 240–247.

Fillmore, C. J. The Case for Case. In E. Back and R. G. Harms (eds.), *Universals in Linguistic Theory.* New York: Holt Rinehart and Winston, 1968.

Frederiksen, C. H. Effects of Context-Induced Processing Operations on Semantic Information Acquired from Discourse. *Cognitive Psychology,* 1975, *7,* 139–166.

Kintsch, W. *The Representation of Meaning in Memory.* Hillsdale, N.J.: Erlbaum, 1974.

Lehnert, W. *Question Answering in a Story Understanding System.* Research report #57, Yale University Department of Computer Sciences, 1975.

Lindsay, P., and Norman, D. *Human Information Processing.* New York: Academic Press, 1972.

Meyer, B. J. Organization in Prose and Memory: Research with Application to Reading Comprehension. In Pearson, P. D. (ed.), *Reading: Research, Theory, and Practice,* the Twenty-Sixth Yearbook of the National Reading Conference. Clemson, S.C.: National Reading Conference, 1977, 214–220.

Minsky, M. A Framework For Representing Knowledge. In P. Winston (ed.), *The Psychology of Computer Vision.* New York: McGraw Hill, 1975.

National Institute of Education. *Request for Proposal for a National*

Center for the Study of Reading. Washington, D.C.: Department of Health, Education and Welfare, 1976.

Pearson, P. D. The Effects of Grammatical Complexity on Children's Comprehension, Recall and Conception of Certain Semantic Relations. *Reading Research Quarterly,* 1974–75, *10,* 155–192.

Pearson, P. D., and Studt, A. Effects of Word Frequency and Contextual Richness on Children's Word Identification Abilities. *Journal of Educational Psychology,* 1975, *67,* 89–95.

Rumelhart, D. E. Notes on Schema for Stories. In D. Bobrow and A. Collins (eds.), Representation and Understanding: *Studies in Cognitive Science.* New York: Academic Press, 1975.

Schank, R. C. Identification of Conceptualizations of Underlying Natural Language. In R. C. Schank & K. M. Colby (eds.), *Computer Models of Thought and Language.* San Francisco: Freeman, 1973.

4
UNDERSTANDING CONCEPTS

THERE ARE several reasons for beginning a discussion of comprehension tasks with concept (word) level comprehension. First, words are important to comprehension. Davis (1974), Spearritt (1971), and several other researchers have repeatedly demonstrated the importance of vocabulary knowledge (word meanings) as a component of comprehension. Second, concept level comprehension is more straightforward than comprehension of longer discourse. By beginning with the concepts, we hope to establish some clear patterns of relations among ideas that will apply to sentences, paragraphs, and passages as well. Third, by beginning with concepts, we follow a pattern established in Chapter 3.

WORD LEVEL COMPREHENSION TASKS

We have selected nine concept level relations in our taxonomy. They fall in three categories, as listed in the chart in Table 4.1. The three major breakdowns—simple associations, complex associations, and ambiguous words—are categorically different from one another. Simple associations are fairly similar to the types of relations among concepts we have discussed in Chapter 3. For example, we would expect to find synonym or antonym pairs fairly close to one another in a semantic map. Antonym pairs, such as heat-cold, analysis-synthesis, man-woman, usually share many attributes and class relations and differ in only a few attributes and class relations. Our third relationship item, associations, provides many pairs of concepts that are related by an attribute link: dog-bark, grass-green, blue-sky, hit-ball. Classificatory associations obviously involve what we referred to as class-example (isa) relations in Chapter 3. But in Chapter 4, the notion of classification is expanded to include classifying by attribute, for example, things that crawl or things that are green.

When we move from simple to complex associations, we move a bit further away from the simplicity of our semantic maps. Analogous relations are rarely portrayed directly on our maps; however they are derivable from them. For example, in the analogy *dog* is to *bark* as *cat* is to *meow*, two attribute relations, dog-bark and cat-meow, are being compared. On the other hand, when we discuss connotative-denotative relations, we move more directly back onto the map. Take the set of words—walk, stroll, stride, saunter, trudge—all these words denote walking but connote different feelings or tones. We would expect to find

TABLE 4.1 Concept Level Comprehension

Category	Relation	Examples	Task
Simple Associations	1. synonymous (synonyms)	Assist-help	Recognize that two words have similar meanings
	2. antonymous (antonyms)	help-hinder	Recognize that two words can have opposing meanings
	3. associative (associations)	green-grass run-fast walk-slow	Recognize that pairs of words often occur together in the language (often the words are linked by an attribute relation)
	4. classificatory (classes)	animal-dog cat horse	Recognize that a class label has various examples that belong to that class
Complex Associations	5. analogous (analogies)	dog is to bark as cat is to meow	Recognize that two pairs of words can be related in a similar way
	6. connotative-denotative	I strolled walked sauntered	Recognize that words that denote the same class of things or behaviors connote different meanings or feelings
Ambiguous Words	7. multiple meanings	fly—to soar fly—an insect	Recognize that a given word can refer to different concepts (have different meanings)
	8. homographic (homographs)	proJECT— PROJect	Recognize that words alike in spelling can differ in pronounciation and meaning
	9. homophonous (homophones)	fair-fare	Recognize that words alike in sound differ in spelling and meaning.

all members of this set fairly close to one another in a semantic map for *perambulating,* perhaps.

Finally, when we move to the category of ambiguous words we move "off the map" entirely. We seriously doubt that homophones or homographs or multiple meanings of a given label, like *bear*, would appear close to one another on a semantic map. Yet we feel an obligation to deal with these relations because they constitute important aspects of comprehending words.

SIMPLE ASSOCIATIONS

Synonyms

Is it possible for two words to be truly synonymous? Compare, for example, the pairs big-large and walk-stroll. Somehow big and large appear to be more alike in meaning than walk and stroll. So pairs of synonyms differ in terms of their degree of synonymy. There is a point of view suggesting that no two words are exactly synonymous; if they were, one word would drop out of the language. Such a view assumes that languages are optimally economical; that is, there are no redundant words. Words which appear to be synonymous really elicit *shades* of interpretation. For many alleged synonyms this is true, as we will see when we talk about the whole denotation-connotation issue later in this chapter. Perhaps what we want students to learn, when we ask them to complete synonym exercises, is to recognize the *similarity* not the *identity* of two words.

We believe, especially for younger students, that synonym activities are very important. And we are willing to postpone shades of interpretation instruction until sometime in the intermediate grades. Here are several types of synonym activities we and our colleagues have found useful.[11]

1. Circle the word that means the same as the key word.

big: small   large   hope

2. Circle the word that means the same as the word italicized in the sentence.

Joan has a *big* bike.
small   large   hope

3. Draw lines between words that mean the same.

big   bicycle
little   large
run   race
bike   small

4. Once antonyms and associates have been introduced, the following type of activity can be used to practice all three tasks at once. Clas-

[11] Whenever an activity should be delayed until a certain developmental level, we have indicated an approximate grade level to begin the activity. Otherwise, assume that all types of activities are appropriate at all levels.

sify each pair of words as about the same in meaning or opposite in meaning; indicate words that "go together" (you would likely find them together in the same sentence) and words that are *not* at all related. See Table 4.2. This activity can be started as low as grade 3. If you use just same and opposite words, you can begin it at an even lower grade. You have to be liberal in your scoring of "go together" words.

TABLE 4.2

Pair	Same	Opposite	Go Together	Not Related
big-large	X			
hot-cold		X		
green-grass			X	
guitar-north				X
redwood-elect				X
happy-sad		X		
run-ever				X
afraid-scared	X			

Antonyms

Like synonyms, antonyms are not so simple a matter as most of us might want to believe. Unlike synonyms, there probably are real antonyms—words truly opposite in meaning. The problem is that there are many kinds of "opposition."

For example, one kind of opposition is called *contradiction*. If a thing is true then it cannot be partly false. You are either in or out. You agree or you disagree. You are alive or you are dead. A diamond is perfect or it is imperfect. A thing can be near perfection; but if it is not there, it is not perfect. The terms are what logicians call mutually exclusive. There are not too many such antonyms. Besides the pairs that have been mentioned, a few that come to mind are right-wrong, complete-incomplete, finished-unfinished, correct-incorrect. One note about contradictory terms. In common usage, we often talk about something being partially correct, half finished, half dead, or partly true. Such modifiers do not change the picture. A half-dead horse is still alive. A partly true statement is still false. A half-finished project is unfinished.

Contradictory pairs differ from *contrary* pairs, another term borrowed from the logicians. They may be thought of as true diametrical opposites. For example, hot and cold lie at precisely the same point on opposite ends of a heat continuum, equidistant from some midpoint that is neither hot nor cold. Warm and cool are not at the extremes, but we probably think of them as equidistant from the same midpoint. Unlike contradictory terms, contrary terms allow for a range of values in between. Good and bad are extremes on a quality continuum with many values in between, including fair, mediocre, and poor. There are a fair number of these contrary pairs.

white-black	superior-inferior	prodigal-parsimonious
dark-light	easy-difficult	deep-shallow
empty-full	happy-sad	noisy-quiet
loud-soft	heavy-light	wet-dry
love-hate	shy-bold	fast-slow
sharp-dull	fat-thin	

A third category of antonyms might be called *reverse* terms: one term is more or less the undoing of the other. There are many clear examples:

admit-reject	help-hinder
constructive-destructive	aboveboard-underhand
build-raze	arrive-leave
go-stop	go-come
alleviate-aggravate	analyze-synthesize
fear-hope	

A fourth type of antonymy might be called *counterparts*. Some are what logicians call *relative* pairs, pairs where one term implies that the other also exists: parent-child, send-receive, husband-wife, predecessor-successor, employee-employer, tenant-landlord, seller-buyer. Other counterpart terms denote pairs where the two words are alike in all aspects but one: brother-sister, mother-father, aunt-uncle, actor-actress. Still others are *complementary* terms; when you encounter one, you expect to encounter the other or you expect that the other has or will occur. They are, in a sense, *reciprocal*. For example, an answer implies a question. If one party attacks, another defends. Stimuli elicit responses. If one gives, another takes.

The last category is usually called *contrasted* terms. It hides a multitude of sins; that is, it includes many terms that do not really clash with one another in the way that contradictory or contrary terms do. Here are some examples:

top-bottom	night-day	begin-end
floor-ceiling	morning-evening	keep-abandon
stop-start	heaven-hell	open-close
awake-asleep	quell-foment	rational-irrational
cloudy-sunny	relative-absolute	strict-lenient
raw-ripe	religious-secular	laud-revile
relaxed-stiff		

In the strictest sense, only contradictory, contrary, and reverse terms are true opposites. However, there are so many other terms that are contrasted on some feature that we think all the categories should be included in instructional activities for antonyms.

You may feel as though we have dwelt too long on this topic and made some unnecessarily fine distinctions. There are three reasons for going into such detail about antonyms. First, all of us have intuitively recognized these distinctions among antonyms. We know that hot is not the opposite of cold in the same way that husband is the opposite of wife or that build is the opposite of raze. Second, we would like teachers to have a clear understanding of the issues concerning opposites even if they do not communicate these fine points to their students. We think it will help you when you are trying to think of examples to build a particular lesson on or to amplify some example of opposites a student has offered in class. Third, in the secondary years we see no reason why, at least for better students, teachers should not build lessons in which the various types of antonyms are contrasted. Opposition is an important part of vocabulary instruction; there is no reason to hide its secrets from capable secondary students. As an invaluable resource (for teachers as well as secondary students), we suggest a copy of *Webster's New Dictionary of Synonyms* (1973). Not surprisingly, it has many excellent synonyms, too.

Many of the activities suggested for synonyms can be applied to antonyms. In addition here are some others we have found useful.

1. Change the italicized word in the sentence to make the sentence mean the opposite.

John *hates* to go fishing.
Hazel *destroyed* the chair.
That diamond is *imperfect*.
That is an *ugly* horse.

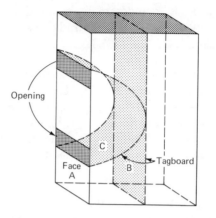

Fig. 4.1.

2. Make a computer box. See Figure 4.1.

Using a laundry soap carton, make two openings on the narrow face (A). Remove the top. Then insert a vertical piece of tagboard (B), against which you can lodge a bent piece of tagboard (C) to make a slide for 3 × 5 index cards to run through. Fasten all pieces with tape or glue. Replace top. When cards slide through they will flip over.

On the 3 by 5 cards, write a term on one side and its antonym on the other. When the students operate the computer, they take a card from a stack, read a word, guess its opposite, insert the card, and check their guess against the computer's answer. This can be modified for any game where two things—synonyms, antonyms, associations, definitions, and so on—are to be compared.

3. See activity 5 under synonyms.

4. A concentration game can be modified to allow for practicing antonyms. Instead of asking students to match the same word in two different locations, ask them to match antonyms. Notice that this works equally well for synonyms.

5. For any contrary pair, make a continuum, and place words along it, as in Figure 4.2. Students may disagree about exactly where certain terms should go. Nurture such disagreement and discussion. It will help to sharpen their concepts for these words. Be certain to reward good reasoning; do not look for "right" answers. This activity can be used for grades 5 and up.

Associations

We have tried to find a better term to denote this task because the term *associations* is so general. In fact, it could apply to any of the tasks listed thus far. But the other terms we could think of do not capture the

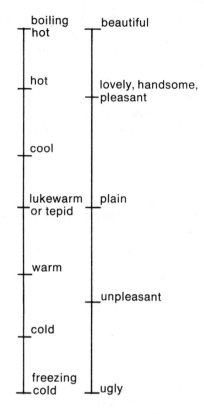

Fig. 4.2.

essence of this task. So we have selected the term association, recognizing full well that it is ambiguous.

What we mean by associations are words that "go together," words that would naturally occur in the same sentence or paragraph, words that you might find adjacent to one another in running discourse. Psychologists discuss two kinds of associations—*paradigmatic* and *syntagmatic*. Paradigmatic associations are words of the same part of speech that are commonly associated—tiger-lion, collie-spaniel, peas-potatoes. Syntagmatic associations are words of different parts of speech that might appear adjacent to one another in a sentence—green-grass, ferocious-tiger, hit-ball. Notice that all synonymous and antonymous associations would be classified as paradigmatic; the members of any pair are always the same part of speech. The term paradigmatic (from paradigm) is used to denote the fact that the two words come from the same *class* of words. Syntagmatic (from syntax) denotes a bond established by the *syntax* (word order) in which the words commonly occur. Green (adjective) often modifies grass (noun); ferocious (adjective) often modifies tiger (noun); hit (verb) often takes ball (noun) as an object; swim (verb) is an action which is often located in a pool (noun). Notice that many of these syntagmatic associations are like the attribute relations described in Chapter 3: dogs *do* bark, grass *is* green, and so on.

At this point it would be fair to ask us why we have selected such a vague task to include in our instructional program. It is included because it is such a pervasive influence on comprehension and in instructional programs. How, for example, does a reader decide which word fits into the blank in the typical fill-in-the-blank activity?

What a beautiful _____ sky!

We believe that the reader's accumulated store of knowledge, including associations of the type we have described, enables him or her to complete such a task. The contextual *fit* a reader achieves in such a task is a direct function of the wealth of syntagmatic and paradigmatic associations brought to the task.

The following set of instructional activities can be used to promote children's ability to manipulate associations.

1. *Fill-in-the-blank activities.* There are so many ways of structuring fill-in-the-blank exercises that we could not possibly discuss all the alternatives. Here are a few alternatives.

A. No choices.
   The sky is so _____ it looks like the ocean.
B. Choices that are semantically different.
   The sky is so _____ it looks like the ocean.
   blue   red   orange
C. Choices which are syntactically different.
   John _____ the race yesterday.
   ran   runs   running
D. Choices with are graphically similar.
   The sky is so _____ it looks like the ocean.
   blue   glue   blur

Notice that the set of choices given determines the other skills which must be employed to solve the task. In tasks (1A) and (1B) word knowledge is emphasized; in (1C) word knowledge plus knowledge of inflection endings; in (1D) initial and final letter-sound relations are emphasized in addition to word knowledge. The point is this: typical fill-in-the-blank activities, especially when choices are given, tap something besides word knowledge and associations between pairs of words. Hence you must have a clear objective in mind when you select or create a fill-in-the-blank activity.

2. Simple matching activities.

green	building
blue	tiger
ferocious	light
electric	sky
tall	grass

3. Free associations. When you introduce vocabulary use the free association technique described and exemplified in Chapter 3. The associations you get from the children can form the basis of a vocabulary lesson for the new words in a selection. First, ask each student to jot down the first word that comes to mind when you hear the word _____. Afterward, pool all the associates from the group. Then discuss the meaning of the new word as it relates to the associates offered by the group. Well, it is like a _____, it is different from _____, and so on.

4. The Concentration game (after the television show) can be modified for instruction in associations. Simply make the criterion for a match, a pair of words that go together; the matching pairs might be blue-sky, green-grass, tall-building, run-race, hit-ball, rapid-transit, and so on.

5. Sentence writing. Give students a list with pairs of associated words; for each pair, ask them to create a sentence using both words.

A note about association activities: we believe that this comprehension task, as well as most comprehension tasks in this chapter, require a flexible attitude toward "correct" answers; there are many reasons why two words can *go together;* as a teacher you have to be willing to accept deviant responses for which students can offer plausible justification.

Classification Activities

Thinking back to Chapter 3, remember that one of the important aspects of concepts was the *class relation;* that is, concepts belong to classes, and the nature of that relation is captured by the compound, *isa*. A dog *isa* mammal; a mammal *isa* animal; a cat *isa* pet. We believe that classifying is the most common and certainly one of the most important forms of human thinking.

Consider what happens to you when you encounter a strange creature for the first time. You wonder, What is it? Is it dangerous? Will it hurt me? Then someone tells you, Oh, it is just a stange kind of dog you have not seen before. Somehow knowing it is a type of dog allays a whole set of fears; it is not a wild boar, or a frisky porcupine, or a frightened skunk.

As soon as we can identify the class of things to which a new stimulus belongs, we are able to assign all the attributes of that class to the new stimulus. To use the language of Chapter 3, we assimilate the new information. As a consequence, we are able to call up from our memory a whole range of experiences for comprehending and dealing with the new information. We pet the new thing instead of running away from it. We expect it to bark; we are surprised if it moos. Classification is not only convenient, it is absolutely essential for dealing with one's world; if we had to treat each new stimulus as a unique entity, our memory stores would surely reach overload very soon.

It is our contention that classification activities are among the most helpful a teacher can direct or assign to students; further, we believe it is a task that can be used at any developmental level from preschool through graduate school.

As a teacher there are a variety of ways that you can structure classification activities. There are several factors that will influence the difficulty of the classification task. Among these are: (1) whether or not the concepts used are familiar, (2) whether or not the class labels and the examples to be classified are provided for the student *or* whether they must be self-generated, (3) whether or not the categories used are mutually exclusive (mutually exclusive means that each example to be classified fits into one and only one category), and (4) whether the category labels represent true classes (for example, animals) or categories based upon a common attribute (for example, things that bark).

While we would not argue that there is an optimal sequence for introducing classification activities, the following sequence is one that we and our colleagues have found useful.

1. As early as kindergarten, begin by asking children to categorize pictures that represent familiar concepts that clearly belong to a single category. Food and clothing, animals and plants, fruits and vegetables, furniture and tools are pairs of classes that might be used at this early stage. (Stay away from the category, toys; almost anything can be a toy—truck, car, hammer, saw, chair, or workbench.) Begin with the labels for the categories and ask children to place the examples in the appropriate category.

2. Reverse the procedure: place cards with pictures of clothing and tools into two rows. Ask which row has clothing; which row has tools.

3. Mix the clothing cards and the tool cards. Without giving the labels, ask students to place the cards into the two categories. Assist them if they have difficulty. Once the pictures are in the correct categories, ask them how the groups differ from one another. Try to elicit a class label. Be flexible with responses. Clothing may turn out as things to wear or things to go into a washing machine; tools, as building things or things in a garage.

4. As students begin to be able to read words, these same three steps can be repeated with words rather than pictures. Notice that the third step is always the most difficult; somehow, without the label for the category, the task is much more difficult. We recommend that, until

about grade 3, only clear cases should be used—types of animals, plants, common real-world objects, games. After that time categorizing by attribute (things that have wings, things that have handles, things you could tear) can begin.

5. Next begin asking students to categorize by attribute, as mentioned in point 4. The minute you start children categorizing by attribute, you increase the likelihood that you will not have mutually exclusive categories. Suppose, for example one of your categories is *things that have wings* and another is *things you can ride in*. Notice that airplanes can fit into either category. At least in the initial stages, you should select or create your activities carefully to avoid confusion. Another problem with categorizing by attribute is that it is more difficult to discover the commonality than it is when categorizing by class membership. Contrast, for example, the set, collie, spaniel, dachshund, and poodle (all dogs) with the set, cow, dog, chair, and table (all four-legged items). Until grade 5 or 6 it is probably wise to use category labels when asking students to categorize by attribute.

6. The next factor to add into the categorization sequence is categories that are not mutually exclusive, requiring that students be able to identify those words that belong to more than one category. Consider the categories, *types of animals, games to play,* and *things you might find on a golf course*. Because of their multiple meanings, words like donkey, fish, birdie, eagle, and horse fit into more than one category. Notice that a concept like snake fits into more than one category, not because of multiple meanings, but because it is an animal *and* you could find it (and other animals) on a golf course.

There are a host of useful categorization activities, many of which you undoubtedly already use. The following are some formats that we have found useful.

1. Straightforward categorization. Give the students a worksheet with a set of scrambled words and three category labels at the bottom of the page. Ask them to write the words under the appropriate category labels.

struggled	jump	lumbered
asphalt	brontosaurus	charge
roamed	stuck	triceratops
creature	meat eaters	trap
sticky	oil	gripped
stiffened	dinosaurs	walked
tyrannosaurus	deposit	beast
striding	pits	tar
ankylosaur	gas	stretched
black pools	lizards	saber-toothed tiger

Write the topics on your paper. Put the words under the right topics.

Prehistoric   Tar Pit Terms   Animal Body
   Animals   Movement

2. Place an additional constraint on the task by asking students to categorize by class and by initial letter. See Table 4.3.

TABLE 4.3

	Jobs	Flowers	Tools	Games	Sounds
R	Radio Operator	Rose	Rake	Racketball	Roar
E	Engineer				
A	Accountant				
D	Dairy Farmer				

Ask the students to discuss their choices, and have those who have omitted spaces fill in the blanks with suggestions from other students.

3. Omission. In this activity, students are presented lists of words which contain one word that does not fit. They are to decide on the misfit and explain why it does not fit within the others. If this is done as an independent activity, it should be followed by a discussion. Often the discussion will lead to a category label.

elbow	cheek
jaw	nose

fly	bee
mosquito	raisin

4. Vocabulary review. Several secondary teachers have found that classification can be an effective technique for vocabulary review. Somehow, it helps to tie things together. For example, a unit on the federal system might end by placing the following words into categories.

stare decisis	Senate	amicus curiae
filibuster	House of Representatives	committee system
advise and consent	appeal	cabinet
gerrymander	hearing	enforces laws
Supreme Court	makes laws	bureaucracy
interprets laws		
Legislative	*Executive*	*Judicial*

5. Common elements. You have probably all played the parlor game called, "What do these things (or people) have in common?" Here are some examples:

lettuce, tomatoes, and olive oil (salad ingredients)
rabbits, turtles, and grasshoppers (characters in Aesop's fables)
Thomas Dewey, Adlai Stevenson, and Hubert Humphrey (they all lost presidential elections).

6. Giant pyramid. As a take off on a popular television game show, this can be an entertaining group activity. Make ups cards with a category label and other cards with members of the category. The guesser gets the category cue; the other person gives cues about each member of the category to help the guesser identify each word. Set a time limit. Divide the class into groups if you like competition.

7. Concentration. You can modify the concentration game format to accommodate category activities. A match is achieved when a person can locate a pair consisting of a card with the category label and a card with the members of that category. See Figure 4.3.

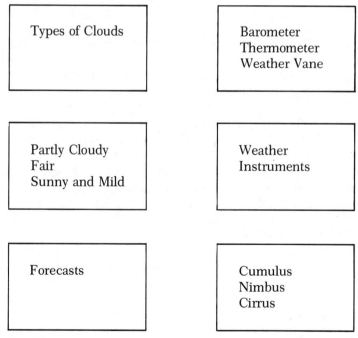

| Types of Clouds | Barometer
Thermometer
Weather Vane |

| Partly Cloudy
Fair
Sunny and Mild | Weather
Instruments |

| Forecasts | Cumulus
Nimbus
Cirrus |

Fig. 4.3.

COMPLEX ASSOCIATIONS

Analogies

Many of you have probably had the dubious privilege of taking an aptitude test based on analogies at some point in your professional career. You may remember something like:

Science:inductive = Mathematics: _____*

1. data
2. deductive*
3. numerical
4. reductive

If such a test has been your only experience with verbal analogies, you may question their inclusion in a comprehension program for younger students; however, analogies are powerful logical and linguistic organizers and deserve inclusion in a comprehension curriculum at the earliest possible point. Even five-year-olds are capable of completing an analogy like, *dog* is to *puppy* as *cat* is to _____. Interestingly, analogies are usually based upon a comparison of the types of associations we have introduced thus far. For example, Hot:cold = tall:short is an analogy based on two antonymous relations; it could be paraphrased, just as hot is the opposite of cold, so tall is the opposite of short. Flea:insect = dog:mammal is an analogy based upon class relations; it could be paraphrased, just as a flea *isa* insect, so a dog *isa* mammal. Dog:bark = cat:meow is an analogy based upon comparable attribute relations; it can be paraphrased, just as bark is an attribute of dog so meow is an attribute of cat, or just as dogs bark, cats meow.

When can you begin activities in analogies? There is no hard-and-fast answer; but in general, as soon as students know that a dog barks and that a cat meows, then they are ready to learn that barking serves the same function for a dog that meowing does for a cat. In fact, analogy can be a powerful tool when you are trying to introduce new concepts to students. Suppose a group of students know that crickets communicate by sound (it is in fact true that one species of cricket can determine which crickets to mate with on the basis of sound). The comparable communication mechanism for cockroaches is smell (different species sort out their own kind by smell). Thus the analogy, sound:cricket = smell:cockroach, summarizes an important comparison between these two types of insects.

To use another example from science, suppose students know that animals have to intake oxygen to survive; learning that plants need to intake carbon dioxide for survival might be enhanced by establishing an analogous relation such as, oxygen:animals = carbon dioxide:plants.

Here are some activities that can be used to promote practice in handling analogies.

1. Establish a whole list of pairs of words that are related to one another in an analogous fashion. Give a few examples and ask students to add more, either from their own experience or from consultation with a dictionary or encyclopedia.

ADULT:	OFFSPRING	ANIMAL:	SOUND ATTRIBUTE
dog	puppy	dog	bark
cat	kitten	cat	meow
lion	cub	lion	roar
deer	fawn	horse	neigh

BIG:	LITTLE	ANIMAL:	HOME
river	stream	lion	den
ship	canoe	deer	thicket
cadillac	volkswagen	bear	cave
lake	pond	robin	tree nest
horse	colt	pheasant	reed nest
tiger	cat	eagle	aerie
ocean	sea		

2. A teaching colleague of ours has a delightful continuous classroom display, consisting of a giant tagboard ice cream cone into which students pile scoops on each of which is written:

a _____ is like a _____ only bigger.

Students add to the pile of scoops whenever they can create a relationship that fits the constraints of task. Similar displays could be created for relations of length (a _____ is like a _____ only longer), smoothness, or temperature.

3. Do not rule out the traditional format for analogies: simple practice sheets with items consisting of three parts of an analogy for which the students choose or create a fourth.

dog:bark-cat: _____
growl   neigh   meow   roar

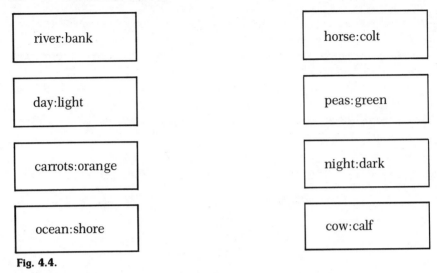

Fig. 4.4.

The activity can be modified by asking students to match one half of an analogy with the other half.

dog:bark =
horse:roar   bear:neigh   cat:meow.

Instead of putting these on worksheets, you can put them onto cards to be used in a game format.

4. We have experienced success using analogies in a concentration format with older students. A match is achieved when two halves of an analogy have been identified (see Fig. 4.4). The task can be made simpler by giving three parts of the analogy on one card.

5. As we continue to indicate, for each of these word level tasks, there are a variety of simple games that can be modified to analogy tasks. Consider the ubiquitous "Rocketship to Somewhere" game typically used for word recognition activities. It can be made into an analogy activity simply by placing an analogy item on each of the game cards.

Connotation-Denotation[12]

For the first few years of schooling, we are satisfied (perhaps delighted) if a child can acquire even a vague notion of what a particular word means. We are happy, for example, if a child is able to figure out that enormous means big. But at some later point (one whose onset is

---

[12] This task is discussed again in Chapter 7 in relation to evaluating bias in writing style.

difficult to specify), we want that same child to know that the phrase, an enormous rock, connotes a different shade of meaning than does the phrase, a big rock.

We are convinced that by the upper elementary years, and especially in the secondary years, students need direct instruction in discriminating the subtle shades of meaning conveyed by words that denote the same object, action, or feeling in the real world. The need for this type of instruction increases as children become more involved in legitimate children's or adolescent literature.

This task is intrinsically bound up with the synonym task. With a few exceptions, it is accurate to state that two words that are synonymous at one level of meaning (denotative) are different at another level of meaning (connotative). This task is also related to categorization tasks; for example, we can ask children to identify the commonality in a set of words—saunter, stroll, stride, march, wobble, teeter, trudge, and ambulate (they are all ways of walking). In fact, a thesaurus is nothing more than a categorical listing of words that all denote a similar experience in the world but connote a different attitude about that experience.

There are many ways of organizing activities to promote the ability to discriminate among denotatively similar words.

1. A first step is to recognize the similarity among such words. Hence categorization activities are appropriate (see page 70).

2. As a group activity, place the following sentence frame on the blackboard. Then insert different words all denoting the activity of walking into the verb slot. Discuss the differences in meaning which result.

Susan _____ through the woods.
(walked, trudged, skipped, strolled, ambled, sneaked, strode, and so on)

3. Assign questions such as the following, asking students to justify their responses.

1. Would you rather *eat* with someone or *dine* with someone?
2. One person *strode* through the park; another *trudged* through the park. Who walked faster?
3. Who is prettier? Someone who is *pretty* or someone who is *gorgeous?*
4. Who is hungrier? Someone who is *hungry* or someone who is *ravenous?*

4. Rank synonyms on a single feature. Ask students to rank lists of words on the basis of intensity, strength, approval, beauty, or any other feature on which they differ in degree. Some sample lists are provided below. A thesaurus is invaluable in generating further lists.

Connotative / Denotative Meanings

TO THE STUDENT:

Sometimes there are many words that can describe an action or a person or a thing. For example,

plod, skip, saunter, wobble

are all words that describe how someone can walk.

For each part below, put an X beside the one choice that tells what the words at the top describe.
The first is done for you.

(1) plod, skip, saunter, wobble are all

___X___ how people walk
_____ how people eat
_____ animal parts
_____ names of bugs

(2) devour, consume, shovel in are all

_____ ways of talking
_____ ways of walking
_____ animal names
_____ ways of eating

ailment	astound	loathe	afraid	love
poor health	astonish	abhor	panicky	like
illness	flabbergast	dislike	terrified	adore
sickness	surprise	hate	scared	admire
disease	predictable	despise	frightened	tolerate

5. For older students, ask them to consult a newspaper or periodical. Ask them to jot down all the different words that are used to denote speaking, for example. Have them discuss differences in meaning that result from words like: said, remarked, exclaimed, discussed, disagreed, argued, and so on. Similar lists could be made for walking or running (the sports section is replete with such examples, however hackneyed they may be).

(3) buddy, pal, acquaintance are all

_____ types of friends
_____ types of enemies
_____ ways of saying hello
_____ ways of crying

(4) brook, stream, creek are all

_____ squeaky noises
_____ bodies of running water
_____ parade parts
_____ football plays

(5) wail, sob, whimper are all

_____ ways of eating
_____ sea animals
_____ ways of crying
_____ kinds of cars

connotative

denotative

meanings

connotative

denotative

6. As a modification of item 2, omit two words in a sentence frame, asking students to select pairs of words that go together.

The _____boy _____through the park.
(frightened, happy, pensive; sneaked, skipped, strolled)

AMBIGUOUS WORDS

The last three tasks fall under the rubric of ambiguous words, implying that the meaning is not always clear. We will deal with three kinds of ambiguous words:words with multiple meanings, homophones (words that sound alike but have different spellings and meanings) and homographs (words that are spelled alike but have different pronunciations and meanings).

Multiple Meanings

Most words have more than one meaning. It is through the use of sentence and paragraph context that we are able to decide which alternative meaning to assign a word (fly = soar versus fly = insect). Furthermore, the more commonly a particular word is used in the language, the more meanings it is likely to have. Contrast common words like run, fly, bear, case, and hit with uncommon words like platypus, microscope, flattery, and van. In the former set each word has several common meanings, whereas in the latter set each word has, at most, a few meanings.

As was the case for the connotative-denotative task, there is a point at which we are happy if a student is able to select a single meaning (hopefully the one associated with a reading selection) for a given word. But there is a later point at which we want that same student to recognize the multiple meanings assigned to a given word.

When can instruction in multiple meanings begin? Again, there is no set time. It hardly seems worth the effort in grade 1, although we have found many five-year-olds who recognize the fact that words have multiple meanings (as in evidenced by their penchant for puns). Certainly beginning sometime in primary years and continuing throughout formal schooling years, such activities are desirable and necessary.

Below are listed several activities that can be used to promote an awareness of multiple meanings.

1. Definition or usage. Ask to provide definitions or sentence contexts for words you wish to stress. For example, you may say, "Use each of the following words in three (or four or five) different sentences which show the different meanings of the word."

plant	run	watch
ring	check	bank
order	stand	swing

2. Definition matching. Write the word in various sentences and ask the pupils to match the appropriate sentence and definitions.

(a) She wore a wedding *ring*.	(a) Sound of a bell.
(b) The boxer left the *ring*.	(b) A number of objects in a circle.
(c) Do you see that *ring* of trees?	(c) Circular band worn on finger.
(d) I heard a loud *ring*.	(d) Site of a boxing match

3. Sentence matching. This activity is the same as the one above except the task is to match sentences which portray the same meaning of the word.

(a) His *watch* keeps good time.
(b) Are you going to *watch* television?
(c) The guard had a quiet *watch*.

(a) His relief came before the end of the *watch*.
(b) My *watch* is at the jewelers.
(c) Did you *watch* the parade?

4. Sentence writing. In this case the meaning of the word is shown by its use in a sentence. The pupil's task is to write a new sentence which shows the same meaning.

1. My sister got a job·at the *plant*.

_____

2. They brought me a *plant* when I was in the hospital.

_____

3. Tomorrow we will *plant* the shrubs.

_____

5. Illustrations. Primary-grade children in particular enjoy drawing pictures to demonstrate concepts. One such activity looks like this.

Double Trouble

Many words have double meanings. Draw pictures to show the double meanings of some of these words!

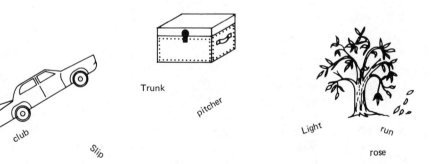

6. The narf game. Use a nonsense word like *narf* to substitute for a real word missing in three or four sentences. Each time "narf" is used, it is used with a different meaning of the intended word in mind. When students think they know the real word, have them locate the page in the dictionary where the word is found (this feature allows the game to go on even after the faster students have found the word). After a few

examples, students at grade 3 and above can generate their own examples.

1. A *narf* is not the kind of animal you would like to meet alone in the woods.
2. That apple tree should *narf* fruit this year.
3. The burden was too much to *narf*.
4. The stock market was in a *narf* cycle. (narf = bear)

7. The narf game can be translated into an independent activity by allowing students choices to select from when they encounter the item on a worksheet. For example in number 6, the choices might be, wolf, give, take, and bear. Notice that each choice fits at least one of the sentences, but only bear fits all four.

Homographs

Homographs are words that are spelled alike but differ in both pronunciation and meaning, words like read (rhymes with heed) and read (rhymes with red) or CONtent (material) and conTENT (happy). Homographs could be a potential problem in reading comprehension if there were enough of them in our English writing system to cause confusion. Fortunately there are not very many. We have listed the most common below.

aged	contract	minute	stingy
arch	desert	mow	subject
august	digest	nice	tarry
bases	do	object	tear
bass	does	patent	tier
blessed	dove	permit	transfer
bow	entrance	present	use
bower	excuse	primer	vice
buffet	forte	project	wind
close	gallant	read	wound
collect	gill	record	bowed
colon	herb	refuse	converse
commune	hinder	retail	convert
compact	incense	row	frequent
conduct	intern	seer	kinder
conjure	intimate	sewer	leading
conserve	invalid	shower	perfect
console	job	singer	putter
consort	lead	slaver	prayer
content	live	sow	relay

We have not encountered a host of instructional activities for deal-ing with homographs; however, the following can be used starting in the intermediate years.

1. Definition matching. Students match a sentence using one of the members of the homographic pair with an appropriate definition.

John will *lead* us into the mine. _____   1. guide
Watch out for the *lead* pipe. _____   2. a metal

2. Sentence construction. Encourage students to construct sen-tences using both members of a homographic pair.

John will lead us into the lead mine.
I hope the garbageman will not refuse our refuse.
I would like to record your new record on my tape machine.
Without a permit, they will not permit us to enter the park.

Homophones

There is considerable dispute regarding the positive or negative in-fluence of homophones—words that sound alike but differ in spelling and meaning. On the one hand, their existence forces us as readers to learn that two different spellings can yield the same pronunciation; on the other hand, the different spellings provide an additional cue to meaning. For example, when we see the word *fly,* we do not know whether it is the insect or the soaring that is referred to; however, when we see *reed,* we know the referent is a tall grass and not what we do with words (read). Consider what our writing system would be like without homophones. Read the three versions of a paragraph which follow.

Ether the none oar the buoy herd the bell, butt the bell told four sumwon else.

ēthər the nŭn ōr thə boi hurd thə bĕl, bət thə bĕl tōld for sŭmwŭn ĕls.

Either the nun or the boy heard the bell, but the bell tolled for someone else.

The point is that homophones are not necessarily negative influ-ences on reading comprehension. They may confuse the decoding task, but they may help the comprehension task in reading.

The following types of activities may be used to help students deal with homophones.

1. Definition matching. As with homographs, students can match a member of a homophonous pair with appropriate definitions.

Sarah *threw* the ball at the wall. _____   1. hurled
He is *through* with the job. _____   2. finished

2. Sentence construction. Have students construct sentences using both members of an homophonous pair.

The thieves tried to steal the steel pipes.
George felt weak all week.
She just sits there and stares at the stairs.
The boat went straight through the strait.
You mean she dug the whole hole.
I thought the bus fare was fair.
She threw the ball through the window.
She taught us how to tie a taut knot.
We were not allowed to read aloud.

3. "Hinks hinks." Remember the old hink pink game. One person gives a definition, the other person supplies the answer, to which is a pair of words that rhyme. For example, a fruit thief is a *melon felon,* or a sign for a horse ranch might be a *stable label.* Well, hink hinks are simply the same word used twice. Sometimes they are homophones; a *cannon canon* is a law governing the use of large guns or a bargain on iron might be a *steel steal.* Other times they are multiple meanings of the same word form: a *fair fair* might be defined as a mediocre exposition, or a person who sells property boundary markers on the black market might be called a *fence fence.* You may want to use some from the list below as a way of starting students on building a classroom collection.

1. A person who sells stolen property boundary markers on the black market (hink hink).
2. A post mortem discussion following an arithmetic exam (hinkity hinkity)*
3. A law governing the use of large guns (hinky hinky)
4. The correct answer as to the identity of a mystery liquid in a chemistry class (hinkity hinkity)
5. A quick diet involving complete abstention (hink hink)
6. A serious tomb (hink hink)
7. 20 runs in base ball (hink hink)
8. 144 hink hinks (hink hink)
9. A crude class (hink hink)
10. A tie in a shoving contest (hink hink)
11. Someone who entertains scads of people (hink hink)
12. A groovy bodyjoint (hink hink)
13. Someone who monitors the output of a factory producing a game played a lot on park benches (hinky hinky)
14. Someone who monitors the people in 13 (hinky hinky hinky)
15. A great apartment manager (in the east) (hinky hinky)

16. A fantastic large firewood holder (hink hink hink)
17. A unique work of fiction (hinky hinky)
18. A lawyer's portfolio (hink hink)
19. The outcome of overindulging in brinesoaked cucumbers (hinky hinky)
20. A tentative plan for conscription (hink hink)
21. Construction of an edifice (hinky hinky)
22. A stand-in below water machine (hink hink)
23. An unusual accomplishment with one-s hindlimbs (hink hink)
24. A more sunburned leather processer (hinky hinky)
25. A device for spying on insects (hink hink)
26. A matching partner (hink hink)
27. A spare special edition of the newspaper (hinky hinky)
28. A sixth tire for a car (hink hink)
29. The head of the Goodyear Company (hink hink)
30. A period of time when everyone's into motor bikes (hinky hinky)
31. A high quality group of students (hink hink)
      or
    A high quality course
32. A reasonable amount to pay for a bus ride to a mediocre exposition about explosives (hink hink hink hink hink)
33. Floating billards (hink hink)
34. The night before the night before (hink hink)
35. A contest to determine which company makes the best fire lighters (hink hink)
36. A box for storing torsos (hink hink)
37. A lousy hobo (hink hink)
38. A really *in* place to stay temporarily in the woods (hink hink)
39. A lousy citrus fruit (hinky hinky)
40. A farm animal stricken with laryngitis (hink hink)
41. A footprint on a sprinter's oval (hink hink)
42. A common aircraft (hink hink)
43. A stove on the prairie (hink hink)
44. An attack on your car's source of electrical power (hinkity hinkity)

1. fence fence
2. aftermath aftermath
3. cannon canon
4. solution solution
5. fast fast
6. grave grave
7. score score
8. gross gross
9. coarse course
10. push push
11. host host
12. hip hip
13. checker checker
14. checker checker checker
15. super super
16. great great grate
17. novel novel
18. brief brief

19. pickle pickle
20. draft draft
21. building building
22. sub sub
23. feet feat
24. tanner tanner
25. bug bug
26. turn turn
27. extra extra
28. spare spare
29. blimp blimp
30. cycle cycle
31. class class
32. fair fair fair fare
33. pool pool
34. eve eve
35. match match
36. chest chest
37. bum bum
38. camp camp
39. lemon lemon
40. hoarse horse
41. track track
42. plain plane
43. range range
44. battery battery

4. No section on homophones would be complete without suggesting the proverbial "pair tree" display for a classroom. As students come up with homophonous pairs, they write the pair on a paper pear and add it to the "pair" tree constructed of tagboard or the like.

5. As a resource for structuring activities in homophones or homographs, we suggest that you add a copy of *A dictionary of American homophones and homographs* to your library (Whitford, 1966).

A FINAL WORD

In this chapter we have attempted to specify the set of concept level comprehension tasks that we consider worthy of teaching. For the most part, those tasks represent simple and complex relations (or associations) among concepts. Of the nine tasks presented, the first six are closely bound to the comprehension model presented in Chapter 3; that is, those six are examples of ways in which teachers can manipulate instruction in order to modify and expand the kinds of semantic maps students carry around in their heads. The last three, characterized as ambiguous words, are not so directly integrated with that same model of comprehension. Nevertheless, we feel that it is important for you to emphasize those tasks because they represent possible complications in the process of reading comprehension. We have also tried to offer examples of specific activities that you can use to begin an instructional program for each of these tasks.

In closing this chapter it is appropriate to highlight a few points that have been implied throughout.

1. At least for word level comprehension tasks, the number of formats in which they can be presented or practiced is virtually unlimited.

Most of the game formats that are so widely used for word identification activities can be modified for word level comprehension tasks. Note, for example, how many times we suggested a concentration format for different tasks. Also, the computer box activity could be used for several of these tasks.

2. Simply giving students worksheets or games and allowing them to practice on their own is not sufficient. Discussion and feedback are important to clarification of many of these tasks. We will have more to say about specific interaction strategies later in Chapter 9. But we underscore their importance here, lest you get the impression that we advocate a paper-and-pencil curriculum.

3. As we introduce longer discourse level tasks (in Chapter 5 and 6), we will often use the constructs we have built in this chapter as analogues of sentence level comprehension tasks.

REFERENCES

Davis, F. B. Fundamental Factors of Comprehension in Reading. *Psychometrika,* 1944, 9, 185–197.

Gove, P. B., Editor. *Webster's New Dictionary of Synonyms,* Springfield, Mass: G. C. Merriam Company, 1973.

Spearritt, D. Identification of Subskills of Reading Comprehension by Maximum Likelihood Factor Analysis. *Reading Research Quarterly,* 1972, 8, 92–111.

Whitford, H. C. *A Dictionary of American Homophones and Homographs.* New York: Teachers College Press, 1966.

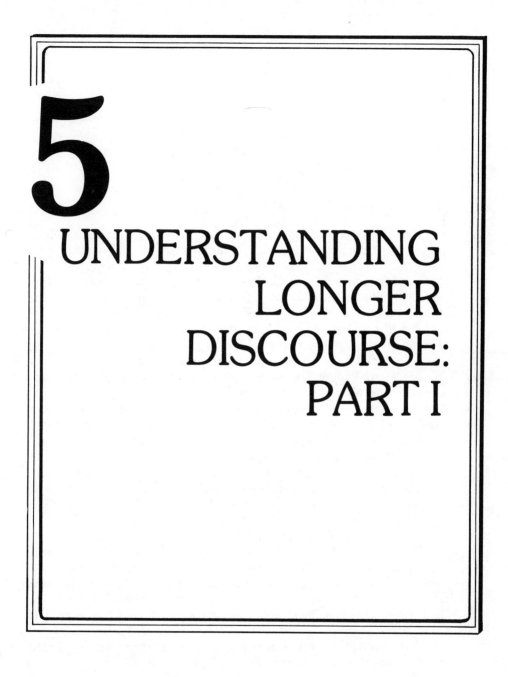

5
UNDERSTANDING LONGER DISCOURSE: PART I

"I don't have any trouble with the sentences; it's the words that get in my way."

—*Anonymous quote allegedly attributable to a nine-year-old boy*

IN CHAPTER 3, we began our discussion with concepts and then moved on to the propositions typical of longer discourse; in Chapter 4, we treated instructional techniques for developing concepts. Now we move to instructional methods that will help students better understand and deal with longer discourse such as, propositions, sentences, paragraphs, passages.

It will take two chapters to complete the task. We admit that the division between Chapters 5 and 6 is somewhat arbitrary. But we wanted to provide this information in two short chapters rather than one long chapter. Part of our motivation is consistency in length across chapters, but most of it stems from our own realization that what is in Chapters 5 and 6 is "tough sledding." The chapters were the hardest to write; we suspect they are the hardest to read. We encourage you to read them carefully, partially because of their difficulty and partially because of their centrality to comprehension.

In Chapter 4, we presented you with a taxonomy, a chart of relations that exist between concepts. We will begin our treatment of longer discourse with a similar chart entitled, Propositional Level Comprehension (Table 5.1). As noted in Chapter 3, the term proposition is borrowed from another discipline, logic, and is commonly used by psychologists to discuss relations of ideas in written discourse. While it has a more precise logical definition, a simple definition will serve our purposes. A *proposition* is an assertion about the world that typically takes the form of a clause (sometimes a phrase) or a sentence (Thorndyke, 1977). All sentences contain at least one proposition, but a sentence may have more than one proposition.

The goals of this chapter are to describe (1) how readers comprehend relations among propositions, (2) what types of relations among propositions readers must understand, and (3) how teachers can structure lessons to facilitate students' comprehension of such relations.

While understanding relations among concepts (and teaching vocabulary) is an important aspect of comprehension, understanding relations among propositions is a more central aspect of comprehension. The activities in this chapter deal with comprehension of text—real written discourse. Most of us would agree that acquiring information from written discourse is the ultimate goal of all comprehension instruction regardless of whether it deals with words, clauses, sentences, paragraphs, or passages. In this sense, this chapter is really the heart of this book.

If you have not read Chapter 4, which concentrates on understanding concepts typically expressed as words, it will be useful for you to do so before you read this chapter. Whenever possible, we have listed concept level analogues (from Chapter 4) of the proposition level tasks described in the present chapter. We use these because we have found that those concept level analogues (which are relatively easy to understand) serve to clarify proposition level tasks (which are not always so easy to understand). Unfortunately, there is not a one-to-one match between concept level and proposition level tasks. Some concept level tasks, like homophones and homographs, have no substantial propositional level counterparts; conversely, certain propositional level tasks, like causal relations or time relations, have no concept level analogues. Nevertheless, whenever comparisons can be made between these two levels, we will make them in the spirit of trying to clarify and simplify some seemingly complex relations.

PROPOSITION LEVEL TASKS

Table 5.1 lists the basic propositional level comprehension tasks, along with descriptions, examples (where feasible), and concept level analogues. In Chapters 5 and 6, we will deal with each in the order listed. For each task, we will describe the nature of the task, justify its inclusion in the list, and specify instructional activities or guidelines you can use to help students deal with discourse expressing such relations. We remind you, once again, that these activities are suggestive not inclusive. We know there are many other activities equally as appropriate as those we list. We hope you create some even more appropriate than ours.

Paraphrase

Asking students to identify or construct a paraphrase for a proposition is similar to asking them to identify a synonym for a word. The commonality is in recognizing the equivalence in meaning between two linguistic elements.

There are two aspects to recognizing propositional paraphrases—

TABLE 5.1 Propositional Level Comprehension

Task	Word Level Analogue	Example	Description
1. Paraphrase	Synonym	The lady shut the door = The door was closed by the woman.	Recognize the equivalence in meaning between two or more sentences.
2. Association	Association		Student reads paragraph. Selects the one sentence that is out of place in the paragraph.
3. Main Idea— Details	Classification		Student reads paragraph. Then 1. Selects the main idea, or 2. Selects details that support a main idea.
4. Comparison	Analogies	One paragraph is about bicycles, a second about canoes. Question: How are the pedals on a bicycle like the oars in a canoe?	After reading a paragraph, student compares relationships therein to relationships in another paragraph, story, or experience.
5. Figurative Language	Connotation-Denotation	1. John is a veritable gazelle = John can run fast.	1. Recognizes the equivalence between a figurative and a literal statement, and 2. Recognizes the difference in tone and feeling communicated by the two sentences.

6. Ambiguous Statements	Multiple Meanings	Flying planes can be dangerous = 1. It can be dangerous to fly planes. 2. It can be dangerous to be around where airplanes are flying.	1. Recognizes that a single sentence can have more than one meaning, *and* 2. Selects the appropriate meaning for a given paragraph context.
7. Causal Relations		The people revolted because the new king was a tyrant. 1. Why did the people revolt? 2. What happened because the new king was a tyrant?	1. Can identify causes or explanations (answer *why questions*), *or* 2. Can identify effects (answer *what happened because or what will happen next* questions).
8. Sequence		John went into the store. He bought a new tire. Then he went home to put it on his bike. What happened after John bought a new tire?	After reading a paragraph, 1. Places events in the sequence explicated in the paragraph, *or* 2. Answers *when* or *what happened after* or *what happened before* questions.
9. Anaphora		*John* is my friend. *He* is kind. *I play ball. So does* Henry.	Recognizes the logical equivalence between an anaphoric (substitute) term and its antecedent.

syntactic and semantic. Remembering the introduction to syntax and semantics provided in Chapter 2, two propositions can be equivalent if they have different syntactic forms (surface structure) but the same underlying meaning (deep structure). Hence sentences (1) and (2) are paraphrases of one another.

(1) The slender lady shut the door.
(2) The door was shut by the slender lady.

Similarly, two propositions can be paraphrases of one another because one proposition contains words that are semantically equivalent to the words in another proposition. Hence (3) is a paraphrase of (1).

(3) The thin woman closed the door.

Combining these two factors, then, (4) is a paraphrase of (2), differing only in the words used in the sentence.

(4) The door was closed by the thin woman.

And we would probably want to argue that sentences (1), (2), (3), and (4) are all paraphrases of one another, that is, they all communicate a similar (if not identical) underlying meaning.

(5) The lady who was slender shut the door.

The word *similar* needs to be emphasized. Recall our discussion of synonyms: no two words are ever truly synonymous; if they were, there would be no need for one of them, and one would, accordingly, drop out of the language. Similarly, there are probably no two propositions that are exact paraphrases of one another. For one thing, whenever synonyms are used, precise paraphrase is automatically ruled out. But even with syntactic paraphrases, such as the pairs (1)-(2) and (3)-(4), and (1)-(5), there is a subtle different in focus communicated by shifts in the grammatical arrangement of words on the page. In (1) the focus is on the *lady* whereas in (2) the focus is on the *door*. The phrase *the slender lady* somehow implies that her slenderness is an important attribute of her being; in contrast, *the lady who is slender* implies little more than that her slenderness serves as an identifying attribute (enabling us to distinguish her from other ladies in the room, perhaps).

These qualifications are important but they need not discourage us from presenting students with paraphrase tasks. The ability to paraphrase and to recognize paraphrase is one of the best available indexes of comprehension. In a more global sense of the word *paraphrase,* the ability to restate something "in your own words" is a true test of understanding. Furthermore, English is a language with many options, many ways of expressing a given idea—a fact which has given many writers fitful nights ("I just cannot find the right way to say what I want to say"). To be a competent listener or reader, one must acquire this paraphrase ability.

Along with many teachers with whom we have shared ideas, we have found the following activities to be useful.

1. Match a sentence. Students are given a standard sentence and two or three choices from which they are to select the one sentence that means the same as the standard. Sets of instructional items can be placed upon a ditto master for independent practice, or the items can be placed on index cards for use in a game format (see Chapter 4). The task can be sequenced in difficulty by first including only syntactic paraphrases, then semantic paraphrases, then both.

Syntactic Paraphrase: *Susan hit the ball.*

1. The ball was hit by Susan.
2. Susan was hit by the ball.
3. Susan was hit ball by.

Semantic Paraphrase: *Susan napped on the carpet.*

1. Susan slept on the tacks.
2. Susan rubbed on the rug.
3. Susan slept on the rug.

Both semantic and syntactic paraphrases: *The tortoise beat the hare in a race.*

1. The rabbit was defeated by the turtle in a race.
2. The wig was whipped by the turtle in a contest.
3. The hare beat the tortoise in a race.

2. Indicate the sentence that does not match. A variation of the first activity, equally as amenable to a variety of formats, involves selecting the one sentence that does not mean the same as the others. Again both syntactic and semantic variation can be used.

1. Unless you get an *A* in arithmetic, you cannot play football.
2. If you do not receive an *A* in mathematics, you cannot play football.
3. If you get an *A* in football, you cannot play mathematics.

3. Say it another way. Exposed to a discussion about different ways to communicate the same idea and armed with a thesaurus or synonym dictionary, students can be given lists of sentences to rewrite on their own. Sometimes complex statements can be simplified; other times, simple statements can be made more complicated. One classic examples comes to mind. "Do not numerically iterate your Australorps prior to the point in their development when they mature from intraovum to extraovum stages." *Or,* "don't count your chickens before they hatch."

Association

If you recall our discussion of associations among concepts in Chapter 4 (grass-green, dog-bite), you will remember the difficulty we had clarifying the function of concept association tasks, even though we were convinced that it was essential for students to engage in association activities. We have a similar difficulty here; again, we are convinced that such tasks merit your instructional time and effort. In fact one of the virtues of such tasks stems from their value in helping so-called remedial readers, although we would not limit the activities to remedial students.

Intermediate and secondary students who have failed to learn to read exhibit certain characteristics. One such characteristic is that they have learned that what you read need not make sense. They do not expect that words on a page should make sense to them in the same way that speech makes sense. A successful reconditioning approach has involved inserting anomolous (nonsensical) clauses and sentences into paragraphs and stories, instructing students to search for ideas that do not make sense, do not fit with the rest of the paragraph.

First, we operate entirely in a listening mode, asking students to stop the speaker (or the tape recorder) whenever they hear a sentence that seems out of place in the story or paragraph. Then we move to the written mode, asking students to underline or cross out statements that seem out of place. If you think back to our discussion of schemata (Chapter 3), you will recognize how such an activity fits into our over-riding notion of comprehension as building bridges between the new and the known.

It is not too difficult to structure such activities. What you need to begin with is some paragraphs that make sense, ones in which all the component sentences fit an overall theme. Then you insert a sentence related to a totally different topic. Students are asked to underline the sentence that does not fit with the rest of the paragraph. Sentence (c) in (6) illustrates such an anomoly.

(6) (a) Birds build nests in a variety of places. (b) Robins build nests in trees. (c) Caterpilars spin cocoons. (d) Pheasants build nests in bushes. (e) Eagles build nests on rocky cliffs.

The task can be adjusted to different levels of ability and sophistication by varying the degree to which the anomolous sentence (or sentences) "misfits" the paragraph. For example, had we inserted (f) in place of (c), the task would have been easier. But (g) would have made the task more difficult.

(f) What a nice new table!
(g) Bluejays like to eat worms.

Main Ideas—Details

We know of no aspect of comprehension so universally accepted yet so often confused as the notion of "Finding the Main Idea." One can find such exercises in materials written for kindergarten and first-grade students as well as for college students. And in intermediate and secondary reading programs, no comprehension activity is complete without a main idea item.

Yet we find much confusion when we examine the range of available instructional items. Sometimes it appears as though the main idea is the most general idea in a paragraph or passage, a *theme* that logically subsumes all the other sentences in the paragraph or paragraphs in a passage. Other times, what is called for is really little more than a topic, perhaps a category label like, Trains, that generally describes what the paragraph *is about*. Still other times, what appears to be called for is the most *important* thought in the paragraph—not the most general, not a topic, but the most *significant* statement. Finally, "finding the topic sentence" for a paragraph and "choosing the best title" for a passage find their way into the maze of main idea activities.

The notion of "details" is also ambiguous, especially as details relate to main ideas. Comprehension of factual details is often taken to mean that a student can answer specific detail questions such as, Who opened the door? or When did Sam get his reward? In other circumstances, comprehension of details means that a student recognizes the details that support a main idea or the examples that support a generalization. In this latter sense, details assume greater importance as a legitimate aspect of comprehension. In the former sense, comprehension of details (often called factual recall) has conveniently served as a professional "straw man" for those critics of comprehension instruction who like to point out that the teachers spend most of their time asking detail questions (Guzak, 1967) when they really ought to be dealing with higher-order comprehension tasks.

We will take the point of view that comprehension of details is an important aspect of comprehension *if and only if* detail questions are used to help students identify facts that support broader generalizations, main ideas.

Earlier we referred to a rampant confusion in main idea activities. It is a surface confusion. What all but one (finding the most important thought) of those examples have in common is a logical relation between more general and more specific propositions. In this regard, finding a main idea, or a topic, or a topic sentence is similar to finding a category label for a list of words (see Chapter 4). Finding the main idea requires the reader to recognize that some of the propositions are *examples* of the most general proposition intended to serve as *the main idea*. An example will help. In paragraph (7), propositions (a), (b), and (c) serve as examples of proposition (d), in much the same way as collies, dobermans, and spaniels serve as examples of dogs (see Chapter 3, the section on semantic maps).

(7). (a) Robins build nests in trees. (b) Pheasants build nests in bushes. (c) Eagles build nests in rocks. (d) Birds build nests in a variety of places.

In fact, we believe that it is wise to use examples of word (really concept) categorization as an introduction to main idea activities, especially with elementary school children.

SOME GUIDELINES FOR TEACHING MAIN IDEAS. In working with teachers and students to try to make sense out of main idea instruction, we have developed the following set of guidelines.

1. Not all paragraphs have main ideas, either stated explicitly or implicitly. Much fictional material and even some expository material is simply an enumeration of detail. Consider paragraph (8).

(8) John Smith stood in the hot afternoon sun. He pushed his straw hat back on his head. Leaning on his shovel, he peered underneath a large grapevine. Out of a hole in the ground, two large eyes peered back at him.

We might be able to generate a cute title for the paragraph, such as, Eyeball to Eyeball. But only the last two propositions in the paragraph fit neatly under that idea. A plausible but meaningless main idea might be, Some things that happened to John Smith. Students, especially in the early stages of instruction, should not be asked to find the main ideas for a paragraph without clear-cut main ideas explicitly stated in the text. Students at any age level should not be asked to find main ideas for paragraphs that do not have main ideas, explicit or implicit. In short, you have to be very careful about your selection of paragraphs for main idea instruction. Begin with clear cases. If the main idea is not obvious to you, chances are it will not be obvious to your students.

2. Some main ideas are more important than other main ideas. Contrast the main idea in paragraph (9) with the main idea in paragraph (7).

(9) Because robins eat insects, worms, and other creatures found in wooded areas, they build their nests in trees. Pheasants feed on marsh grasses and grains. So they build their nests in grasslands or grainfields. You can find an eagle's nest (called an aerie) high among the arid rocky crags that hide snakes, rodents, and jackrabbits. Where a bird builds its nest depends upon its main source of food.

To us the main idea at the end of paragraph (9) is intuitively more important than the main idea in paragraph (7). It says something substantive about the world. It gives you a rule or a generalization for dealing with the world. The main idea in paragraph (7), by contrast, is almost vacuous. We have developed an operational test to rate the importance of main ideas. We call it the "Aha!–So What!" test. If the main idea elicits an Aha! reaction, it is probably a meaningful conclusion, generalization, or rule about an event, type of event, or kind of behavior. If it elicits a So What! reaction, it is probably a relatively vacuous summary label for a set of events or behaviors.

If our intuitions (and yours) are correct, there are some instructional implications. First, you should include a large proportion of Aha! main ideas among the items you ask your students to complete, lest they get the impression that all main ideas are largely unimportant, irrelevant summary statements. Second, at least by junior high school, it might be useful to ask students to try to distinguish between So What! and Aha! main ideas—if not for their reading comprehension, at least for their composition skills.

This Aha!–So What! test is probably related to the distinction between so-called topics and main ideas. Topics tend to communicate little substantive or important information. They simply prepare the reader for what is to come. Consider your reaction to a speaker who says, "Now I am going to talk about phonics." Your internal reaction is probably something like, "Oh! That's great! But get to it. Now that we know what you are going to talk about, tell us what you are going to *say*." The speaker might give several examples of children who did and did not benefit from phonics instruction, concluding, "Phonics should be taught only to those children who do not seem to be able to pick it up on their own through sheer exposure to print." The last statement is more like the main idea of his talk, and may elicit an Aha! reaction on your part. Furthermore, the examples that were presented along the way (the details) likely served to support that main idea.

We are not saying that you should not ask your students to identify topics and to use topics and topic sentences when they write. We are suggesting that topics be recognized for what they are (thematic cues to let the reader know what parts of his or her knowledge store, what schemata, to use) and that they not be confused with what we are calling main ideas. In fact, we believe that instruction in finding topics should probably precede instruction in finding the main idea. First, while we have no direct evidence, we suspect that it is easier to recognize that a paragraph is about birds and their nests than it is to reach (and remember) the concluding main idea in paragraph (9). Second, finding a topic is probably more like finding a category label for a set of words, a skill that younger readers are likely to be familiar with when you begin main idea instruction.

3. There are a limited number of ways in which text can be organized, and teachers can vary text organization to facilitate students' development in dealing with main idea–detail relations.

First, main ideas can be stated (explicit) or unstated (implicit). Second, main ideas can be stated early in a paragraph or they can be stated at the end of a paragraph. Third, the main idea–detail relation can be one of two types: label-list or rule-example. A label-list relation is illustrated by the paragraph in stage 1 (birds build nests in a variety of places). A rule-example relation is illustrated by the paragraph in stage 3 (where a bird builds its nest depends upon its main source of food). We believe that main idea instruction can be facilitated if these three factors are combined to generate the following sequence:

Stage 1: Explicit main ideas are stated at the beginning of a paragraph for label-list relations.

> Birds build nests in a variety of places. Robins build nests in trees. Pheasants build nests in bushes. Eagles build nests in rocks.

Stage 2: Same as stage 1, except that the main idea comes at the end of the paragraph.

> Robins build nests in trees. Pheasants build nests in bushes. Eagles build nests in rocks. Birds build nests in a variety of places.

Stage 3: Explicit main ideas are stated at the beginning of a paragraph for rule-example relations.

Where a bird builds its nest depends upon its main source of food. Because robins eat insects, worms, and other creatures found in wooded areas, they build their nests in trees. Pheasants feed on marsh grasses and grains. So they build their nests in grasslands or grainfields. You can find an eagle's nest (called an aerie) high among the arid rocky crags that hide snakes, rodents, and jackrabbits.

Stage 4: Same as stage 3, except that the main idea comes at the end of the paragraph.

Because robins eat insects, worms, and other creatures found in wooded areas, they build their nests in trees. Pheasants feed on marsh grasses and grains. So they build their nests in grasslands or grainfields. You can find an eagle's nest (called an aerie) high among the arid rocky crags that hide snakes, rodents, and jackrabbits. Where a bird builds its nest depends upon its main source of food.

Stage 5: Implicit main ideas for label-list relations.

Robins build nests in trees. Pheasants build nests in bushes. Eagles build nests in rocks.

Stage 6: Implicit main ideas for rule-example relations.

Because robins eat insects, worms, and other creatures found in wooded areas, they build their nests in trees. Pheasants feed on marsh grasses and grains. So they build their nests in grasslands or grainfields. You can find an eagle's nest (called an aerie) high among the arid rocky crags that hide snakes, rodents, and jackrabbits.

Within each stage, the task can be made easier by giving the students a set of choices from which to choose. Obviously, then, it can be made more difficult by asking the students to find (or, in stages 5 and 6, create) the main idea. Set 1 would be appropriate for stages 1, 2, and 5; Set 2, for stages 3, 4, and 6.

Set 1:

1. Robins build nests in trees.
2. Birds do things.
3. Last summer.
4. Birds build nests in a variety of places.

Set 2:

1. Robins eat insects.
2. Birds like to eat.
3. Jackrabbits.
4. Birds tend to build nests near their food source.

We encourage you to use these four factors (explicitness, position of main idea, type of relation, and item format) as an aid in building your own main idea programs or as selection criteria in choosing materials for your students.

4. Main idea instruction is not an entity unto itself. It is, as we have implied, intrinsically related to other comprehension activities, such as categorizing. It is also closely related to activities that some would label study skills, such as outlining and summarizing. Consider what you do when you make an outline of a chapter in a book. Remember all those indentings with roman numerals, capital letters, arabic numerals, and lower-case letters. Essentially what you are doing is placing ideas (propositions) in logical relation to one another. Bigger (more general) ideas occupy farther left positions than do smaller (more specific) ideas. An outline is not unlike a semantic map (Chapter 3) for a text segment. Later in this section, we will suggest that outlining provides a useful visual model for illustrating to students how main ideas and details fit together.

5. To teach main ideas, you cannot rely on the principle of sheer practice—the more practice activities students complete, the better they will perform. Direct teaching, modeling and feedback, and discussion are necessary. Here are some techniques we have found to be useful.

Try a visual model to explain how a main idea relates to the details that support it. (See Figures 5.1 and 5.2.) Or try an outline format.

I. MI_1
   A. Detail 1
   B. Detail 2
   C. Detail 3
II. MI_2
   A. Detail 1
   B. Detail 2

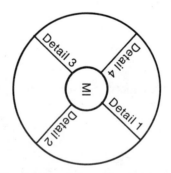

Fig. 5.1.   A hub and the spokes that keep it off the ground.

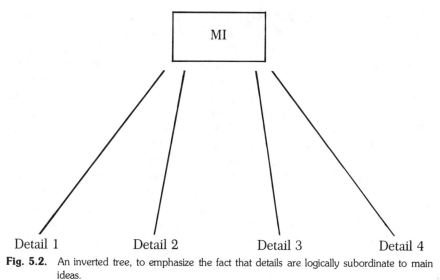

Fig. 5.2. An inverted tree, to emphasize the fact that details are logically subordinate to main ideas.

Try a key lexical item analysis of a paragraph with a group of students. For the paragraph on stage 1, ask older students to underline each subject noun, then each verb. Then ask students to look for a relationship between the nouns and the verbs. The net result for that paragraph is *Robins, Pheasants, Eagles, Birds* for the nouns; for the verbs, *build, build, build, build.*

Do not keep paragraph organization a secret. Encourage students to examine first and last sentences of a paragraph to see if the main idea is contained therein. If the main idea is stated at all, it will usually be in one of these two places.

Most multiple-choice test items are built in a particular format. Some choices are too general; some are too specific; some are irrelevant; and some are just right. Examine and discuss choices with students, pointing out the various categories of incorrect responses. Here is an example based upon the paragraph in stage 1.

What is the main idea of this paragraph?

1. Robins build nests in trees—too specific.
2. Birds do things—too general.
3. How Janet spent her weekend—irrelevant.
4. Birds build nests in a variety of places—right level of generality.

Comparison

Like association, the comparison task is included to account for a small but important facet of the comprehension of longer discourse.

Furthermore, we admit at the outset that comparison in the most general sense of the term is involved in many of the other tasks in our propositional level list of tasks. For example, you cannot complete paraphrase tasks without *comparing* the two propositions whose equality you are judging. Figurative language involves comparisons. When we say that John is as slow as a snail, we are *comparing* John's speed with a snail's. You must *compare* alternative interpretations of an ambiguous statement to determine whether or not they are acceptable. In its generic sense, comparison is involved in many comprehension tasks.

However, we mean something more specific. A reader is exposed to one text segment, then another. Finally the reader is asked to determine how aspects of the one segment were alike or different from the other. Alternatively, a reader is exposed to one text segment, then asked to compare it with his or her own experience. For example, (10) and (11) require such a comparison between a text segment and a reader's experience.

(10) What did Susan and Henry study that you also study?
(11) What do you do in school that is similar to (different from) what Susan and Henry did?

Comparisons between two text segments might be probed by (12), (13), or (14).

(12) How was the Civil War like the Revolutionary War?
(13) Were the weapons of the Civil War different from those used in the Civil War? How?
(14) Henry had a pet bear whom he told his troubles to. In the story about Susan Johnson, what did she have that was like Henry's pet bear?

Referring back to the concept level tasks in Chapter 4, this comparison task is similar to both the analogy task and the category task. In the analogy task, students are asked to *compare* and find the similarity between two pairs of concepts: the relationship between a bear and a cub is *comparable* to the relationship between a cow and a calf. In the category task, students were asked to categorize concepts by *common attributes*. At the propositional level, comparing text segments often involves identifying common attributes. Asking how the Civil War was like the Revolutionary War is akin to asking a student to identify the common attributes of the two wars. Incidentally, using comprehension probes that require students to draw comparisons between events, episodes, or stories is probably one of the best techniques a teacher can use to assist students in building strong schemata or scripts. Just as comparison of a number of different types of dogs is necessary for a child to develop a concept for dog, so comparison of different wars, governments, or revolutions is likely to help students abstract, or sort out, the attributes common to these phenomena. In short, comparison exercises aid in the development of appropriate scripts.

We do not have a large number of unique suggestions for comparison activities. The questions interspersed as examples in the last few pages serve as models for the kinds of questions we find useful in directing exercise comparisons. To foreshadow a point we will expand in a later chapter, much comparison instruction must emanate from a discussion format. The give-and-take among teacher and students helps to maximize the likelihood that appropriate points of similarity and difference will emerge. Nevertheless, we have found the following activities to be useful in helping students make comparisons.

1. Use visual displays to sharpen contrasts. Charts, graphs, and tables often help to highlight contrasts. For example, in a chart of the planets you might make the comparisons in Table 5.2.

TABLE 5.2

	Distance from Sun	Orbital Duration	Number of Moons
Mercury			
Venus			
Earth			
Mars			
Jupiter			
Saturn			
Uranus			
Neptune			
Pluto			

Three South American countries might be compared on the characteristics in Table 5.3.

TABLE 5.3

	Major Product	Area	Type of Government	Population
Brazil				
Argentina				
Chile				

Charts like these can be distributed either before or after reading, depending on your purpose.

2. Augment texts. If you have consumable materials available, you can facilitate comparisons like those in Tables 5.2 and 5.3 by providing cues in the text. Suppose you have three short segments on Chile, Brazil, and Argentina. In each segment, you might underline the statements specifying the major product, circle the statements for area, asterisk the statements indicating type of government, and so on. Later you can train students to perform this task themselves.

Figurative Language

"I'm so hungry I could eat a horse!"
"Susan is as slow as a snail!"
"Tom is a real gazelle!"
"I have a frog in my throat!"
"George chatters like a monkey!"

These examples are typical of the kind of figurative language we hear and read daily. Oral language—especially casual conversation, certain forms of literature, and humor—is filled with examples of figurative language: metaphor, simile, and hyperbole. And figurative language is not limited to any educated elite. In fact, one of the distinctive features of colloquial speech or regional dialect is its peculiar set of metaphors, similes, and hyperboles—colorful language, we call it.

There is an irony about figurative language. People seem to enjoy clarifying a point by using language that is not at all clear. To say, "I'm so hungry I could eat a horse" makes the point clearer to your audience than does, "I'm very hungry." To say "Tom is a real gazelle," gives your audience a better feel for his speed than does, "Tom can run fast." One of our favorite examples is the figurative use of the word literal by television sportscasters: "He literally tore up the field." In short, we use figurative language because we believe it aids our communication.

People use figurative language because it amuses them. We cannot hear someone say, "I've got a frog in my throat," without getting at least a fleeting image of a green creature peeking its head out of the speaker's mouth. And when we hear, "My love is a red, red rose," we can appreciate the beauty of the metaphor, but, at least, the more perverse among us can conjure up an image of a "floramaniac." It is not simply amusement that motivates the continued use of figurative language; perhaps it is cleverness more generally. We appreciate a speaker or writer who can "turn a good phrase." We often reveal our envy by saying to ourselves or others, "I wish I had thought of that," or "That's a good way to look at it."

Intuitively we expect figurative language to be confusing to students. Our impulse is to believe that they will interpret the message literally. Unfortunately, there is little research on the development of figurative language comprehension and production. Hence it is difficult to refute intuitions on the basis of clear-cut data. However, we encourage you to listen to a conversation among a group of six-year-olds. Hyperbole—exaggeration—runs rampant, even if sometimes it is directed toward frivolous ends: "He's so fat, he can't move!" "That car is so fast, it looks like a flash goin' down the street."

We believe in direct instruction in figurative language. We think it should parallel the type of activity recommended in Chapter 4 for the connotation-denotation task. In many ways, the difference between the concepts *walk* and *stride* is comparable to the difference between the propositions, "John runs fast," and "John is a veritable gazelle." A figurative statement is a loose paraphrase of a literal statement. Basically, students need to learn two things about figurative language: (1) They need to be able to assign an appropriate literal interpretation to the figurative statement, and (2) They need to discriminate the differences in interpretation that are elicited by a literal proposition and one or more figurative statements. As in the case of synonyms, students need to know how these statements are alike and how they are different.

There are three kinds of figurative language that deserve attention: simile, metaphor, and hyperbole. Hyperbole, as we indicated earlier, is simple exaggeration, as in (15), (16), and (17). Metaphor and simile are similar devices.

(15) Henry is so thin that he makes a cornstalk look fat.
(16) Paul Bunyan was so big he used to pull up a pine tree to use as a toothpick.
(17) Ina eats enough for a whole army.

For example, similies (18) and (19) and metaphor (20) are decent paraphrases for one another, all references to Susan's speed.

(18) Susan is as slow as a snail.
(19) Susan is just like a snail.
(20) Susan is a snail.

Sentence (18) represents the classic form for a simile, but similes often appear with the word *like* as a comparator, as in (19). Sentence (20) gives the classic form for a metaphor. The obvious formal distinction between similies and metaphors is that metaphors do not contain the comparative terms, such as *like* or *as . . . as,* that are found in similes. Despite these formal differences, the intent of simile and metaphor is similar. In fact, at least one instructional approach to teaching simile and metaphor (Science Research Associates, 1967) regards a metaphor as a grammatical transformation of a simile going from the *as . . . as* form to the *like* form to the metaphor form, as in the sequence in (19), (18), and (20).

Figurative language can be an exciting part of a reading comprehension program. Students of many ages enjoy the humor associated with the sometimes outrageous comparisons. Here are some instructional activities you may wish to incorporate into your own program.

1. Emphasizing the comparative nature of figurative language. Begin your lesson on figurative language with a few examples like these. Say, *"Henry is tall. A tree is tall.* If we want to emphasize Henry's tallness, we might combine these statements to say, *Henry is as tall as a tree.* Here's another, *George eats a lot. An army eats a lot.* To emphasize the size of George's appetite, we might say, *George eats enough for a whole army."* Emphasize two aspects of figurative language: (1) We usually draw comparisons in figurative language, and (2) we select the second item in the comparison because it (a tree or an army) naturally possesses the attribute (tallness or volume of food consumed) we want to emphasize about the first item in the comparison (Henry or George).

2. Comparing metaphors and similes. While you need not use the terms until the secondary grades, the similarity between metaphors and similes can be emphasized by asking students to complete exercises similar to the following.

Henry is as slow as a snail.

_____ _____ like _____ _____.

_____ is a _____.

Henrietta runs _____ fast _____ a gazelle.

Henrietta runs _____ a gazelle.

_____ is a _____.

3. Recognizing the literal meaning of figurative language. Give figurative statements, and ask students to select (or in later grades, create) a literal interpretation for them.

Vicky said, *"It's raining cats and dogs!"*

1. Cats and dogs were falling out of the sky.
2. It was sprinkling lightly.
3. It was raining quite heavily.

Andre eats enough for an army!

1. Andre eats about 1000 pancakes for breakfast.
2. Andre eats a lot.
3. Andre barely touches his food.

That car is so old it might have a heart attack any day.

1. The car is in danger of heart failure.
2. The car might stop running soon.
3. The car is in great shape.

An enjoyable follow-up activity involves asking students to draw pictures illustrating what the expression would mean if we interpreted it literally. While a bit "silly," such activities are enjoyable for students and do serve to highlight the strength of the comparisons.

4. Using context to determine literal meanings. Paragraphs such as this allow students to use context to fix the meaning of the figurative statement.

> Susan was enjoying her stroll through the woods. *As agile as a cat,* she leaped over fallen logs and traversed the rocks peeping out of the shallow brook.

5. Rewriting literal statements. Put a standard sentence on the blackboard, such as, *Susan walks slowly*. Then encourage the group to generate as many figurative statements of the standard as they can. For example,

1. Susan is a turtle.
2. Susan walks as if she were a snail.
3. If Susan walked any slower she'd be standing still.
4. I've known some trees that moved faster than Susan.

Ambiguous Statements

A word that has more than one dictionary meaning is ambiguous out of context. If I ask you the meaning of *bear,* you will probably ask me the sense in which I am using the word before you respond. But if I give you sentence (21), you will have little trouble specifying the meaning of bear.

(21) I saw a *bear* in the woods.

So it is with sentences. Sentence (22) has at least fifteen or twenty meanings out of context, but there is only one in paragraph (23).

(22) The shooting of the hunters was terrible.
(23) A great tragedy occurred in Woodcrest last week. On the opening day of deer-hunting season, fourteen hunters were accidentally shot by a troop of reserve soldiers from Camp Noway on bivouac in the hills near Woodcrest. Apparently the hunters wandered too close to the troop's target range. The shooting of the hunters was terrible.

Hence this propositional level task, ambiguous statements, is analogous to the multiple meanings task at the concept level. In both instances, readers must learn to assign one of several possible meanings to a linguistic element. Context serves as the medium for clarifying ambiguous words and propositions.

Some would argue that ambiguous language is simply the result of poor writing. Hence, this topic properly belongs in a book dealing with composition rather than comprehension. We disagree. Ambiguity is an inherent part of our language, one we would like to see preserved, not destroyed. Ambiguity allows a poem to be interpreted on several levels of meaning. Ambiguity is an essential part of humor. We are amused by an ambiguous headline, such as (24).

(24) Colonel asks military police to stop drinking on base.

It is the ambiguity of word meanings that accounts for the lowest (and most popular) of all forms of humor, the pun: Did you run this morning? No, but my stocking did. Rather than eliminate ambiguity, we believe that students should be taught to interpret and enjoy it.

At the level of propositions, there are two sources of ambiguity—syntactic and semantic. Propositions (25) and (28) illustrate syntactically ambiguous statements. Proposition (25) can be paraphrased as (26) or (27); (28), as (29) or (30). Notice that planes and flowers can be either the subject or the object of the verbs flying and growing.

(25) Flying planes can be dangerous.
(26) It can be dangerous to fly planes.

(27) It can be dangerous to be in an area where planes are flying.
(28) Growing flowers can be a joy.
(29) It can be a joy to observe flowers that are growing.
(30) It can be a joy to grow flowers.

Propositions (31) and (32) are semantically ambiguous because there are at least two possible meanings for each of the italicized words. Proposition (33) is both syntactically and semantically ambiguous. Shooting can refer either to guns or cameras (or perhaps, rapids), and hunters can be either the subject or the object of the verb, shoot.

(31) John *took* the medicine.
(32) The sentry guarded the *bank* all night long.
(33) The shooting of the hunters was terrible.

We have avoided giving you a tight scope and sequence specifying when each of the tasks presented should be introduced into a school's reading program. We have avoided this, because we believe most of these tasks can be presented at any grade level *if* you accommodate by using content appropriate for students at that level. However, with ambiguous statements, we see no reason to begin instructional activities until about fifth-grade level (on the other hand, multiple meanings can be started in grade 1).

Like figurative language, ambiguous language lends itself to creative teaching and learning. Here are a few activities we believe are worth inclusion in your program.

1. Identifying alternative meanings. There is a humorous way to introduce students to ambiguous statements. Students match two pictures to each ambiguous statement, (Science Research Associates, 1967), as in Figure 5.3.

The activity can also be done entirely with words. Give students an ambiguous sentence, then ask them to select (or for older students, create) sentences which offer alternative meanings.

The sentry guarded the bank all night long.

1. The sentry guarded the bank building all night long.
2. The sentry guarded the bank of the river all night long.
3. The sentry deposited some money in the bank.

2. Using context to clarify an ambiguous statement. Headlines are notoriously ambiguous. Examples such as the following encourage students to use context to unravel the real meaning of the headline. (Examples from Minnesota Statewide Assessment Test.)

Each sentence has two pictures which match it. Write the numbers of the pictures on the lines in front of the matching sentence.

_____ _____ Everyone was pleased that Mrs. Wilson was cooking.

_____ _____ Carol took the pills when no one was looking.

_____ _____ Larry couldn't seem to get his part right.

_____ _____ David discovered that drawing water was difficult.

_____ _____ That night the policeman guarded the bank.

80

Fig. 5.3.   Each sentence has two pictures which match it. Write the numbers of the pictures on the lines in front of the matching sentence.

From the SRA Reading Program, Workbook, Level J. © 1967, Science Research Associates, Inc. Reprinted by permission of the publisher.

CITY COUNCIL DISCUSSES PROBLEM WITH MAYOR

Last night in a closed-door session, council members met with Mayor Frisbee to discuss the problem of traffic tie-ups in downtown Circusville. The meeting, which lasted til 2:00 A.M., resulted in a set of recommendations for changing downtown traffic patterns.

According to the article, the *headline* means that:

1. The city council had a problem with the mayor, and they met without the mayor to discuss it.
2. The city council met with the mayor to discuss a problem of mutual interest.
3. The city council held a meeting which lasted until 2:00 A.M.
4. Traffic will soon be speeding along in Circusville.

JOHNSON MAKING GOOD MONEY IN NEW JOB

Officials at the Plattersville Government Mint awarded a special citation to E. J. Johnson, a former prisoner. One official was quoted as saying that the Plattersville Mint now produces the best quality currency of any mint in the nation.

According to the article, the *headline* means that:

1. Johnson has a new job for which he receives a good salary.
2. Johnson makes high-quality counterfeit money in his new job.
3. Johnson makes high-quality legitimate currency in his new job.
4. Johnson is a good worker, so he gets a special citation.

3. Collecting headlines. Older students should be encouraged to scan the daily newspaper for ambiguous headlines and share them with the class. Here are a few we found in one section of a single issue of the *Minneapolis Tribune* (a daily newspaper).

"KOREA PAID FOR CLUB IN D.C."
"MTC TOLD TO PROVIDE HANDICAPPED ACCESS"
"U.S.–RUSSIAN RELATIONS SENSITIVE"
"FIRM RECALLS PACEMAKERS"

4. Identifying the ambiguous element. After a few samples have been discussed with the group, ask students to complete a worksheet by underlining the portion of each sentence that creates the ambiguity.

1. At Central High *the teaching of the students* is excellent.
2. *The drawing of the lad* made people stop and stare.

3. The sentry guarded the *bank* all night long.
4. Henry *took* the pills.
5. The *turkey was ready to eat.*

A FINAL WORD

In Chapter 5, we began our treatment of comprehension of longer discourse and dealt with six of the nine propositional level tasks in Table 5.1. These six share a common feature: each has an analogue in the concept level taxonomy in Chapter 4.

At the end of Chapter 6 we will give our expanded summary of the longer discourse issue. Suffice it to say that as we move from Chapter 5 to Chapter 6, we move from the simpler to the more complex aspects of longer discourse.

REFERENCES

Guszak, F. J. Teacher Questioning and Reading. *Reading Teacher,* 1967, *21,* 227–34.

The SRA Reading Program-Level J Workbook. Chicago: Science Research Associates, 1967.

Minnesota Statewide Assessment Tests, Department of Education, St. Paul, Minnesota.

Thorndyke, P. Cognitive Structures in Comprehension and Memory of a Narrative Discourse. *Cognitive Psychology,* 1977, *9,* 77–110.

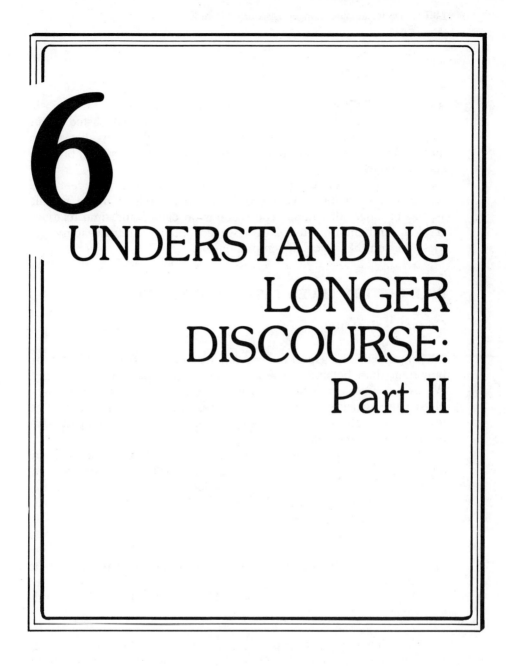

6
UNDERSTANDING LONGER DISCOURSE:
Part II

THIS CHAPTER is both a continuation and an extension of Chapter 5. In the first part of Chapter 6, we treat the last three tasks listed in our propositional level taxonomy in Table 5.1. Then we apply all tasks in that taxonomy to relations among units of discourse larger than propositions or sentences.

As we move from Chapter 5 to Chapter 6, we lose our concept level (Table 4.1) analogues. We move from more stable to more volatile aspects of longer discourse. The sections on causal and time relations are long and multifaceted. Again we encourage careful reading, for these are central aspects of comprehension.

PROPOSITION LEVEL TASKS (CONTINUED)

Causal Relations

In principle, no aspect of comprehension instruction could be more important than helping students to understand relations of causality. We live in a society preoccupied with a search for causes. Scientists, physicians, sociologists, auto mechanics, and even remedial-reading teachers are motivated by a desire to find "the real cause" of a particular event or instance of behavior.

On the surface, comprehending causal relations might seem straightforward. After all, our language is filled with special terms to denote causal relations between propositions: because, since, as, for, hence, so, therefore, as a result, and so on. These signal words provide explicit cues that the connected propositions are causally related, as in examples (1) and (2).

(1) The settlers left Heavenly Valley, because the soil was too rocky to cultivate.
(2) The soil was too rocky to cultivate. Hence, the settlers left Heavenly Valley.

Causality is not that simple. First, many causal relations are not signaled at all, as in example (3). And it is quite common for causally related propositions to be connected by a simple conjunction, as in (4).

(3) The soil was too rocky to cultivate. The settlers left Heavenly Valley.
(4) Susan cleaned her room, and her mother gave her a piece of cake.

Second, many causal relations are disguised as time relations. On first glance, (5) and (6) appear to express time relations between two events. But upon closer examination, the relation is really causal: the primacy of the causal relation is intuitively verified by the fact that question (7) makes

(5) After Susan cleaned her room, her mother gave her a piece of cake.
(6) When Susan cleaned her room, her mother gave her a piece of cake.

as much, if not more, sense than question (8) as a comprehension probe for either (5) or (6).

(7) Why did Susan's mother give her a piece of cake?
(8) When did Susan's mother give her a piece of cake?

Third, there are often multiple causes for a single event. Consider paragraph (9) and question (10). The explicit answer appears in the last sentence of paragraph (9).

(9) When products made of rubber first came out, there were many problems. People found that the rubber became like glue in the summer and brittle in the winter. Storekeepers had to bury piles of rubber products. Because many people lost a lot of money, rubber products were not well liked.
(10) Why were rubber products not well liked?

Because many people lost a lot of money. Yet when students were asked to answer question (10) after reading paragraph (9), many students gave responses like (11)–(16) (Pearson, Boesen, and Carr, 1970).

(11) They had to bury their goods.
(12) They got like glue.
(13) They turned brittle.
(14) There were too many problems.
(15) The rubber wasn't any good.
(16) People wouldn't buy any.

The events in paragraph (9) are ordered in a causal chain, like a set of dominoes. Each event is, in a sense, a prerequisite to the next. To use the language of logicians, each step is a *necessary* condition for the steps following it. Each, then, is a partial cause, a partial explanation, of the final effect. One other point: note that neither response (15) nor (16) appear in the text of the paragraph, yet both represent reasonable answers to question (10). They reveal an important point about comprehension and written discourse: writers rarely include all the possible details they could when they develop a logical argument; by reference to their own knowledge store, readers often dredge up those omitted details. Often they are as sensible as those explicitly stated in the text, and, if one were to develop a *complete* causal chain for a set of events, these omitted details would probably be included.

A fourth complication in causal relations focuses on the distinction between true physical causation and two other kinds of relations that we will call explanation and enablement. In (17) the cause and effect are fairly clear.

(17) The car stopped because it ran out of gas.

Two events occurred in sequence. The first event was a sufficient condition for the occurrence of the second event. By contrast the relations in (18) and (19) are more explanatory than causal.

(18) John did not do his homework, because he is lazy.
(19) Because Susan is a girl scout, she sells cookies.

There is nothing about being a girl scout or lazy that compels one to sell cookies or to fail to do homework. However, running out of gas compels a car to stop. Even though there is a distinction between these two kinds of "causation," they are similar in that it makes just as much sense to ask why Susan sells cookies as it does to ask why the car stopped.

Enablement is different altogether. Examine paragraph (20) and question (21). Response (22) makes good sense, even though the causal relationship is not explicit in the paragraph.

(20) "Helen's birthday is tomorrow," Timothy remembered. He got out of his chair and walked into the kitchen. Then he started to bake a triple layer Devil's Food cake.
(21) Why did Timothy bake a cake?
(22) Because it was Helen's birthday.

Responses (23) and (24) make no sense as an answer to (21), even though Timothy could not have baked the cake until and unless he performed the actions in (23) and (24).

(23) Because he got out of his chair.
(24) Because he walked into the kitchen.

Those actions *enabled* him to bake the cake, but they did not *cause* him to bake the cake. To use the language of logicians, they were *necessary* but not *sufficient* conditions for Timothy's cake-baking activity.

The fifth piece of this puzzle we call causal relations leads us into the realm of conditional relations, if . . . then . . . statements. We discuss them in the context of causality because we consider them a sort of "suspended causality." Consider (25) and (26). We do not know whether or not (25) has occurred.

(25) If Susan cleans her room, her mother gives her a piece of cake.
(26) Because Susan cleaned her room, her mother gave her a piece of cake.

It is a rule explaining a general condition under which Susan can satisfy her confectionary needs. It may never occur! Susan may become a lean but messy person. In contrast, (26) has already occurred. In a sense it is an actual example of the general rule stated in (25). And our intuition about (26) leads us to suspect that Susan may become plump and neat rather than lean and messy. But the reason we call conditionality a sort of suspended causality is that it is *suspended* in both time and space, suspended from reality; it has not necessarily happened. It simply tells us the general conditions under which A will cause B to happen. And if we tell you A has occurred (Susan really did clean her room), you can legitimately infer that B has also occurred (her mother gave her the cake), or will occur soon.

We raise this issue not to confuse causal relations, but rather to point out the extent to which these seemingly separate types of relations are intrinsically intertwined. One other point about conditional relations. Like causal relations, they often appear disguised as time relations. Sentences (27) and (28) are acceptable paraphrases of (25).

(27) When Susan cleans her room, her mother gives her a piece of cake.
(28) After Susan cleans her room, her mother gives her a piece of cake.

Sixth, we bring up two traditional comprehension tasks that usually deserve a separate listing in a taxonomy of comprehension skills—*drawing conclusions and predicting outcomes*. The only difference we can see between what we have talked about as causal relations and explanatory relations and these two new terms, centers on whether or not the cause-effect relation is explicitly stated in the text. Hence, we discuss them here rather than in a separate section.

How do you predict an outcome? Suppose we tell you that a car ran out of gas. Then we ask the inevitable question, What will happen next? How do you respond? On what basis? Clearly you might reasonably infer that the car stopped running. The only reason you can do that is because somewhere in one of your mental schemata you have stored a conditional relation something like (29).

(29) If a car runs out of gas, the car will stop.

However, you would not stop there. You would also infer that the driver would try to find some gas to get the car running again. If we told you that it happened on a deserted desert road, you would make a different set of inferences than if we told you it happened on a city street at 2:00 P.M. on a Thursday. Remember our discussion of scripts in Chapter 3? Depending upon the information we gave to you, you would call up different scripts to make the appropriate inferences. But the true basis of your inferences—the content of your scripts—would be a set of "suspended causality" rules, a set of propositions specifying what kinds of events typically lead to (cause) other events. Predicting outcomes then, is a type of *future* causality, based upon your stored knowledge about what kind of *effect* the explicitly stated *cause* usually elicits: Drivers usually try to find gas when their cars run out of gas. Recall that we borrowed the term scripts from computer science (Schank, 1973). We borrow another from the same source. Computer scientists call this kind of reasoning *forward inferencing*. We like the term because it creates a clear image of what a reader must do when he or she is asked to predict an outcome.

How about drawing conclusions? Let us examine paragraph (20) once more, now (30). Suppose we ask you to speculate about Helen and Timothy's relationship.

(30) "Helen's birthday is tomorrow," Timothy remembered. He got out of his chair and walked into the kitchen. Then he started to bake a triple layer Devil's Food cake.

Are they brother and sister? Father and daughter? Husband and wife? Neighbors? Friends? Suppose we ask you whether or not Timothy liked Helen, or why Timothy is baking a birthday cake for Helen. As with forward inferencing (predicting outcomes), you are forced to delve into your store of scripts to derive plausible explanations. You ask yourself under what conditions—in what circumstances—does one person bake a birthday cake for another (by the way, it is never explicitly stated that Timothy is baking a birthday cake, let alone a birthday cake for Helen; but it is compelling to believe that he is). Again, you search for "suspended causality" rules. But in this instance they deal with motivations rather than clear-cut physical causes. Notice also that instead of going forward from a cause to a plausible effect, you are forced to move backward from an effect (Timothy's making a birthday cake for Helen) to a cause (or more accurately, an explanation). Not surprisingly, computer scientists call such reasoning *backward inferencing*.

We want to underscore the similarity between forward and backward inferencing and more straightforward comprehension of causal and conditional relations. The only difference is in the data base that the reader uses. When the relation is explicit in the text, the reader can (but need not) use that information to answer the question. When there is no explicit cause-effect statement, the reader is forced to use whatever data—"suspended causality" rules—that are stored in his or her mental scripts. But the reasoning processes are similar whether the data are on the page or in the head.

A seventh aspect of causality is usually called purposive relations. It is characterized by cue words such as *in order to* and *so that;* sentences (31) and (32) express purposive relations.

(31) John went to town in order to buy a new car.
(32) John went to town so that he could buy a new car.

The fact that they are related to more typical causal relations can be verified by the fact that (33) is a roughly acceptable paraphrase of (31) or (32).

(33) John went to town because he wanted to buy a new car.

Purposive relations, however, appear to be limited to expressing relations between an action (like going to town) and some internal state of motivation (that is, a purpose or goal like, to buy a new car). It makes no sense at all to paraphrase (34) as (35).

(34) The machine stopped because the chain broke.
(35) The machine stopped so that the chain could break.[13]

Purposive relations can be probed by asking questions like (36) or (37).

(36) Why did John go to town?
(37) What did John do in order to buy a new car?

Before we turn to instructional activities, let us summarize the points we have tried to make.

[13] An anomalous sentence.

1. We have belabored this aspect of comprehension, because we believe that it is a pervasive part of human reasoning. If our treatment seems complex, it must be so to match the complexity of the problem. We believe that teachers must understand these issues if they are to guide students in understanding causal relations.

2. While causal relations are often explicitly cued in text materials, there are instances in which both cause and effect are stated but the relationship is not explicit. There are instances in which *only* the cause *or* the effect is stated, and readers will be forced to engage in forward or backward inferencing in order to complete the requirements of the comprehension task. In such instances, readers are forced to use their available mental scripts.

3. At times causal relations are disguised as time relations or conditional relations. With respect to the latter, they represent a "suspended causality," independent of time and space.

And now we give some instructional guidelines and activities.

Causal relations lend themselves to a variety of exercise formats: Most are mundane; a few are unique.

1. Use question formats. There are a number of question formats one can use to probe students' understanding of causal relations after they have read a text segment. (Conditional relations, "suspended causality," are somewhat awkward to test. Questions (4) and (5) should probably not be used until grade 5 or 6.)

1. Why:\ Why did John have to go downtown?
2. What did because: What did John do because his mother needed a needle?

3. Supply a reason: John had to go downtown because _____?

   His mother needed a needle. So _____.
4. Under what condition: Under what condition will Susan's mother give her a piece of cake?
5. Under what circumstances: Under what circumstances will Susan's mother give her a piece of cake?
6. Using when as a paraphrase: When will Susan's mother give her a piece of cake?
7. What will happen: What will happen if Susan cleans her room?

8. Supply a condition: If Susan cleans her room, _____

   Susan's mother will give Susan a piece of cake if _____

2. Paraphrase. Most of the activities outlined in the paraphrase section of this chapter can be applied to causal relations. For example, students can be asked to find two matching statements.

In order to buy ham and eggs, Henry walked three miles to the restaurant.

1. Henry walked three miles to the restaurant so that he could buy ham and eggs.
2. After he walked three miles to the restaurant, Henry bought ham and eggs.
3. In order to walk three miles to the restaurant, Henry bought ham and eggs.

Because John missed the bus, he walked to school.

1. John missed the bus after he walked to school.
2. Because John walked to school, he missed the bus.
3. John missed the bus. So he walked to school.

Before our ship was sunk by an iceberg, it tossed in waves twenty feet high.

1. Because it tossed in waves twenty feet high our ship was sunk by an iceberg.
2. Our ship was sunk by an iceberg. Then it tossed in waves twenty feet high.
3. After our ship tossed in waves twenty feet high, it was sunk by an iceberg.

3. Supply the cue word. Given two propositions, students select a cue word to connect them sensibly.

1. The machine stopped _____ the chain broke.

_____so _____because _____unless

2. John wanted an ice cream cone. _____he went to the ice cream parlor.

_____so _____because _____if.

4. Predicting outcomes (forward inferencing) and drawing conclusions (backward inferencing) can be assessed by using formats similar to the first three questions in exercise 1; however, the questions should be made more tentative by inserting words like *probably, in your opinion, what do you think.* . . .

1. Why might Timothy bake a cake for Helen?
2. What will probably happen when the car runs out of gas?

5. Game formats. As must be obvious to you by now, we have not, in contrast to the chapter on understanding concepts, recommended many game formats in this section on understanding propositions. It is not that these tasks cannot be put into a game format; it is simply that we wonder whether it is worth the effort to do so. For example, we could develop a concentration game in which students would have to match propositions which are paraphrases of one another. However, the memory load would probably be too great (students would have difficulty holding so much information in their working memories). Furthermore, we doubt that there would be enough transfer value of the stimuli used in the game to merit the effort one would have to expend to create the stimuli. In short, we suggest that you would be better off to put your efforts into a reusable kit of activities with several exercises per page or into a set of ditto masters that you can reuse from one year to the next.

Sequence

We recall, as classroom teachers, that no skill seemed as difficult for our intermediate-grade students as placing a list of events from a story in the sequence in which they occurred. Nearly as difficult was the task of answering *when, what happened before . . . , and what happened after . . .* questions. Why should such tasks have posed such difficulty? What is there about the nature of chronology (time relations) or the nature of children that can explain this difficulty?

E. Clark (1971) has found that young children use temporal order in speech (and, we suspect, spatial order in text) as the only indicator of sequence. Hence, a sentence like, Before John ate lunch, he watched television, would be interpreted as, first he ate lunch and then watched television. Young children do not seem to be aware of time markers like before and after. The logical relationship between two events also seems to influence children's comprehension of time relations. In a series of informal studies, Pearson (1977) found that first- and second-grade students have much more difficulty placing events in order or answering what-, when-, or where-type questions (wh-questions) when the two events presented as a pair were reversible rather than irreversible. A reversible pair of events can logically occur in either order, as in (38). An irreversible pair can, under normal circumstances, occur in only one order, as in (39).

(38) John watched television before he ate dinner.
(39) John closed the door. Then he bolted it.

We suspect that the reversibility of events is the greatest source of difficulty in comprehending time relations. Once more, we invoke our notion of scripts to explain this assertion. What makes the order of a set of events irreversible? Expectations based upon experience. Remember the restaurant story in Chapter 3. The order of events in a restaurant story are quite predictable, if not reversible. Hence you are able to answer questions about event order or retell the correct sequence without great difficulty. If, however, we were to ask you to read a short story detailing the steps in a Chinese Tea Ceremony, we expect you would have difficulty recalling the order of the steps. You do not have a well-developed script for such an episode.

Put yourself in the place of a student trying to remember the chronology of battles in the Civil War or the order of events in a biographical sketch about Charles Lindbergh. There is nothing compelling about the particular order in which the battles were fought, Why Gettysburg before Vicksburg? Episodes in a person's life, with the exception of birth, schooling, and death can occur at many different stages. Lindbergh could have flown the Atlantic when he was twenty-three or fifty-three.

Essentially, we should be very careful in selecting and creating time-relation instructional activities for students. A good rule of thumb would be to begin time-relation activities in the early grades using only irreversible sets of events, gradually introducing predictably ordered sets of events, then, at about age ten, insert sets of events, the order of which is reversible, arbitrary, and particular to a text segment.

In the section on causal relations, we indicated that two propositions may appear to be linked by a time relation, as in (40), when what is really important is the causal relation implicit in the statement.

(40) After Mary cleaned her room, her mother gave her a piece of cake.

For such statements, avoid the time-relation question, (41), in favor of the causal question, (42).

(41) When did Mary's mother give her a piece of cake?
(42) Why did Mary's mother give her a piece of cake?

It is only incidental that a time cue (after) rather than a causal cue (because) was used. Such decisions are not difficult to make. You need only ask yourself whether or not it makes sense to ask the *why* question. It does for statement (40) but not for (43).

(43) After Mary cleaned her room, her mother gave her a list of groceries needed for dinner that night.

Students' comprehension of time relations varies according to how these relations are stated, in particular how they are cued, and whether or not the order of presentation matches the order of occurrence. Examine the set of sentences in Table 6.1. The yes-no responses are answers to the three questions in the upper-left-hand corner. Essentially all these sentences (except those that are footnoted) are paraphases of one another; that is, they all communicate the same sequential relationship between the two propositions. And, eventually, students must learn to comprehend all the different syntactic forms in which time relations can occur. We have found, however, that primary-grade children have difficulty with those structures in which the order of presentation (on the page) does not match the actual order of occurrence (examples 4, 5, and 6). Furthermore, Pearson (1977) has found that example (1) is easier

TABLE 6.1   Variations in the Presentation of Time Relations

Does the order of presentation match the order of occurrence?	Is there a marker to cue the order?	Are the propositions in two separate sentences?	
Yes	Yes	Yes	1. John worked on his bike. Then he ate lunch.
Yes	Yes	No	2. John worked on his bike before he ate lunch.
Yes	Yes	No	3. After John worked on his bike, he ate lunch.
Yes	No	Yes	John worked on his bike. He ate lunch.[a]
Yes	No	No	John worked on his bike, and he ate lunch.[a]
No	Yes	Yes	4. John ate lunch. Earlier, he worked on his bike.
No	Yes	No	5. Before John ate lunch, he worked on his bike.
No	Yes	No	6. John ate lunch after he worked on his bike.
No	No	Yes	John ate lunch. He worked on his bike.[a]
No	No	No	John ate lunch, and he worked on his bike.[a]

[a] These sentences, while grammatically acceptable, do not really communicate the correct sequence of events unambiguously.

than (2) or (3). Hence, as children develop in their reading skill, introducing these structures in the order from one to six has some merit.

Furthermore, in line with what we recommended in the section on paraphrase (Chapter 5), starting in grade 3 or 4, students should receive paraphrase instruction so that they will become aware that all these structures can be used to communicate the same time relation between two propositions.

Quite often the time relations between propositions or events is not explicitly pointed out in the text. The only cue provided is the order in which the events are presented on the page. For example, we would probably all agree that the actual sequence of events in (44) matches the order of presentation.

(44) Susan fixed her bike, watched television for a while, ate lunch, and went to a movie.

We are not used to presentation of events that are out of order. We expect authors and speakers to give them in the actual order in which they occurred, unless we are told otherwise, as in (45).

(45) Before Susan went to the movie, she fixed her bike, watched television for a while, and ate lunch.

This tendency is especially strong in younger children (ages six to eight), who will often ignore cues that signal that the first listed event occurred last, as in (45), steadfastly contending that the first listed event occurred first (E. Clark, 1971; Pearson, 1977). The arguments in this paragraph reinforce the earlier point that it is best to begin with time relations in which the order presented on the page matches the actual order of the events.

The following are instructional activities for time relations.

1. Answering wh-time questions. While question answering is not the most imaginative behavior, it needs to be included in an instructional program because it is widely used (in standardized tests) and represents a reasonable type of comprehension probe. After reading a passage, containing at least two sequenced events, students can be asked three types of wh-questions:

1. When did John do X?
2. What happened before John did Y?
3. What happened after John did X?

Whenever the paragraph or passage includes several sequenced events, you need to be careful about scoring students' answers. Suppose three events are sequenced, A then B then C. Suppose the question is, What happened before C? Notice that both A and B are acceptable even though there may have been a sentence which placed B before C. We caution you, because we all have a tendency to accept the most obvious answer when there may be several that satisfy the logical requirements of the task.

2. Indicating what happened first, A. or B. A variation of exercise 1, this question format usually proves simpler, especially for younger students. For students who have difficulty with the typical *wh*-time questions, we recommend questions of this type:

1. What happened first, A or B?
2. What happened second, A or B?
3. Did A happen before B? Yes or No?
4. Did B happen before A? Yes or No?

3. Paraphrasing. Students are given a standard statement expressing a time relation. Then they are given three or four choices from which they are to select one or more paraphrases of the standard statement (alternatively, they could be asked to select the one choice which is *not* a paraphrase of the standard statement).

After the man slammed the car to a stop, he honked the horn several times.

1. After the man honked the horn several times, he slammed the car to a stop.
2. Before the man honked the horn several times, he slammed the car to a stop.

In Table 6.1, there are examples of different paraphrase alternatives. For older students, ask them to create rather than select paraphrases.

4. Placing events in order. A common workbook activity, it can be a useful exercise if certain precautions are taken. Do not list the events and ask students to number them in the order in which they occurred in the selection. The problem with such exercises is that a student can err on only one of the events but end up missing several. In other words, if you get one event out of order, all those that follow will appear to be out of order. Let us illustrate. Suppose that the actual order of events A through E is C, D, B, A, E. Student X marks A3, B2, C5, D1, and E4. As indicated, the correct order is A4, B3, C1, D2, and E5. Student X appears to have missed the order of all five events. In reality, student X only has one event, *C1*, out of order. But the nature of this exercise format has penalized him unfairly. As alternatives, we suggest two possibilities. First, if you use this format, be liberal in your scoring

practices. Second, list the five events in random order, assigning a letter designation to each event:

A

B

C

D

E

Then give students a set of choices from which they are to select the one choice that lists the events in the correct order:

1. B C D E A
2. A E B D C
3. C D B A E
4. C D B E A
5. D C B E A

5. Placing cartoon frames in order. We have seen some clever sequencing activities using cartoon frames from the Sunday funnies. The frames are cut out and laminated. Then students are asked to examine the pictures and the bubbles and place the frames in their original sequence. This can be an enjoyable and worthwhile activity if you are careful in selecting the cartoons. What you want to avoid is cartoons whose frames can be placed in more than one sensible order. Or, if you choose ambiguously ordered cartoons, then you will have to give the "benefit of the doubt" to students who can give a plausible argument for a deviant order.

6. Filling in the cue word. Using only irreversibly ordered pairs of events (events that can occur only in one order), leave a blank space for the time-cue word. Students select from a set of choices, the word that completes the statement.

1. John started the car _____he shifted it into *drive*.

_____after _____before _____earlier.

2. _____Hazel woke up, she fixed a big breakfast.

_____after _____before _____then.

This exercise can be used with predictably ordered or even reversible events if you allow students first to read a passage revealing the correct order.

Anaphoric Relations

We encounter anaphoric relations more than any other relation we have discussed so far. It is difficult to read more than two sentences without having to deal with one. The sentence you just read contains two anaphoric relations—*it* and *one*. *It* refers to the nominal proposition, *to read more than two sentences,* and *one* refers to the adjective-noun term, *anaphoric relation* in the first sentence of this paragraph.

The Random House Dictionary of the English Language (1966, p. 53) defines anaphora as, "the use of a word as a regular grammatical substitute for a preceding word or group of words. . . ." Anaphora, therefore, includes all the basic personal pronouns (I, me, we, us, you, he, she, it, they, him, her, them) and demonstrative pronouns (this, that, these, those). But it also includes *pro-verbs* (not proverbs), such as *do, can, will, would, could, should has,* and many nouns which serve the function of pronouns.

Menzel (in Bormuth, 1970) has provided a complete taxonomy of anaphoric relations. Our analysis, presented in Table 6.2 is drawn up on Menzel's work but is simplified for our purposes. After identifying each type of anaphoric relation, we provide examples as well as comprehension probes one might use to assess whether or not students have been able to relate the anaphoric term to its appropriate referent in the sentence, paragraph, or passage context in which it occurs.

The relative difficulty of various types of anaphora has been investigated in at least two studies (Bormuth *et al.,* 1970; Lesgold, 1974). Unfortunately, the two studies yield variant results. For example, Bormuth *et al.* found personal pronouns (our category 1) to be among the most difficult of anaphora, whereas Lesgold, using a different measure of comprehension, found them relatively simple. However, one finding common to these two studies, subsequently corroborated by Richek (1976–1977), is that intermediate-grade students are only somewhere between 60 percent and 80 percent accurate in assigning antecedents to anaphora. Furthermore, there is a wide variation among subjects and among various anaphora. These findings suggest that (1) systematic instruction in anaphoric structures is probably necessary, and (2) some students and some structures will require more attention than others.

Here are some instructional activities that merit your attention.

1. Question probes. We refer you to Table 6.2 for question probes that can be used in written or oral exercises to allow students to practice relating anaphora to their antecedents (words they refer to). We must, however, offer a note of caution. When you create written assignments, asking, *Who* did X, and so on, students will sometimes respond, *He* did, or, *The boy* in the story did. To prevent this type of response you need to tell students to respond with a name or a noun, and so on.

2. Antecedent matching. A paragraph or a list of sentences can be constructed with numbers placed over (or in front of) various anaphora. Students are instructed to write the same number over (or in front of) the antecedent for each anaphora.

(1)
John and his cousin went to the fair last week. *They* had a great time
(2)   (3)   (4)
there. First, *they* took the roller coaster. *It* was really fast. John got sick.
(5)   (6)
So did his cousin. Then they went to see the gorilla. What a crazy *animal!*
(7)
First, it threw peanuts at the crowd. Then *it* pounded its chest. Then they
(8)
went on six more rides, but they only liked three of *them*. John ate four
(9)
foot-long hot dogs. His cousin ate *seven!* Finally they went home and were
(10)
glad to be *there*.

3. Anaphora substitution. This is more or less the reverse of the previous activity. Students are instructed to find words to substitute for the italicized words in the paragraph. The task can be made simpler by providing a list of anaphora from which students can select.

John and his cousin went to the fair last week. *John and his cousin* had a great time *at the fair*. First, they took the roller coaster. *The roller coaster* was really fast. John got sick. So did his cousin. Then they went to see the gorilla. What a crazy *gorilla!* First, it threw peanuts at the crowd. Then the *gorilla* pounded *the gorilla's* chest. Then they went on six more rides, but they only liked three of *the rides*. John ate four foot-long hot dogs. His cousin ate seven *foot-long hot dogs*. Finally, they went home and were glad to be *home*.

PROPOSITIONAL LEVEL TASKS APPLIED TO LARGER UNITS OF DISCOURSE

Time, Causal, and Main Idea Relations

So far we have dealt with eight propositional level tasks, ranging from straightforward paraphrase to rather complex causal and time relations. All of those tasks apply equally as well to relations that prevail between units of discourse longer than a proposition or a sentence. For example, paragraph (46) presents the details of a lavish dinner. Paragraph (47) presents a subsequent nightcap episode. The events described in each paragraph are chronologically related, (46) occurred before (47). But the order of events within each episode is unclear.

TABLE 6.2 Anaphoric Relations

Relation	Example	Possible Comprehension Probe
1. Pronouns: I, me, we, us, you, he, him, they, them.	Mary has a friend named John. *She* picks *him* up on the way to school. *They* walk home together too.	Who gets picked up? Who picks him up? Name the person who gets picked up.
2. Locative (location) pronouns: here, there.	The team climbed to the top of Mt. Everest. Only a few people have been *there*.	Where have only a few people been. Name the place where only a few people have been.
3. Deleted nouns: usually an adjective serves as the anaphora.	The students scheduled a meeting but only a *few* attended. Apparently *several* went to the beach. *Others* attended a dance in the gym. *Only the most serious* actually came to the meeting. (Notice that each adjective phrase or adjective refers to students.)	Who went to the beach? Who attended the dance in the gym? What does the word *others* refer to?
4. Arithmetic Anaphora.	Mary and John entered the building. The *former* is tall and lovely. The *latter* is short and squatty. The *two* make an interesting couple.	Who is tall and lovely? Who makes an interesting couple?
5. Class inclusive anaphora: a superordinate word, substitutes for another word.	1. The dog barked a lot. The *animal* must have seen a prowler. 2. The lion entered the clearing. The *big cat* looked graceful as it surveyed its domain. 3. John was awakened by a siren. He thought the *noise* would never stop.	1. What animal must have seen a prowler? What does the word animal refer to? 2. What cat looked graceful? What does the word *cat* refer to? 3. What noise did John think would never stop?

6. Inclusive Anaphora: that, this, the problem, these reasons. Can refer back to an entire phrase, clause, or passage.

1. (After twenty pages discussing the causes of the Civil War.) For *these reasons*, the South seceded from the Union.
2. Someone was pounding on the door. *This* (or *it*) surprised Mary.
3. Crime is getting serious in Culver. The police have to do a better job with *this problem.*
4. "Do unto others as you would have them do unto you." *Such an idea* has been the basis of Christian theology for 2000 years.

1. Why did the South secede from the Union?
2. What surprised Mary?
3. What do the police have to do a better job with?
4. What has been the basis of Christian theology for 2000 years?

---

7. Deleted predicate adjective: so is, is not, is too (also), as is.

1. John is dependable. So is Henry.
2. John is dependable. Susan *is not.*
3. The lion was large but graceful. The tiger *was too.*
4. The lion, *as is* the tiger, is large but graceful.

1. Is Henry dependable?
2. Is Susan dependable?
3. Describe the tiger.
4. Describe the tiger.

---

8. Proverbs: *so does, can, will, have,* and so on (or), can, does, will *too* (or); can, does, will *not, as* did, can, will

1. John went to school. *So did* Susan.
2. John went to school. Susan *did too.*
3. Henry will get an A. *So will* Theresa.
4. Amy can do a cartwheel. Matthew *cannot.*
5. Mom likes bologna. Dad *does not.*
6. John likes, *as does* Henry, potato chips.

1. What did Susan do?
2. What did Susan do too?
3. What will Theresa do?
4. Can Matthew do a cartwheel? What can't Matthew do?
5. Does Dad like bologna?
6. What does Henry like? Does Henry like potato chips?

(46) What a dinner we had at Tom's house last night! Susan brought a case of 1959 Trockenberenauslese. Abe cooked Beef Wellington. Theresa created a unique caesar salad. And, last but not least, Matthew made bananas foster.

(47) Afterward, we all went over to Josh's place for Havana cigars and VSOP cognac. Josh played his favorite Beethoven Symphonies, Numbers 5 and 7.

As indicated, there are no specific cues to the order of the cooking or eating events. As such, the relation between paragraph (46) and paragraph (47) is analogous to the relation between the two propositions in (48).

(48) After we ate a lovely dinner at Tom's house, we went over to Josh's place for cigars, cognac, and music.

The difference of course, lies in the amount of detail included in the description of the two basic episodes, the dinner and the nightcap. The analogy between (46) and (47) and the propositions in (48) is further indicated by the fact that comprehension probes (49), (50), and (51) make equally good sense after (46) and (47) or after (48).

(49) When did they go over to Josh's?

(50) What happened before they went over to Josh's?

(51) What happened first? Dinner at Tom's or cognac and cigars at Josh's?

We suspect (but have no evidence to support our suspicion) that students would answer (49), (50), or (51) more accurately after (48) than after (46) and (47). First, we suspect that the sheer load of detail in (46) and (47) will interfere with some students' ability to store the chronological relation or to locate it in the text. Second, the relationship between the two basic episodes, while specifically cued in both versions, is more explicit in (48) than in (46) and (47).

A similar analysis can be applied to causal relations. Examine (52) and (53) and then (54).

(52) At Trader Vic's last night, the six of us had to wait two hours to be seated at the dinner table. Tom ordered twenty-seven trays of hors d'oeuvres, including cheese bings, broiled shrimp, fried shrimp, boiled shrimp, sweet and sour pork, and barbecued pork. Needless to say, we ate all twenty-seven trays.

(53) Finally, we were seated at the dinner table. Everyone ordered the heavily curried chicken entrée. When it came, we were all too full to eat a single bite.

(54) Because we ate twenty-seven trays of hors d'oeuvres while waiting to be seated, we were all too full to eat a single bite of our chicken curry entrée.

There is an implicit causal relation between the appetizer fiasco and their inability to eat the entrée. Most of us have no trouble inferring the cause-effect relation. But it is embedded in a context of other detail, and it is not explicitly cued, in contrast to the relation in (54).

As with the previous example of a time relation, we suspect that the added detail and the reduction in explicitness will make it more difficult for students to answer questions (55) and (56) after reading (52) and (53) than after reading (54).

(55) Why couldn't anyone eat a single bite of the entrée?
(56) What happened because they ate twenty-seven trays of hors d'oeuvres while waiting to be seated for dinner?

A third example. Suppose we were going to end this section right now (we are not) with statement (57).

(57) In short, the added detail plus the greater difficulty of making inferences between textually distant propositions makes comprehension more difficult at the longer discourse level than at the propositional level.

In a real sense (57) serves as a main idea for all that has been stated up to this point. And the examples of causal and time relations serve as details to support (57). But note that within the time and causal sections there were also main ideas. Statement (57) is the main idea of main ideas. Diagrammatically it looks like Figure 6.1. The numbers in parentheses refer to examples elucidated thus far in the text. The paragraph numbers refer to the actual ordinal number of paragraphs included thus far in this section (Hint: We are now in paragraph 5).

We are less certain that the main idea–detail relation between (57) and the previous paragraphs will be more difficult for students to comprehend than the main idea–detail relations between paragraph 2 and examples (46), (47), and (48) or between paragraph (4) and examples (52), (53), and (54). Granted, the main idea in (57) is more general and includes more detail; however, the reader has now been given two doses of it, once in paragraph (2) and once in paragraph (4). But one other point about main ideas is quite similar to time and causal examples. Relations that exist between propositions (as we defined them in Chapter 5) can also exist between longer units of discourse such as paragraphs and passages.

Having discussed three propositional level relations that also apply

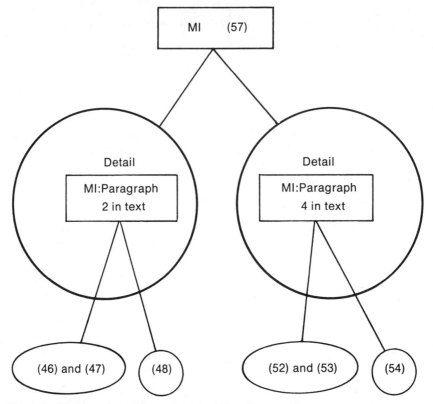

Fig. 6.1. Diagram of main idea and detail relations.

at the longer discourse level we will now discuss the application of our other five propositional level tasks, namely, paraphrase, association, comparison, figurative language, ambiguous statements, and anaphoric relations. Before we do however, we offer a single instructional guideline for time, causal, and main idea relations at the longer discourse level: the activities outlined for each of these tasks can be used at the longer discourse level; but because of added detail and an added inference load, you can expect them to cause more difficulty for students.

Paraphrase

At the concept and propositional level, paraphrase meant that students were required to recognize the equivalence in meaning among two or more linguistic units. One could require students to recognize the equivalence in meaning between two paragraphs; however, we do not recommend it as an instructional activity. We believe that recognizing equivalence in meaning at the paragraph level involves little more than recognizing the equivalence in meaning of the component propositions of the two paragraphs. Our belief stems from the fact that both concepts and propositions have been demonstrated to be *basic units* of discourse, whereas paragraphs have not. Kintsch (1974), for example, concludes from his own research that propositions are basic units of discourse; that is, they are psychologically real units that people use in comprehension and memory. The psychological reality of concepts has been demonstrated by Collins and Quillian (1969). In short, practicing paraphrase at the paragraph level would not differ from practicing it at the propositional level.

There is, however, an extension of paraphrase that does merit attention at the level of longer discourse—retelling or summarizing. Sometimes used as an assessment technique (Durrell, 1955, Goodman and Burke, 1972), asking a student to retell or summarize a selection in his or her own words is a reasonable practice activity. Invoking our new to known principle, retelling provides an overt measure of what a student has done with the information presented in a selection, indicating what has or has not been assimilated into existing schemata or scripts.

Association

Association activities can be practiced at the level of longer discourse. Just as students can be asked to identify a sentence that does not fit the rest of a paragraph, so they can be asked to select a paragraph that seems out of place in a longer selection. The constraints that apply at the propositional level also apply at the level of longer discourse.

Comparison

There is no substantial difference between comparison tasks at the propositional level and at the longer discourse level. The reason: the task as presented in Chapter 5 was already at the level of longer discourse. Recall that we suggested that students research for commonalities and differences between text segments or between a text segment and information already a part of their mental scripts. We cheated a bit in Chapter 5. It is rare to find the propositions for comparison relations adjacent to one another in text. It is more common to find them interspersed in several paragraphs of running discourse. To answer Question (58), a student is likely to have to search several parts of at least two selections.

(58) How was the Civil War like the Revolutionary War? How was it different?

The guidelines and activities suggested in Chapter 5, therefore, serve well for comparison activities at the level of longer discourse.

Figurative Language and Ambiguous Statements

We see no good reason to concern yourself with special instruction for these two tasks at the level of longer discourse. First, like paraphrases, these are really propositional concerns. That is, it is a proposition that is a simile or a metaphor, not a paragraph. It is a proposition that is ambiguous, not a paragraph. A paragraph may be unclear to a reader, but that does not necessarily mean that it is semantically or syntactically ambiguous. And it may contain ambiguous statements or figurative language, but again, it is the component propositions that are ambiguous or figures of speech, not the paragraph itself. Second, we have, in a sense, already suggested longer discourse activities for these tasks. Recall that for each of these tasks we suggested that children be exposed to them as they appear in paragraph contexts because the context helps to provide a *literal* meaning for a figure of speech and a *single clear* meaning for an ambiguous statement.

ANAPHORIC RELATIONS. Since the anaphoric relations discussed earlier include examples that cut across sentences and paragraphs, we do not include a special section here. We should, however, point out that category 6 in Table 6.2, inclusive anaphora, is particularly important when guiding student's work in comprehension of longer discourse.

A FINAL WORD

In Chapters 5 and 6 we have enumerated a set of relations that can exist between propositions that occur in connected discourse. For each propositional relation we have tried to (1) explain the logical nature of the relation, (2) justify its importance as a part of an instructional program in comprehension, and (3) specify some instructional guidelines and instructional activities which teachers can use to help students handle the relation.

A few conclusions seem appropriate.

1. While we have treated each of the nine types of relations as though they were separate entities, a great deal of overlap exists among them. We have specified some of the areas of overlap: (1) causal, conditional, and time relations often appear in one another's clothing, (2) comparison is involved in many of the other tasks, and (3) many of

these relations can be taught by asking students to engage in para-phrase tasks.

Despite this inevitable overlap, we encourage you to deal with each of these relations as separate instructional components, recognizing, of course, their inherent interdependence. We make this recommendation as much for the sake of instructional convenience as for any logical or research-based reason. As a teacher, you cannot deal with the universe of comprehension all at once. You have to start somewhere, with some piece of the puzzle that you can deal with instructionally. All we would require is that over the course of your instructional program, you deal with all of the tasks in the taxonomy.

2. With the exception of the figurative language task, we see little reason to concern yourself with any strict scope and sequence for the tasks in this chapter or for the tasks in Chapter 5. From time to time we have suggested some guidelines for sequencing activities within a par-ticular task, for example, categories, main idea, time relations. However, in general, we believe that most of the tasks we have included can be presented to students of any age if you are able to (1) adjust the content to match the students background and reading ability, (2) vary the cues you give (for example, creating versus choosing a main idea), and (3) adjust your expectations regarding the sophistication of the responses students are able to give. With respect to (3), you expect a fifteen-year-old to offer a more sophisticated explanation of Timothy's cake-baking motivations than a seven-year-old. Yet each should be able to derive a plausible response consistent with his or her background. With compre-hension, you may not have a scope and sequence of skills. Instead, you may have a *scope* of tasks appropriate at all ages and a *sequence* that is scaled in terms of the sophistication of responses students are able to provide at various stages of development.

3. Somewhat related to our second conclusion, just as we have dif-ficulty specifying hard-and-fast starting points for these tasks, so we have difficulty specifying termination points. We cannot imagine why you would want to terminate instruction in main idea, categorization, comparisons, or causal relations. In other words, we cannot imagine what it would mean to *master* any comprehension task to the degree that a student could no longer benefit from practicing it. Show us a fourth-grade student who has achieved the mastery criterion on your fourth grade main idea test, and we will show you that he has not mas-tered main idea. All we have to do is to alter the content drastically.

4. We continue to remind you that our instructional suggestions are just that—suggestive. They are not meant to provide an exhaustive list of appropriate activities. We are contended if they serve as stimuli for the kinds of creative assignments that thoughtful teachers have generated for decades, or perhaps, centuries.

REFERENCES

Bormuth, J. R., Carr, J., Manning, J., and Pearson, P. D. Children's Comprehension of Between- and Within-Sentence Syntactic Structures. *Journal of Educational Psychology*, 1970, *61* (5) 349–357.

Clark, E. V. On the Acquisition of the Meaning of 'Before' and 'After'. *Journal of Verbal Learning and Verbal Behavior*, 1971, *10*, 266–275.

Collins, A., and Quillian, R. Retrieval Time from Semantic Memory. *Journal of Verbal Learning and Verbal Behavior*, 1969, *8*, 240–247.

Durrell, D. *Durrell Analysis of Reading Difficulty*. New York: Harcourt, Brace and World, Inc., 1955.

Goodman, Y., and Burke, C. L. *Reading Miscue Inventory: Procedure for Diagnosis and Evaluation*. New York: Macmillan, 1972.

Kintsch, W. *The Representation of Meaning in Memory*. Hillsdale, N.J.: Erlbaum, 1974.

Lesgold, A. M. Variability in Children's Comprehension of Syntactic Structure. *Journal of Educational Psychology*. June, 1974, *66*, 333–338.

Menzel, P. Anaphora. In Bormuth, J. R. *On the Theory of Achievement Test Items*. Chicago: University of Chicago Press, 1970.

Pearson, P. D. *Children's Comprehension of Sequential Relations Among Events*. Unpublished paper. University of Minnesota, 1977.

Pearson, P. D., Boesen, M., and Carr, J. *A Rationale for Scoring Constructed-Response Items*. A paper read at IRA Convention, Kansas City, 1969.

Richek, M. A. Reading Comprehension of Anaphoric Forms in Varying Linguistic Contexts. *Reading Research Quarterly*, 1976–77, *12*, 145–165.

Schank, R. C. Identification of Conceptualizations Underlying Natural Language. In R. C. Schank & K. M. Colby (eds.), *Computer Models of Thought and Language*. San Francisco: Freeman, 1973.

Woolf, H. B., Editor. *Random House Dictionary of the English Language*. Springfield, Mass.: G. C. Merriam Company, 1973.

7

MAKING
JUDGMENTS
ABOUT THE
WRITTEN WORD

As WE went from Chapter 5 to Chapter 6, we cautioned you that we were moving from stability to volatility. In entering into an area that many people call "critical" reading, we continue in the same direction. In fact, as we have moved through all these instructional chapters, beginning with Chapter 4, we have increasingly tred on less stable ground; we continually address issues of decreasing certainty and exactness. It is probably also true that we increasingly consider issues more central to the process of developing capable and thoughtful readers.

Nowhere is this thoughtfulness more needed than in the issues discussed in Chapter 7. One may legitimately question the virtue of preparing students who can read correctly but cannot evaluate the accuracy of what they read. The purpose of this chapter is to assist you in helping students make better and more critical judgments about what they read.

FACT AND OPINION

We invite you to take the following test. For each of the following statements, make a determination regarding whether it is a fact (F) or an opinion (O); by writing F or O in the blank. If you cannot decide, put a question mark (?) in the blank.

1. Benjamin Franklin should have behaved more respectably in Paris.

   ———

2. Benjamin Franklin probably did more for this country than any of the other so-called Founding Fathers. ———

3. Benjamin Franklin did more for this country than Thomas Jefferson. ———

4. Benjamin Franklin wrote more books than Thomas Jefferson.

   ———

5. Benjamin Franklin was a remarkable man. ———

6. Benjamin Franklin was fat. ———

7. Benjamin Franklin was fatter than Thomas Jefferson. ____

8. Benjamin Franklin weighed 217 pounds. ____

9. Benjamin Franklin weighed 918 pounds. ____

10. Thomas Jefferson thought that Benjamin Franklin was a remarkable man. ____

11. Benjamin Franklin liked French women. ____

12. Benjamin Franklin drank a lot. ____

13. Benjamin Franklin drank two quarts of port a day. ____

14. On most days Benjamin Franklin drank two quarts of port. ____

15. It is a well-established fact that Benjamin Franklin drank too much. ____

16. Benjamin Franklin was more popular than Thomas Jefferson. ____

17. Benjamin Franklin was controversial. ____

18. The Bears beat the Tigers, 37–14. ____

19. The Bears trounced the Tigers, 37–14. ____

20. The Bears edged the Tigers, 37–14. ____

Here's a tentative answer key. The following are statements of fact: numbers 4, 7, 8, 9, 10, 13, 14, and 18. The following are clearly opinions: numbers 1, 2, 3, 5, 12, 15, 16, and 17. That leaves 6, 11, 19, and 20 as unclear, at least in our minds. With respect to the statements of fact, 4, 9, 13, and 14 are either incorrect or open to question. Whether or not that makes them opinions, we shall discuss later.

What makes a fact, a fact, and an opinion, an opinion? We quote from a widely used rhetoric text (Gorrell and Laird, 1967, p. 53) intended for use in a freshman English course.

> They (opinions) characterize or classify; they express approval or disapproval; they make a general statement. Their truth or falsity cannot finally be demonstrated. The facts report what has happened or exists; they result from observation or measurement or calculation; they can be tested or verified.

These distinctions may make sense to us, but they are probably too abstract to present to students in the upper elementary or early secondary years, the point at which fact and opinion activities are usually initiated. Later we shall present some guidelines that we think eleven- and twelve-year-old students can understand.

Verifiability

But back to the distinction between fact and opinion. Surely verifiability is one test we can apply. For example, there are probably records that would help us to decide whether (1) or (2) is correct. We can probably dismiss (3) on the basis of our inspection of portraits, a form of evidence.

(1) Benjamin Franklin weighed 217 pounds.
(2) Benjamin Franklin weighed 290 pounds.
(3) Benjamin Franklin weighed 817 pounds.
(4) Benjamin Franklin was fatter than Thomas Jefferson.
(5) Benjamin Franklin was fat.
(6) Benjamin Franklin was overweight.

Likewise, by reference to portraits, we can probably verify the truth or falsity of (4). But (5) presents a different problem because we cannot prove or disprove it without reference to a standard of fatness. We have less trouble with (6) because standards of overweight are intuitively clearer to us than standards of "fatness." Besides, fat is an emotionally loaded term, whereas overweight is more objective, almost neutral. One other aspect of verifiability deserves emphasis: *statements* of fact are often wrong. Simply because something is stated *as if* it were a fact does not make it a fact in the sense that it is a true statement about the world. Statement (3) is a statement of fact; it is just incorrect. Examine (7), (8), and (9)—all responses to the trivia question, who won the 1976 World Series?

(7) The Yankees won the 1976 World Series.
(8) The Phillies won the 1976 World Series.
(9) The Reds won the 1976 World Series.

While all are stated as though they are facts, only (9) is true. To call (7) and (8) opinions would be misleading. To characterize incorrect or uninformed statements of fact, we use the term, *guesses.*

Qualification

There are specific cues that place a statement more to the fact or more to the opinion end of the continuum.[14] Qualifiers like, *I believe, I think, In my opinion, It is my opinion that,* almost certainly introduce an opinion. For example, when *I believe* is inserted in front of (7), it becomes an opinion, as in (10).

(10) I believe that the Yankees won the 1976 World Series.

(As an aside, notice that the whole of statement (10) is a fact; presumably, the writer knows what he believes. However, we will leave this kind of complication to the metaphysicists.) Other words like *probably, likely,* and *usually* are indications that the writer is not certain of the truth of the statement; hence, they indicate opinions, as in (11) and (12).

(11) Benjamin Franklin usually did drink a lot.
(12) Benjamin Franklin probably was controversial.

Words like *should, ought, must,* and *have to* denote opinions (or judgments); they all indicate obligations, and obligations are rarely facts, as is evidenced by (13), (14), and (15).

(13) Tom should not drink so much.
(14) Benjamin Franklin should have behaved more respectably in Paris.
(15) You ought to try my new diet.

Quality versus Quantity

In general, adjectives that deal with qualities indicate opinions; those that deal with quantifiable phenomena indicate facts that can be tested for truth or falsity. Contrast (16) and (17).

(16) Susan is nicer than Amy.
(17) Susan is faster than Amy.

The empirical test for "niceness" has, as far as we know, yet to be developed. A simple foot race will allow us to test the truth value of (17).

---

[14] The notion of a continuum is appropriate. The distinction between fact and opinion is not clear-cut. A statement either *is more of a* fact or *more of* an opinion.

There are some fuzzy in-between categories. Take *popular,* for instance. Given modern polling procedures, we can test the truthfulness of (18).

(18) Early in their presidencies, Carter was more popular than Nixon.

General versus Specific

Other things being equal, the more general a statement the more likely it is to be an opinion; the more specific, the more likely it is to be a statement of fact. We have all been taught to avoid sweeping generalizations and categorical judgments. Yet they seem to remain a real part of our oral and written language traditions. Contrast (19) with (20), (21) with (22), and (23) with (24). The second statement in each pair lends itself to the verifiability test more readily than the first. Both testimony and evidence could be gathered to ascertain the truth value of (20), (22), and (24). It is less likely that (19), (21), or (23) could be so easily confirmed or disproved.

(19) Texans talk funny.
(20) Texans usually speak with an accent typical of their regional dialect.
(21) Willmer is a murderer.
(22) Two witnesses saw Willmer shoot at Johnson last night.
(23) Benjamin Franklin liked French women.
(24) While in Paris, Franklin was seen in the company of French women on 310 separate occasions.

There are some exceptions to this general rule, but they often deal with statements that are true by definition rather than observation. Contrast, for example, (25) with (26).

(25) All men are mortal.
(26) All men like potato chips.

Statement (25), while true, is not even in principle subject to verification, whereas (26) could conceivably be tested (although no one would want to try).

Objectivity

Other things being equal, statements that use neutral language are more likely to be factual in character than those that use emotionally laden terms. Contrast (27), (28), and (29). Statement (27) is more a statement of fact because the test for one team *beating* another is clearer and more objective than the the test for *walloping* or *edging*. Now if we add the phrase, "49–0", to each of the three statements, then (28) becomes more plausible as a factual statement because we are probably nearer whatever criterion exists for deciding when we have reached a genuine "walloping."

(27) The Vikings beat the Packers.
(28) The Vikings walloped the Packers.
(29) The Vikings edged the Packers.

Thus far we have suggested five criteria that can be used to help decide whether a statement is a statement of fact or a statement of opinion. We wish that they were clearer and more precise. Such is not the case. And because of this imprecision we anticipate that instruction for this task will not be simple.

We offer these guidelines.

1. In the early elementary years, students can start on the road to discerning fact from opinion by attempting to distinguish between make-believe stories and stories that could really have happened. Granted such discriminations differ from the fact-opinion distinction, yet practice in deciding whether a story is real or make-believe requires attention to evidence and detail (How do you know that this is a make-believe story?), a mind set that will be helpful at a later point in making fact-opinion discriminations.

2. In the later elementary years, you can begin systematic exercises in distinguishing fact and opinion. At first present only clear-cut facts and opinions. Use cue words such as *ought, must,* and so on, to signal the opinions. Make the facts specific and clearly testable. In these early stages, the task will be easier if the content is familiar to the students so that they can use prior knowledge in helping them to make these judgments.

3. As students demonstrate success in dealing with clear-cut examples, you can begin to expose them to the fuzzier cases (see the sections on objectivity, general versus specific, and quality versus quantity).

4. Distinguishing fact from opinion is not the kind of task that should be left to chance. It requires thoughtful guidance on your part as a teacher. Such guidance includes generous modeling, numerous examples, and substantive feedback. As each new facet of this task is introduced, offer numerous examples of fact and opinion statements. Ask students to give reasons for their judgments. Offer your own reasons (well, I decided that (7) was an opinion because . . .) when appropriate. Above all, offer substantive feedback—ask students to discuss their responses and their reasons for them—while correcting the assignment.

An expanded example of a modeling-feedback lesson appears in Chapter 9.

EVALUATING BIAS IN WRITING

If all writers (and all speakers) used only the most objective of language, if they used facts rather than opinionated sweeping generalizations, if they tried to inform rather than persuade, there would be little need for a section like this in a book about comprehension. As with the section on fact and opinion, there is a feeling that a section on recognizing bias is out of place in a book on reading comprehension. For in such a section, we go beyond comprehension—understanding the author's message—to evaluation—understanding the author's intent, however ignoble it might be.

We could invoke an argument made earlier in the section on ambiguous statements (see Chapter 6); just as we should not allow writers to write ambiguous statements so we should not allow them to write biased accounts. Yet we would not really want that. For one thing, it is illegal, a violation of First Amendment rights. For another, as long as man remains a political and economic animal, persuasion will be an important part of our written and oral traditions. Persuasion necessarily involves taking a point of view, a particular slant on an issue. It thrives on half-truths (or stretching the truth), sins of omission (leaving out critical details—not out and out lying, mind you), and emotionally loaded words and phrases (a walloping rather than a simple victory). Indeed, detecting bias and point of view is almost like a game of wits between writer and reader, speaker and listener, advertiser and consumer. And after a 2500-year history we should probably admit that it is a part of our political and economic linguistic tradition. But its existence creates an educational need. If writers (and speakers) are going to work within that tradition, the readers (and listeners) must learn the conventions.

What are the conventions? What are the devices used by writers that result in what we have called biased points of view.

Emotionally-laden Words

Examine the following instructional activity, originally written for a junior high audience (from Minnesota Statewide Assessment Test),

Writer 1

At 2:30 A.M. four courageous police officers braved darkness and the gunfire of three gangland mobsters to overtake the vicious criminals in their warehouse hideout near the waterfront.

Writer 2

In an early-morning shootout–fist fight, three suspects were captured by four city police officers in their warehouse hideout near the waterfront.

Writer 3

At 2:30 A.M. four burly and brusque city cops burst in on three helpless alleged burglars. Using unnecessary brute force, the police subdued their victims in a warehouse hideout near the waterfront.

1. Which writer is least sympathetic to the police?

Writer 1.
Writer 2.
Writer 3.
I don't know.

2. Which writer is the most objective?

Writer 1.
Writer 2.
Writer 3.
I don't know.

3. In the account of writer 3, which set of words listed below gives you clues to his point of view?

Four, city, hideout.
Brusque, brute, victims.
Waterfront, burglars, warehouse.
I don't know.

Writer 2 clearly is most objective, writer 1 favors the police, and writer 3 seems to dislike the police. But what makes the three accounts differ is the connotative value (the emotional loading) of the particular words selected in each account (see Chapter 4, Connotation-Denotation). There is little doubt that each description *denotes*, or refers to, the same incident. Yet each leaves us with a distinctly different impression about precisely what happened and who the villains and heroes were. Compare these terms in Table 7.1. The contrasts are revealing about the point of view of the writers.

TABLE 7.1

Denoted Term	Writer 1	Writer 2	Writer 3
policeman	courageous police officers	city police officers	burly and brusque city cops
suspects	gangland mobsters, vicious criminals	suspects	alleged burglars, victims
the action	braved, overtake	captured	burst in, subdued

While adjectives seem particularly to lend themselves to inspiring bias, verbs, nouns, and adverbs contribute their share. Contrast the following pairs of words:

politician-statesman
enlightens-confuses
official-bureaucrat
orator-demogogue
colorful-gaudy
expose-slander
lawyer-mouthpiece
suspect-alleged assassin

It is not difficult for a writer to achieve a particular slant by judiciously selecting words that contribute to the impression she wants to achieve.

Implication by Association

We remember a television advertisement, popular during the 1976 and 1977 car-advertising seasons that clearly illustrates the principle of implication by association: "Baseball, hot dogs, applie pie and Chevrolet." Presented in the pictorial context of pleasant All-American people having an All-American time, what could be more All-American than these four things: the All-American Sport, food, dessert, and, of course (but only by implication), car. Just as there is *guilt by association,* so there is *praise by association.*

Advertisements, particularly television commercials, make extraordinary use of this principle. Popular athletes endorse products. Why? Because the companies think that customers will believe that if a champion wins with the product, so will they. One commercial says as much for a tennis racket, "I play with it. I win with it." Praise by association!

In a less obvious manner, the principle is used in the naming of an object: Executive Ball Point Pens, Titleist Golf Balls, Devastator Tennis Rackets. Products have features like space-age circuitry or computer-precision tuning.

Another application of implication by association is a propaganda device commonly called appeal to authority, especially scientific authority. You have all seen the actor dressed in medical garb who comes on to tell you that he has found that a certain aspirin is remarkably effective in relieving headache pain. And there is the survey technique: sixty-four percent of all television repairmen own BXL sets, the implication being that television repairmen must know which set is best. We are both educators, and we assure you that we do not know which kind of school or which method of teaching beginning reading is best. But we could imagine a commercial for open schools or traditional schools in which it was reported that 64 percent of educators (who must know) surveyed sent their own children to open schools.

Implication by association is not limited to advertisements. Speakers use it all the time. A presidential candidate who may have never mentioned his war record once in the campaign thus far, makes certain that he tells a few appropriate war stories when he speaks before the American Legion convention. When college professors talk to a group of classroom teachers, they manage to tell a few stories about their days in the classroom. They believe it helps to establish credibility. Praise by association. Yet it has little to do with the message they may present. We too have used this device. If you look carefully in Chapters 4 and 5 you will find allusions to *our* classroom experiences.

Just as there is praise by association, so there is guilt by association. Sometimes disguised as a joke, a harmless story, or an aside, it is among the most insidious of rhetorical devices: "I'm not saying Smith is disloyal, but I hear he wears pink pajamas, even in the winter."

The witch hunts of the McCarthy era are too recent to allow us to forget the terrible cost of applying this principle to public figures in lieu of the due processes of our legal system. Perhaps the most damning of all was the implication that any witness who used his or her legally guaranteed right of protection from self-incrimination (the Fifth Amendment) was, by implication, hiding something. Invoking one's constitutional right was taken as prima facie evidence of communist leanings. The individual was accordingly drummed out of his or her profession. Guilt by Association!

Half-truths and Conveniently Omitted Details

Politicians, actors, and athletes—really anyone in the public eye—often complain of being misquoted in the paper. And some sensationalist newspapers seem to make a living by using quotations out of context. Compare the following original statement with the subsequent quotation.

John Smith: "In the field of secondary reading, Jones's book is the best I've ever read."
Quotation: ". . . Jones's book is the best I've ever read."

The quotation has conveniently omitted details that place a significant qualification on the statement. We are always suspicious when we see those three little elipses (omission) in a quotation (but perhaps we should be equally as suspicious when we do not see them. At least the writer who uses the three dots is admitting that something was omitted).

The half-truth is a clever device and is really an extension of our last principle, implication by association. A half-truth consists of two propositions, one true and the other either false or unverifiable. Examples (30) and (31) illustrate half-truths.

(30) Politicians give a lot of speeches, and they rarely tell the truth.
(31) The Bears beat the Vikings, but they had to resort to dirty football to do it.

The first proposition in each sentence is subject to verification; we can gather data or consult records to determine the truth of each. But the second proposition in each is more of an opinion; in (30) it is an overgeneralization while in (31) it is a value judgment. But by conjoining each opinion with a fact, the writer is hoping for a halo effect: if you accept the first statement, maybe you will accept the second in the same uncritical glance.

Overgeneralization

Clever polemicists use overgeneralizations in conjunction with factual statements, hoping that their audiences will regard the facts as ample support for the generalizations, even though the facts may only support a more modest generalization. Examine (32), (33) and (34). The factual statement in (33) would provide some support for generalization

(32) Phonics generalizations are not worth teaching.
(33) For example, the *ea* diagraph rule only works 52 percent of the time.
(34) Some phonics generalizations apply about as often as they do not apply.

(34) but we would need much more evidence before we could appropriately evaluate (32). Perhaps the most important question we can teach students to ask in the face of generalizations like (32) is, What is your evidence?

SOME INSTRUCTIONAL GUIDELINES.   1. Like the activities for fact and opinion tasks, we see no urgent need to deal systematically with bias and point of view until the late elementary or middle school years. We believe that it should receive increasing emphasis through junior and senior high school.

2. Instruction need not, and should not, be limited to the printed word. Since bias, propaganda, and persuasion are so characteristic of advertisements and commercials on television, we can imagine (indeed there are secondary teachers who do this) bringing a television set into a secondary reading or English class to view and evaluate the devices used in commercials to convince consumers of the superiority of their product.[15]

3. Like so many other comprehension tasks, this set of tasks requires teacher guidance. It ought not to be relegated to an independent activity strategy without introduction, discussion, and feedback. Instead, discussions in which students (and the teacher) share their judgments and the reasons for their judgments are needed (cf. Chapter 9, Modeling and Feedback section).

4. For introducing a lesson about emotionally loaded words, there is an old but delightful article by Hellman (1955) called "Time Lumbers On." It would be appropriate for an English class in the junior or senior year of high school.

5. Lest students think that all these devices are figments of their teacher's imagination, have them search newspaper and magazine articles and advertisements for examples. You should be allowed to contribute to the collection also. The examples can be categorized and displayed on a bulletin board if you like. Here are a few examples we collected from a recent daily newspaper.[16]

These headlines all are example of *connotatively loaded words*.

"Sox Slap Twins"
"Cruise Missile Hinders Arms Talks"

---

[15] While we are not in the business of endorsing particular reading materials (and have tried to avoid doing so), we must mention that the Rand McNally *Young America* series (1972) has devoted several pages of their upper-level workbooks to exercises dealing with bias, overgeneralization, and propaganda devices. Later we will include some of their materials as examples of reasonable practice activities.

[16] All these examples were collected from the *Minneapolis Tribune*, Sunday, July 3, 1977.

"The 15 Year Old Girl Made Her Dash for Safety . . ."
"Police Bouncer Question Bounced Around by Council . . ."

These advertising slogans are examples of *overgeneralizations.*

"No matter what the sentiment, sweethearts (roses) say it best."
"Yes, our whole philosophy is really different."

These advertising slogans are examples of *implication by association.*

"Find out why millions are watching this unusual show." (This invites you to get on the bandwagon.)
"It's a fountain of youth."
"Charcoal is used . . . by NASA to freshen the air in space craft . . ." (Tareyton's charcoal filter improves flavor.)

6. Using examples like the following accounts of the basketball game, as an introduction, students can practice writing reports that are biased one way or another or as neutral as possible. Make up teams of three students, assigning each person in the team the biased or the neutral point of view. Later these should be compared to determine how the bias was communicated. (Examples from Minnesota Statewide Assessment Test.)

THE FACTS

The Abbeystown Centaurs defeated the Centerville Boomers 84–72 in a basketball game played on the Centerville High School basketball court last night. The leading scorer for Centerville was Alex Simpson with twenty-four points. James Smith (6'1") led Abbeystown with thirty-one points, followed by Ralph Fritz (5'11") with twenty-six. Abbeystown coach, Gil Shuffle, was quoted as saying, "The Centaurs can beat any team in the state which tries to use a full court press against them. Under pressure, they really come through." Each team was called for twenty-one fouls. The Centaurs made thirty-two of sixty-one field goal attempts; the Boomers made twenty-eight of sixty-nine.

Account 1

Operating on the theory that if you shoot enough times, the ball will eventually go in, the bruising Abbeystown Centaurs squeaked by the Boomers 84–72 last night in the local gym. The finesse of the Boomers was not enough to overcome the sloppy but bruising play of the larger Centaurs, particularly their two Goliaths, Smith and Fritz. Aided by some unfair officiating, the Centaurs threw up enough missiles to capture the game in the last few minutes. The Centaurs arrogant Coach, Gil Shuffle, was quoted as saying that his team can beat any team in the state.

Account 2

The Abbeystown Centaurs used accurate shooting and good ball handling to demolish the tenacious full court press of the Centerville Boomers 84–72. Never in real trouble throughout the game, Smith broke through the press to drive in for easy lay-up baskets. When they could not get the lay-up, Fritz canned fifteen- to twenty-foot jump shots with the grace of a gazelle. According to mild-mannered coach Gil Shuffle, the Centaurs stand a chance of winning the state tournament. Shuffle added that they really come through under pressure.

7. As we indicated earlier, we have found some workbook activities that deal with biased language in a reasonable manner. We have reprinted a few pages for your perusal (pp. 148–151).

A FINAL WORD

In the preceding sections we have turned from comprehension to evaluation of the printed (or spoken) word. Even though such content does not fit neatly into our three-level taxonomy, we feel it is a topic that is important in its own right and, hence, deserves treatment in a book about reading comprehension. In terms of transfer to real-life situations, these evaluative tasks may be more important than more straightforward comprehension tasks. No matter how well or poorly people read, they are still confronted with the need to evaluate claims made by writers, politicians, polemicists, and advertisers (indeed all people in the business of persuasion). Granted, people can and do *survive* in our world without such evaluative skills. But mere survival has never been the only goal of our educational system. Most educators still hold out for goals like an informed electorate, rational decision makers, careful consumers—in short a decent quality of life.

These topics—fact and opinion, bias, propaganda—represent fuzzy aspects of comprehension. They overlap. The criteria for categorizing examples are imprecise. Different readers are likely to make different classifications. The discussions you hold on these topics are likely to generate controversy and disagreement. But despite this fuzziness—or rather because of it—these topics require careful guidance on the part of the teacher. More so than for other areas, teachers must rely on modeling, discussion, and feedback strategies. Granted some good materials exist to aid students in developing these evaluation skills. But much of

Spotting Propaganda Traps

Some kinds of propaganda try to stampede you into thinking or behaving in a certain way. If you aren't careful, you can be drawn into attitudes or actions you probably wouldn't have fallen into had you known how to recognize propaganda traps.

In recent years, with so many kinds of propaganda and so many ways of spreading it, public agencies have tried to educate people to watch for propaganda tricks. One such agency has analyzed a number of often-used kinds of propaganda and given them names, so that you can learn to watch for them. Read through the list of propaganda tricks below. When you think you understand all of them, see if you can tell which ones are being used in the examples on the next page.

1. Name Calling—appealing to hate and fear by giving "bad names" to people, groups, races, nations, or beliefs that the speaker or writer wants us to mistrust or dislike.

2. Glittering Generalities—using impressive and appealing generalizations that "shine" for almost anybody ("truth," "honor," "freedom," "justice") to make us feel that the speaker is a fine man because he has all the same ideals that we do, but without being specific or giving any real guarantee as to how he is going to attain them.

3. Transfer—getting the approval (or *suggesting* the approval) of a respected or honored group or institution for an idea or project, so that the respect we have for that organization transfers, or carries over, to the project, and we accept it because we think a group we respect has accepted it.

4. Testimonial—getting popular people or public heroes to testify that an idea or product is good, so that we will buy or accept it because whatever is good for important or well-known people must be good for us.

5. Plain Folks—suggesting that a prominent or important person is modest and humble, by having him wear clothes, take part in activities, or say things that prove he's really just ordinary like us and, therefore, trustworthy.

6. Card Stacking—Using every kind of trick, deception, half-truth, or false testimony to "stack the cards" against our learning the real truth.

7. Band Wagon—playing on fear of being left out to make us "jump on the band wagon," or follow the crowd in buying, believing, or doing whatever "everyone else" is supposed to be doing.

Write an example of propaganda, using the "Name Calling" approach.

Answers will vary.

_____

_____

Use with "The House in Parsley Street."

Spotting Propaganda Traps

Name the trap or traps used in each example of deceptive propaganda.

1. "Killer" Klein, world's greatest wrestler says: "Slikshave is for MEN!"
   Testimonial

2. "I tell you, fellow citizens, that what our country needs is a return to faith, courage, bravery, loyalty, and the honesty of our forefathers!"
   Glittering Generalities

3. A picture of a top-recording starlet modeling Cuddlesoft pajamas—
   Testimonial

4. "Imperialist war-mongers!" "Communist agitators!"
   Name Calling

5. A picture of Candidate Jones, a Wall Street financier, in overalls and straw hat, chewing on a straw and talking to farmers at a county fair—
   Plain Folks

6. "The latest polls show that our candidate will win by the largest landslide ever seen in this state!"
   Band Wagon (or Transfer)

7. A distinguished and well-known actor giving a commercial for Knoxitquick headache tablets—
   Testimonial

8. "Going fast! Over 2 million already sold. Don't miss out on this bargain!"
   Band Wagon

9. "Again the opposition party offers a slate of power-hungry bosses, bureaucrats, and big spenders."
   Name Calling

10. "Dignity Carpets for your home! Used in churches, synagogues, and temples all over the country!"
    Transfer

11. "If elected, I plan to increase employment, raise wages, build more and better public housing, extend and improve our highways, lower the taxes, and balance the budget."
    Glittering Generalities

Recognizing Prejudice

In an earlier exercise you read news stories that revealed their writers' feelings about the news they reported. Sometimes, of course, merely the headline will tell you.

Below are ten pairs of headlines. Read each pair and then answer the question opposite it by writing the letter of one of the headlines in the blank.

1. (a) Indians Scalp Sox 5-4
   (b) Indians Edge Past Sox 5-4

   Which headline favors the Sox? __b__

2. (a) Candidate *X* Wins by Narrow Margin
   (b) Candidate *X* Triumphs

   Which headline favors Candidate *X*? __b__

3. (a) New TV Show Gets Acclaim
   (b) New TV Show Liked by Some

   Which headline favors the TV show? __a__

4. (a) Plan for New Park Merits Lively Discussion
   (b) Plan for New Park Stirs Heated Debate

   Which headline favors the plan for the new park? __a__

5. (a) Concert Draws Teen-Agers from Wide Area
   (b) Concert Mobbed by Out-of-Town Hippies

   Which headline does *not* favor the people who attended the concert? __b__

6. (a) Author's New Book Expected Soon
   (b) Author's Book Eagerly Awaited

   Which headline favors the author? __b__

7. (a) New Play Takes the Town by Storm
   (b) New Play Is Well Attended

   Which headline favors the new play? __a__

8. (a) Community Fund Fails to Reach Goal
   (b) Community Fund Slightly Below Expectations

   Which headline favors the Community Fund raisers? __b__

9. (a) Weather Perfect for Skiers
   (b) Weather Perfect—If You Happen to Be a Ski Buff

   Which headline does not favor snow? __b__

10. (a) Group Reaches Decision Quickly
    (b) Group Makes Hasty Judgment

    Which headline does *not* favor the decision made by the group? __b__

Use with "The House in Parsley Street."

Recognizing Propaganda

"It's not what you say, it's the way you say it!"—and the words a writer chooses to describe a person or event can be a very significant part of that "way."

Both stories in each pair of news stories below report the same event, but they give the reader different feelings about it. As you read each pair of stories, circle words you think are "loaded" with feelings the writer wants the reader to have. Then answer the questions that follow the stories. **(Answers may vary.)**

A. A lucky last-minute basket by Riverdale nosed out Westville's hard-fighting Warriors in a nonconference meeting Friday. A rough-and-tumble affair from beginning to end, the game was frequently tied, but Westville lost out to heavy fouling and inefficient officiating by both referees.

B. Refusing to give up, Riverdale's plucky heroes fought their way to a two-point victory in a sparkling extra-schedule contest with Westville Friday. Hard-fought right down to the wire, the battle was neck-and-neck all the way. Officials showed understanding for rule infractions caused by the spirited play.

Which do you think appeared in Riverdale's school paper, story A or story B? __B__

If you had read only story A, would you consider the game had been played fairly? __no__

Read these two stories about a political candidate and a political gathering. Answer the questions with the names of the newspapers. **(Answers may vary.)**

From the *Standard*:

A smiling Harold Wilkins and his many loyal followers filled the Gold Room last night for one of their impressive dinner meetings. Nagged by reporters at the door, candidate Wilkins graciously clarified his former relations with speculators, and thoughtfully reserved judgment on the pollution uproar. As always, the charming Mrs. Wilkins was at her husband's side.

From the *Guardian*:

"Happy Harry" Wilkins and his crowd of cronies mobbed the Gold Room last night for still another fifty-dollar-a-plate affair. Questioned by reporters at the door, office-seeker Wilkins denied his long-time association with gamblers and stalled on taking a position on the pollution issue. The ever-present, sugar-sweet Mrs. Wilkins accompanied her husband.

Which newspaper would like to see Mr. Wilkins elected? __Standard__

Which one had reporters at the door to challenge him? __Guardian__

Which one thinks pollution is an important subject? __Guardian__

Would you rely on these papers to help you form a sound opinion? __no__ the material must come from naturally existing sources—newspapers, commercials, magazines, students' compositions.

Finally, we suggest that the ultimate goal of such instruction is to help students build strong schema that they can use when they encounter these devices on their own. Just as one can have a schema for *dog* or a script for what happens in *restaurants* or *wars,* so students can develop schemata for what constitutes a *factual statement,* what characterizes *implication by association,* or what identifies the intent of *connotatively biased words.* What makes this type of instruction particularly difficult is that, in contrast to earlier discussed comprehension tasks, there may not be much *known* to which one can attach the *new.*

REFERENCES

Fay, L., Ross, R. R., and LaPray, M. *The Young America Basic Reading Program Skillbook,* 6. Skokie, Ill.: Rand McNally, 1972.

Gorrell, R., and Laird, C. *Modern English Handbook.* Englewood Cliffs, N.J.: Prentice Hall, 1953.

Hellman, G. Time Lumbers On. *The New Yorker.* April 16, 1955, 34–36.

8

QUESTIONS

Q UESTIONS HAVE been a mainstay of reading comprehension instruction for decades. They appear on most standardized and informal comprehension tests. Workbooks are filled with them, and teachers' manuals provide numerous prereading and postreading questions to use in discussing the selections that students read. Second-grade students are sometimes asked to copy them off the chalkboard and answer them in complete sentences. Middle school students often get as many as fifteen or twenty per selection in the form of a duplicated study guide.

However, simply because questions are widely used is no evidence of their quality, importance, or appropriateness. In fact, Guszak (1967) demonstrated that students were best at answering the types of questions teachers asked most often (factual recall). It is possible that a teacher who focuses on a particular kind of question may develop an undesirable set in his or her students. But Guszak's finding is an argument against particular questioning strategies, not against questions in general. We believe in questions. We see them as a vital part of any discussion activity. We think they are important in both formal and informal assessment procedures. And we believe they have a place in independent practice materials. The issue is not whether or not to use questions, but how, when, and where they ought to be used.

We should point out that we have already devoted considerable discussion to questions. In Chapters 4 to 7 we often suggested appropriate questions as a means for getting students to engage in the comprehension tasks discussed. Furthermore, we will discuss questions again in Chapters 9 and 10. Why, then, a separate chapter devoted to questions? First, their widespread use merits special attention. Second, since our approach to categorizing questions is somewhat unique, we feel obligated to compare and contrast it with other taxonomies. Third, and most important, because it represents yet another perspective we can use to examine the alleged mystery called reading comprehension. Examining reading comprehension is much like trying to diagnose a respiratory disease. A doctor will perform a blood test, looking for an abnormal distribution of white and red blood cells. Then he or she might take an x-ray and attempt to match the patient's x-ray against standards that typically indicate a certain disease—pneumonia, for example. Throat cultures, body temperature measurements, and other vital signs are assessed in order to gather more and more indexes to assist in the diagnosis. But the organism, the human body, being examined remains the same. Each test is a new perspective, not completely independent from the other tests, but adding new information nonetheless. Our approach to "comprehending comprehension" is similar. In each chapter we have examined the same phenomenon—reading comprehension—from a different perspective. The phenomenon has not changed but our perspective has. Hopefully, with each new perspective, you have gained some new insight about comprehension.

Our plan for this chapter differs slightly from the previous four chapters. We will discuss some general issues about questions. Then we will offer some guidelines for using questions in written and oral activities. Finally, we will compare and contrast our categorization scheme with another commonly used taxonomy.

QUESTIONS AND PSEUDOQUESTIONS

What is a question? Most of us would agree that the so-called wh-type interrogative sentences are questions: Who, What, Which, What did, When, Where, Why, How. Examples (1) and (2) illustrate wh-questions.

To this group, linguists (Menzel, 1970) would add yes-no questions—examples (3) and (4), tag questions—examples (5) and (6), intonation questions—examples (7) and (8), and cleft questions—(9) and (10).

 (1) What did John eat?
 (2) Where did Susan go?
 (3) Did John eat the meat?
 (4) Did Susan go to the movies?
 (5) John ate the meat, didn't he?
 (6) Susan went to the movies, didn't she?
 (7) John ate the meat?
 (8) Susan went to the movies?
 (9) What was it that John ate?
(10) Where was it that Susan went?

For our purposes as teachers of reading comprehension we need not be concerned with cleft questions. They differ very little from straightforward wh-questions. We should be concerned about students' ability to understand intonation questions and tag questions when they encounter them in written discourse. But neither is widely used as a way of probing comprehension in discussions, workbook activities, or test items. Yes-no questions are common to classroom discussions but rarely get into tests or workbooks. Wh-questions are the most numerous in discussions, tests, and instructional materials. Hence, they merit your greatest attention.

There are a number of instructional directions that do not meet the grammatical tests for any of the types of questions linguists discuss. Yet they seem to impose the same requirements on students as do questions. We call them pseudoquestions—questions, if you will, in disguise. Compare, for example the pairs (11) and (12), (13) and (14), (15) and (16), and (17) and (18).

(11) What were the causes of the Civil War?
(12) Enumerate the causes of the Civil War.
(13) Where did John go to buy a new fishing rod?
(14) Name the place John went to buy a new fishing rod.
(15) Why did Amy sue the school?
(16) Give a reason explaining why Amy sued the school.
(17) How did Joanna clean the garage?
(18) Describe the way in which Joanna cleaned the garage?

Each probe in a given pair calls for the same response. Hence, we regard the even-numbered probes as pseudoquestions.

Now compare the pairs (19) and (20), (21) and (22), and (23) and (24), where the task in each even-numbered probe is to fill in the blank.

(19) Who went to the store?
(20) ———— went to the store.
(21) When did Susan finish her homework?
(22) Susan finished her homework ———— ————.
(23) Why did Theresa scream?
(24) Theresa screamed because ————————.

These [cloze and modified cloze]¹⁷ questions differ only slightly from the questions they are paired with. We would not want to go to the extreme of claiming that *all* [cloze] activities are questions in disguise. We would not make that claim, for example, for the cloze task where every fifth word has to be filled in. However, many of the so-called completion (fill-in-the-blank) exercises should be regarded as pseudoquestions. One distinction must be made: questions usually provide more information about the form class (part of speech) or grammatical function called for than do completion items. Contrast (21) and (22). In (21) we know that some time word, phrase, or clause is called for. In

---

¹⁷ The term cloze was coined by Taylor (1953). It's relation to the phrase, "reaching closure," is evident. *Cloze* refers to an activity in which a student fills in a blank from experience. *Modified cloze* activities usually require a student to select the correct words from among choices.

(22), a location (where), a time (when), or a manner (how) could all satisfy the grammatical constraints of the sentence. Even so, we find it useful to regard completion items as pseudoquestions.

What is the value of our notion of pseudoquestions? First, it broadens our regard for the general influence of questions as comprehension probes. Second, it allows us to classify heretofore unclassified tasks in convenient and already accessible schemes, that is, existing question taxonomies. Third, it makes good sense to us, intuitively and logically.

A SIMPLE TAXONOMY OF QUESTIONS

Partially because we admit that our taxonomy of comprehension tasks is relatively complicated, and partially because we find the following taxonomy intuitively appealing, we have adopted a question taxonomy with only three categories. As such, it hardly qualifies as a taxonomy. In our estimation its greatest value is its ability to capture the relationship between information presented in a text and information that has to come from a reader's store of prior knowledge (scripts and schema).

We will discuss three kinds of questions (or more accurately, question-answer relations): textually explicit, textually implicit, and "scriptally" implicit. Textually explicit questions have obvious answers right there on the page. Some would call them factual recall questions. Textually implicit questions have answers that are on the page, but the answers are not so obvious. For "scriptally" implicit questions, a reader needs to use his or her script (see Chapter 3) in order to come up with an answer.

As a way of introducing the taxonomy we invite you to read passage (25) and answer questions (26) through (35).

WILL WENDS HIS WAY

(25) Right after the Civil War, many distraught soldiers made their way West to find fame and fortune. Some could not go home because there were no homes to go to. The war had devastated them. One young man, Will Goodlad, made his fortune in the hills of Colorado. He found gold in a little river near Grand Junction. His fortune was short-lived, however. In 1875, he declared bankruptcy and returned to the land of his birth—the Piedmont of South Carolina.

(26) When did Will Goodlad declare bankruptcy?
(27) When did Will Goodlad discover gold?
(28) Where did he discover gold?

(29) Where was Will born?
(30) How did Will make his fortune?
(31) Why couldn't some of the soldiers go home?
(32) Why were there no homes to go home to?
(33) Would a soldier from Boston have had that same problem, that is, no home to go to?
(34) For what side did Will fight during the war?
(35) What was short-lived?

Now let us look at some sample responses to the ten questions and then try to analyze where the responses came from (or could have possibly come from)?

(26) When did Will Goodlad declare bankruptcy? (In 1875.)
(27) When did Will discover gold? (Sometime between 1865 and 1875.)
(28) Where did he discover gold? ([a] In a little river near Grand Junction or [b] in the hills of Colorado.)
(29) Where was Will born? (In the Piedmont of South Carolina.)
(30) How did Will make his fortune? (By discovering gold.)
(31) Why couldn't some of the soldiers go home? ([a] there were no homes to go home to, or [b] the war had devastated their homes.)
(32) Why were there no homes to go home to? (The war had devastated them.)
(33) Would a soldier from Boston have had that same problem? (Probably not because there were no Civil War battles in Boston.)
(34) For what side did Will fight during the War? (The South.)
(35) What was short-lived? (His fortune.)

For which set of questions could the answers be directly, explicitly, and precisely taken from the text? The responses to questions (26) and (35) are obviously derived directly from the text. In fact, if we were to perform a grammatical parsing of the phrases of the target sentences and then put them in wh-words to form questions (26) and (35), the responses "in 1875," and "his fortune" are precisely the words that would have to be deleted in order to add the wh-question words (see Bormuth, 1970). If we were to make a distinction between literal and inferential comprehension, most of us would agree that when these responses are given to these questions, the reader has engaged in literal comprehension. For reasons that we will clarify later, we are going to label "textually explicit" the kind of comprehension that occurs when responses like (26) and (35) are given to questions like (26) and (35). Responses (28a) and (31a) also fall into this category; but notice that responses (28b) and (31b), even though they come from the text, do not quite fit the constraints for this category? There is something qualitatively different about (28b) and (31b).

Responses (28b) and (31b) are really more like the responses to questions (29), (30), and (32). For all five of these question-answer relations, the responses are derived from the text. But one would be hard pressed to argue that the responses were "directly, explicitly, and precisely taken from the text" in the same sense as they were for responses (26), (28a), and (31a), and (35). There seems to be some sort of inference necessary for these responses, however minor and obvious that inference may be.

For example, to derive the response "in the hills of Colorado," the reader must infer that the little river near Grand Junction is in the hills of Colorado. There are two possible sources for such an inference. One is based upon possible prior knowledge—the reader may have known prior to reading the text that Grand Junction is in the hills of Colorado. A second source may have been primarily the text with a little nudge from prior knowledge (scripts). Compare (36) with (37), (38), and (39).

(36) Will Goodlad found his fortune in the hills of Colorado.
(37) He discovered gold there.
(38) He discovered gold there in a little river near Grand Junction.
(39) He discovered gold in a little river near Grand Junction.

Notice the comparability of the term, "there" in (37) and "in a little river near Grand Junction" in (39). In the section on anaphora (see Chapter 6) we discussed the fact that some normal everyday words (nouns, adjectives, verbs, and so on) often serve the same role as pronouns. One way to analyze a response like (28b), "in the hills of Colorado," is to regard it as an anaphoric restatement of the phrase, "in a little river near Grand Junction." In short, just as the reader must infer that "he" refers to Will Goodlad, so he or she must infer that the one specific location *stands for* the other more general location. Notice that a similar argument could be made for the relationship between "fortune" and "gold." It is not totally dissimilar from the clear-cut class inclusive anaphoric relation between deer and animal in (40). There is, however, one important distinction between clear-cut class inclusive anaphora, as in (40), and the examples in (36) and (39).

(40) The *deer* walked into the clearing. The cautious *animal* looked carefully in each direction before drinking from the brook.

In (40) the more specific term comes first; then, the more general term. In other words, the inclusive word, animal, is the anaphora for the antecedent (and the more specific or *included* word), deer. In (36) and (39), the relation between antecedent and anaphora is reversed. Logically, "gold" cannot be the *certain* anaphora for "fortune"; nor can we know *for certain* that "in a little river near Grand Junction" is the anaphora for "in the hills of Colorado." That is, Grand Junction *could* be somewhere else—Utah, for example. To illustrate this point consider the relation between animal and deer in (41). In (41) it is more plausible to assume that there may have been two animals than it is in (40).

(41) The *animal* walked into the clearing. The cautious *deer* looked carefully in each direction before drinking from the brook.

In (41), the deer may have been concerned about the animal that just walked into the clearing.

So much for formal reasoning. Now to pragmatic (practical) reasoning. Even though "deer" might not refer to "animal" in (41), most of us assume that it does. Chances are 995 out of 1000 that it does. It *probably* does. Such is our way of thinking. In fact, we would probably think the author stupid or unskillful if we found out later that "deer" did not refer to "animal." So it is with "gold," "fortune," "in a little river near Grand Junction," and "in the hills of Colorado." We would question the author's craft if the river were not in the hills of Colorado or if gold were not Will's source of fortune. As readers we believe that we have the right to make such inferences even if they are not logically necessary, in a formal sense. To us, they make good sense!

Now to the parallel between anaphoric relations and the inference involved in response (28b). Just as the reader has to decide that *he* refers to Will Goodlad—an inference, no matter how simple it may seem—so, he or she must be willing to take similar risks in deciding that the river and Grand Junction must be in Colorado. The same type of pragmatic reasoning is involved. And mature readers have little difficulty drawing such inferences because they have been conditioned to expect such relations in text. It is almost as if readers had certain expectations (scripts, perhaps) about text organization.[18]

When responses like (28b) are given to questions like (28), we cannot justify labeling this literal comprehension. Granted the question has been derived from the text, as has the response. But it is not obvious that the response is the answer to the question. As we have pointed out, at least one inference (hills of Colorado→little river near Grand Junction) is involved. We call this textually implicit comprehension in order to capture the notion that while both question and answer were *textually* derived, the relation was *implicit* rather than explicit; hence it had to be inferred.[19]

[18] Logically, if a relation is implied in a text, it has to be inferred by the reader. Imply and infer represent a set of complementary terms.
[19] In conversations with colleagues, some have argued that recognizing these anaphoric relations is not an inferential process. Rather, it is a literal process controlled and dictated by the syntactic requirements of the text. Future analysis and research

By invoking this category of comprehension, we put ourselves at odds with the conventional wisdom. As far as we can tell, from a perusal of other question taxonomies and from discussions with teachers, the conventional wisdom dictates that *any* response that comes from the text represents literal comprehension. Our quarrel with the conventional wisdom is both logical and affective. Logically, we do not see how one can deny that inferences are necessary to answer question (28) or (31) with responses (28b) and (31b). Now they may not be qualitatively important inferences, but they are inferences nonetheless. Affectively, we believe that by labeling such comprehension literal, we would be failing to give the student credit where credit is due. Responses (28b), (29), (30), (31b), and (32) represent nifty bits of reasoning. We applaud such responses because they demonstrate that the reader has spent some time trying to understand the text; he has not merely taken the answers verbatim from the text. Once again, we highlight our definition: comprehension is regarded as *textually implicit if* there is at least one step of logical or pragmatic inferring necessary to get from the question to the response *and* both question and response are derived from the text.

We have yet to classify the question-answer relations for (27), (33), and (34). Where do these answers come from? Most of us would answer, from the reader's fund of previous experiences. Given the constructs that we have introduced, we would answer, from the reader's script(s). We assume that a reader could have scripts for "Going West," "Wars (and maybe a special Civil War script) and their Aftermath," "Striking it Rich," and "From Riches to Ruin."[20] We further assume that readers use an appropriate script whenever they confront text (or any other linguistic or sensory stimulus) containing concepts (or associates of concepts) which are part of that script.

Let us go back to responses (27), (33), and (34), and see if we can determine how a reader might have derived them when confronted with questions (27), (33), and (34).

The response "between 1865 and 1875" represents an integration of scriptal data (The Civil War ended in 1865; the text implies that Will did this after the Civil War, hence he did it after 1865) and an inference

---

may validate their claims. However, until such validation occurs, we will persist in regarding these relations as implicit, hence requiring inferences on the part of the reader.

[20] Here, we must admit, is a basic weakness of scripts. It is difficult to specify how many scripts a person has or would need. A related problem is the issue of script and subscript. For example, do I really have a separate Civil War script or is my knowledge of the Civil War subordinated in my generic war script in the form of examples that fit into neat categories like Adversaries, Good Guys, Bad Guys, Weapons, Theaters, and so on?

from textual data (the text says that Will went bankrupt in 1875; he had to have something to go bankrupt from, so it must have been the fortune he made from discovering gold; therefore, he must have discovered the gold between 1865 [the earliest possible date) and 1875 (the latest possible date]). Had the response been simply before 1875, we would have classified it as a textual inference and, therefore, "textually implicit comprehension. We would have altered our classification because the response, "before 1875" does not require the reader to use scriptal knowledge about the Civil War.

The type of comprehension represented by the relation between the question and response in (33) is more clearly scriptal. Question (33) is only incidentally related to the story (it simply establishes the fact that Will—from South Carolina—had no home to go home to). The only way a reader could generate the response, "No, because there were no Civil War battles in Boston," is from his or her knowledge about Civil War battles.

The question-answer relation in (34) is a bit more like (27) than (33). It represents an integration of textual data (Will is from South Carolina) and scriptal data (chances are 999 out of 1000 that a man from South Carolina fought for the South, that is, the Confederacy).

One more example. When we gave this passage to students, several gave response (28c) to question (28), especially when we tested an hour or more after they had read the passage. Clearly such a response represents a scriptal inference.

(28c) Out West.
(28) Where did Will discover gold?

When originally reading the passage, the reader must have connected Colorado with its location in the United States. Later, the specific information had faded, but the general location was still in memory.

Scriptal comprehension, then, occurs when a reader gives an answer that had to come from prior knowledge (it is not there in the text) to a question that is at least related to the text (that is, there would be no reason to ask the question if the text were not there). It is similar to textually implicit comprehension in that an inference is involved; however, it is different in that the data base for the inference is in the reader's head, not on the page.

Operational Rules for Determining Comprehension Categories

We hope that by now it has become obvious to you that we are not classifying questions per se; instead, we have been classifying relations that exist between questions and responses: Essentially, our scheme is based upon the data source that *must have been used* by the reader to generate that particular response.

A question-answer relation is classified as *textually explicit if* both question and answer are derivable from the text *and if* the relation between question and answer was explicitly cued by the language of the text. Hence, if response (44) is given to question (43) after reading the text in (42), the student has engaged in textually explicit comprehension. We like to think of this type of comprehension as "reading the lines."

(42) Up at Basset Lake, a man was ice fishing using minnows for bait. Two pet crows helped him fish. They pulled on the lines with their beaks. And they put their feet on the line to keep it from slipping into the hole. Because the crows were smart, they got a meal. So did the clever fisherman!
(43) Why did the crows get a free meal?
(44) Because the crows were smart.

However, if a student gives response (45), the student has engaged in textually implicit comprehension.

(45) Because the crows helped him fish.

Why? Because there are no explicit textual cues that enable the reader to make response (45). Hence, a question-answer relation is classified as *textually implicit if* both question and answer are derivable from the text *but* there is no logical or grammatical cue tying the question to the answer *and* the answer given is plausible in light of the question. Related to this plausibility criterion, we need to point out that many so-called text inferences turn out to be wrong. Pearson and Nicholson (1976) found that many students seem to select more or less random text segments to give as answers to questions like (43). Some, for example, gave responses like (46) or (47).

(46) Clever fisherman.
(47) Basset Lake.

When we see responses like this, we are reminded of the classic Thorndike (1917) study in which he found that certain words in a passage are what he called "over-potent"; that is, they seem to grab the reader's eye (or mind) and cause her to avoid a careful logical analysis of the task. We label responses like (46) and (47) "textual intrusions": they come from the text, but there is no way that one could generate an argument that they are plausible answers to the questions. To use a harsh phrase, they are wrong. Errors notwithstanding, students often give plausible responses that lead us to infer that they have engaged in textually implicit comprehension. Think of such comprehension as "reading between the lines."

Suppose the student responds by giving answer (48) (a response which was actually given, by the way, in the Bormuth *et al.* 1970 study).

(48) The crows proved their worth to mankind.

Intuitively, most of us would probably want to congratulate the student for such a thoughtful response. It seems to represent higher-order reasoning. But how can a student be given credit for such a divergent response? By recognizing the possibility that the student has taken the text segment and processed it through his or her mental store of scripts and concepts, we could generate a chain of inferences that would allow us to get from the explicit statement, because the crows were smart, to the actual response in (48). It might go like this: Well, how can crows be smart? Maybe by helping a fisherman. A fisherman is a part of mankind; helping is a way to prove your worth. Hence the crows were proving their worth to mankind. Notice that nothing in this chain of practical (pragmatic) logic beyond helping fisherman comes from the test. The rest would have to have come from the reader's mind. But the logic is plausible. It is an inference from the text to the reader's fund of knowledge. We label this type of comprehension *scriptally im-plicit*. It occurs *whenever* a plausible nontextual response is given to a question derivable from the text. We like to think of it as reading "beyond the lines."

Earlier we talked about textual intrusions. Similarly, there are scriptal intrusions, responses that must have come from the students head but for which no plausible line of reasoning can be generated. Example (49) illustrates such a scriptal intrusion.

(49) Because of the scarecrow.

TEACHING IMPLICATIONS OF THE TAXONOMY

What is the point of this method of classifying the question-answer relations? To us, the most important point is that you cannot classify questions in isolation. Questions which on the surface look like they require simple, straightforward, literal recall of factual details may in fact require a complex set of inferences which involve the integration of textual and scriptal information. The implication for teaching is clear—

students who do not possess the requisite scriptal information or who are deficient in their power to draw logical inferences between text segments will not be able to respond accurately to questions without explicit answers in the text. And all the admonitions in the world to "go back and read the text more carefully" will not help. Instructors can help by (1) altering students' scripts—that is, teaching them more about the Civil War and its aftermath, or (2) guiding their growth in the ability to draw inferences between text segments.[21]

Another implication of this taxonomy is that certain questions may appear to require higher-order processes when, in fact, they require only textually explicit comprehension. For example, the question, "Why couldn't some of the soldiers go home," and the response, "Because there were no homes to go home to," represent such a relation. Some experts consider why questions to require higher-order reasoning when, in fact, the cause-effect relation may be explicit to the point of being painfully obvious.

A third implication is that you may not always get the kind of comprehension that you anticipate, even when you ask a "low-level" question which has a textually explicit response. In the Basset Lake story, students were allowed to look back at the story to answer the "free meal" question. Yet many gave responses that indicated textually implicit or scriptally implicit comprehension. We make this point in order to encourage you to adopt a set for diversity when correcting student assignments or discussing a story. To your eye, the question you ask may have an answer that is right there on the page. But the student may have already processed that text segment and integrated it with one of his scripts or schemata.

But perhaps the most important point in this whole treatment is the remarkability of the human brain—its ability to process, integrate, and manipulate sometimes quite disparate bits of information in order to make sense out of its "worlds." And, we think the admonition to you as a teacher is to think through rather carefully the kinds of questions you ask in relation to the "data" you provide your students. Sometimes your scripts are too strong, too well developed. In fact, they are sometimes so strong that you really believe the data are *right there on the page,* when in fact they are really somewhere up in that left cerebral hemisphere of that information processor we call your brain. Other times your scripts are too weak, so that you are unwilling to accept a plausible response that not *right there on the page.* In short, you have to be as aware of *your* data sources as you are of the data sources available to your students.

---

[21] In Chapter 9, we will have more to say about discussion techniques and modeling processes teachers can use to *try* to help students become better inference makers.

REEXAMINING COMPREHENSION OF LONGER DISCOURSE

In Chapters 5 and 6 we discussed various kinds of relations (tasks) that exist between and among propositions in longer discourse. And we often suggested question probes as useful tools for informal assessment and/or practice of the tasks. Now that we have made some more refined distinctions among questions (or, more accurately, among question-answer relations), we can briefly reexamine some of the propositional relations in Chapters 5 and 6 with an eye toward assessing the effect of our question-answer taxonomy on the performance of those propositional relations. In particular, we shall try to make two points: (1) quite often a relation (for example, a causal relation) is stated in such a way that textually explicit comprehension is not possible, and (2) a trade off exists between the grammatical complexity of a propositional relation and the factor we have called textual explicitness.

Consider statements (50) and (51) in relation to question (52).

(50) Susan cleaned her room. Her mother gave her a piece of Devil's Food cake.
(51) Because Susan cleaned her room, her mother gave her a piece of Devil's Food cake.
(52) Why did her mother give Susan a piece of cake?
(53) Because she cleaned her room.

If the causal relation is stated as in (50) then a student is forced to operate at least at the level of textually implicit comprehension. While the inference from question (52) to response (53) may seem so obvious as to be trivial, it is, nevertheless, an inference. And if (50) appeared in a story context, the inference might not seem so trivial because of the search task involved in locating the correct text segment as well as the competition from other information in the story. In contrast the causal relation in (51) is explicit; hence it is possible to engage in textually explicit comprehension in getting from question (52) to response (53). This points to a general rule about comprehension tapped by question probes: if the relation is explicit in the text, all three types of comprehension (textually explicit, textually implicit and scriptally implicit) are possible. If the relation is textually implicit, then textually explicit comprehension is preempted (not possible). And carrying the argument one step further, if the relation is scriptally implicit (that is, there is no plausible response anywhere in the text) then both textually explicit and textually implicit comprehension are preempted. Recall our discussion of predicting outcomes (forward inferencing) and drawing conclusions (backward inferencing) in Chapter 6. Anytime students are asked to predict an outcome, they must engage in what we have labeled scriptally implicit comprehension. The answer simply has not (yet) been presented in the text; hence neither textually explicit nor textually implicit comprehension is possible. Drawing conclusions will always involve either textually implicit or scriptally implicit comprehension. By definition, the task preempts the possibility of textually explicit comprehension.

We might expect comprehension to be more accurate when causal relations are made explicit. Yet, from the standpoint of complexity, (51) is more difficult than (50). In (50), you have two simple declarative statements. The average length of the two sentences is seven words. In (51) the average sentence length is fifteen words. Furthermore, (51) contains a grammatically complex subordinate clause. Readability formulas, which usually use either sentence length or grammatical complexity as an index of difficulty, would lead us to believe that statements like (51) should be more difficult to understand than statements like (50). And some experts (Flesch, 1946) have recommended shortening sentences and removing subordinate clauses as an effective means of increasing the comprehensibility of materials. The research on this issue is mixed. Pearson (1974–1975) found increased sentence length and complexity to be an aid to comprehension; however, Coleman (1964) and Standal (1976) have obtained either mixed or opposite results.

Regardless of the research, the logical trade off is important. Quite often, when you reduce sentence complexity, you place an added inference load on the reader. A person who reads (50) must infer that A is the cause of B. When you increase complexity, you may make a propositional relation explicit but you impose a heavier processing load on the reader. The person who reads (51) must hold more in his or her short-term memory load before the sentence is completely processed. At present, we do not know which of these factors is more important; hence our recommendations are inconclusive. We make the point, however, because we think it is important for you to realize these facts when you evaluate responses given by students to questions you may ask.

We could, but we will not, retrace our steps through Chapter 5, providing examples to illustrate these two points as they apply to several of those propositional relations. Suffice it to say that these points are particularly important for causal relations (including conditionality and purposiveness), time relations, main idea–detail relations, and comparisons.

To summarize, then, (1) a relation can be stated and probed in such a way as to preempt textually explicit and/or textually implicit (but never scriptally implicit) comprehension, and (2) there is an important trade off between explicitness and complexity, such that simple sentences place a heavier inference burden on the reader while complex sentences place a heavier processing burden on the reader.

COMPARING TAXONOMIES

We could compare our three taxonomies (Tables 4.1 and 5.1 and this one in Chapter 8) with any number of comprehension taxonomies; however, we will limit ourselves to Barrett's (1976) taxonomy, because it is, in our judgment, the most widely used in college reading courses and workshops. We shall list each of Barrett's levels in quotation marks. Then we will identify a similar task from one of our taxonomies, pointing out similarities and differences. Whenever Barrett lists skills that we do not address, we shall use the phrase, *not included*.

> 1.0 *Literal Recognition or Recall.* Literal comprehension requires the recognition or recall of ideas, information, and happenings that are explicitly stated in the materials read. *Recognition Tasks,* which frequently take the form of purposes for reading, require the student to locate or identify explicit statements in the reading selection itself or in exercises that use the exlicit content of the reading selection. *Recall tasks* demand the student to produce from memory explicit statements from a selection; such tasks are often in the form of questions teachers pose to students after a reading is completed. Two additional comments seem warranted with regard to literal comprehension tasks. First, although literal comprehension tasks can be overused, their importance cannot be denied, since a student's ability to deal with such tasks is fundamental to his ability to deal with other types of comprehension tasks. Second, all literal comprehension tasks are not necessararily of equal difficulty. For example, the recognition or recall of a single fact or incident may be somewhat easier than the recognition or recall of a number of facts or incidents, while a more difficult task than either of these two may be the recognition or recall of a number of events or incidents and the sequence of their occurrence. Also related to this concern is the hypothesis that a recall task is usually more difficult than a recognition task, when the two tasks deal with the same content and are of the same nature. Some examples of literal comprehension tasks are:
>> 1.1 *Recognition or Recall of Details.* The student is required to locate or identify or to call up from memory such facts as the names of characters, the time a story took place, the setting of a story, or an incident described in a story, when such facts are explicitly stated in the selection.

While we have not dealt directly with details per se (except in the support of main ideas), we would argue that anytime you have a textually explicit statement that can be used as an answer to one of the types of wh- questions (who, what, when, where, why, how, which) outlined earlier in this chapter, a student can (but need not) engage in what Barrett calls comprehension of details. We say *need not* because, as we have argued, students often go "between the lines" or "beyond the lines" to answer such questions.

> 1.2 *Recognition or Recall of Main Ideas.* The student is asked to locate or identify or to produce from memory an explicit statement in or from a selection which is the main idea of a paragraph or a larger portion of the selection.

We believe that nearly all main ideas are inferences, even if the main idea is stated in the text. Why? Because it is not logically or grammatically necessary for a main idea to be a main idea. If a sentence says, "John hit the ball," then the response "John" is a grammatically necessary answer to the question, Who hit the ball? But there are seldom grammatical cues that tell you that a particular statement is the main idea of a paragraph (unless, of course, the text says, "The main idea of this section is . . ."). You have to infer that a particular statement, of all the statements in the paragraph or passage, is the main idea *even when* it is stated in the paragraph. You cannot do so without reference to prior knowledge about the topic or without comparing the statements in a paragraph and inferring that one statement logically subsumed the others. Hence we would not agree with Barrett's inclusion of main idea as a literal comprehension task.

> 1.3 *Recognition or Recall of Sequence.* The student is required to locate or identify or to call up from memory the order of incidents or actions explicitly stated in the selection.

If there are explicit cues (such as before, after, then, next, etc.) then we agree with Barrett that sequence can be assessed at what he calls the literal (what we would call the textually explicit) level. If however, no such cues are provided, then we believe that the student has to infer sequence. Our discussion of time relations in Chapter 6 speaks to this issue.

> 1.4 *Recognition or Recall of Comparisons.* The student is requested to locate or identify or to produce from memory likenesses and differences among characters, times in history, or places that are explicitly compared by an author.

Comparisons are seldom explicitly cued. They can be, however. For example, (54) provides a specifically cued comparison. But suppose we had not provided

(54) Just as Barrett has a level called literal comprehension, so we have
    a level called textually explicit comprehension.

you with statement (54). And then we asked you question (55). You
would have had to infer the comparable category. Hence we conclude
that while it is possible to have literal comprehension of comparison
relations,

(55) What in the Pearson/Johnson scheme is comparable to Barrett's lit-
    eral comprehension level?

it is more common to find them as inferential tasks.

> 1.5 *Recognition or Recall of Cause and Effect Relationships.* The
> student in this instance may be required to locate or identify
> or to produce from memory reasons for certain incidents,
> events, or characters' actions explicitly stated in the selec-
> tion.

Barrett's emphasis is on the fact that the reasons or causes be explicitly stated in the text. He does not speak to the issue of whether or
not the relation *between* the cause and effect must be explicitly cued.
Hence what he calls literal comprehension of cause-effect relations
could, in our scheme, be either textually-implicit or textually-explicit
comprehension of such relations.

> 1.6 *Recognition or Recall of Character Traits.* The student is
> requested to identify or locate or to call up from memory
> statements about a character which help to point up the type
> of person he was when such statements were made by the
> author of the selection.

Character Traits are not directly addressed in our book. Yet we can
account for such activities in two ways. If you ask question (58) after
statement (56), then the student can engage in textually-explicit comprehension. If, however, you ask (58) after (57), an inference must be
drawn. In short, whether recognition of character traits is literal or inferential depends on whether the text is explicit or implicit about the trait.

(56) Tom helped his mother a lot. Tom was a kind person.
(57) Tom helped his mother a lot. He also used to give marbles to the
    kids who didn't have any.
(58) Was Tom a kind person?

2.0 *Inference*. Inferential comprehension is demonstrated by the student when he uses a synthesis of the literal content of a selection, his personal knowledge, his intuition and his imagination as a basis for conjectures or hypotheses. Conjectures or hypotheses derived in this manner may be along convergent or divergent lines, depending on the nature of the task and the reading materials involved. For example, inferential tasks related to narrative selections may permit more divergent or creative conjectures because of the open-ended possibilities provided by such writing. On the other hand, expository selections, because of their content, may call for convergent hypotheses more often than not. In either instance, students may or may not be called upon to indicate the rationale underlying their hypotheses or conjectures, although such a requirement would seem to be more appropriate for convergent rather than divergent hypotheses. Generally, then, inferential comprehension is elicited by purposes for reading, and by teachers' questions which demand thinking and imagination which are stimulated by, but go beyond, the printed page. Examples of inferential tasks related to reading are:

Barrett's notion of inferential comprehension is very similar to our notion of scriptally-implicit comprehension.

2.1 *Inferring Supporting Details*. In this instance, the student is asked to conjecture about additional facts the author might have included in the selection which would have made it more informative, interesting or appealing.

If we were to ask a student to find the details that supported a particular main idea, we would regard his or her ability to do so as evidence of inferential reasoning, *even if* the details were stated in the text. We say this because the relation between a main idea and its details are rarely explicitly cued in a text.

2.2 *Inferring the Main Idea*. The student is required to provide the main idea, general significance, theme, or moral which is not explicitly stated in the selection.

See 1.2. In our scheme if the main idea is stated, then the student has to engage in textually-implicit comprehension in order to select it. If it is not stated then the student must engage in scriptally-implicit comprehension. Barrett's task in 2.2 is comparable to what we would have to call scriptally-implicit comprehension of main ideas (they come from your head).

2.3 *Inferring Sequence*. The student, in this case, may be requested to conjecture as to what action or incident might have taken place between two explitly stated actions or incidents; he may be asked to hypothesize about what would happen next; or he may be asked to hypothesize about the beginning of a story if the author had not started where he did.

What Barrett calls inferring sequence is similar to what we have labeled as drawing conclusions and predicting outcomes. We have discussed these topics under the rubric of causality in Chapter 6; notice that many events that are time related (in a sequence) are also causally related (A occurred earlier than B and also caused B). But Barrett is right in adopting a separate category here. There are certain events which occur in a sequence without being causally related. A person gets up before he brushes his teeth, but getting up does not cause tooth brushing behavior. We address this issue in the causal relations section in Chapter 6.

> 2.4 *Inferring Comparisons.* The student is required to infer likenesses and differences in characters, times, or places. Such inferential comparisons revolve around ideas such as: "here and there," "there and now," "he and he," "he and she," and "she and she."

See 1.4 As we stated earlier we think most comparisons represent inferential reasoning.

> 2.5 *Inferring Cause and Effect Relationships.* The student is required to hypothesize about the motives of characters and their interactions with others and with time and place. He may also be required to conjecture as to what caused the author to include certain ideas, words, characterizations, and actions in this writing.

This is exactly comparable to what we call drawing conclusions and predicting outcomes. See Chapter 6.

> 2.6 *Inferring Character Traits.* In this case, the student may be asked to hypothesize about the nature of characters on the basis of explicit clues presented in the selection.

See 1.6.

> 2.7 *Predicting Outcomes.* The student is requested to read an initial portion of selection, and on the basis of this reading to conjecture about the outcome of the selection.

Obviously we would include this in Barrett's 2.5 category.

> 2.8 *Inferring about Figurative Language.* The student, in this instance, is asked to infer literal meanings from the author's figurative use of language.

We agree with Barrett that recognizing the literal meaning of a figurative statement is an inferential skill (see Chapter 5).

> 3.0 *Evaluation.* Evaluation is demonstrated by a student when he makes judgments about the content of a reading selection by comparing it with external criteria, e.g., information provided by the teacher on the subject, authorities on the subject, or by accredited written sources on the subject; or with internal criteria, e.g., the reader's experiences, knowledge, or values related to the subject under consideration. In essence, evaluation requires students to make judgments about the content of their reading, judgments that have to do with its accuracy, acceptability, worth, desirability, completeness, suitability, timeliness, quality, truthfulness, or probability of occurrence. Examples of evaluation tasks related to reading are:

Barrett's notion of evaluation is quite similar to ours in Chapter 7.

> 3.1 *Judgments of Reality or Fantasy.* The student is requested to determine whether incidents, events, or characters in a selection could have existed or occurred in real life on the basis of his experience.

We deal with this topic in the section on fact and opinion in Chapter 7.

> 3.2 *Judgments of Fact or Opinion.* In this case the student is asked to decide whether the author is presenting information which can be supported with objective data or whether the author is attempting to sway the reader's thinking through the use of subjective content that has overtones of propaganda.

Barrett's notion of fact and opinion subsumes what we have called fact and opinion as well as our topic, detecting bias and point of view. (See Chapter 7).

> 3.3 *Judgments of Adequacy or Validity.* Tasks of this type call for the reader to judge whether the author's treatment of a subject is accurate and complete when compared to other sources on the subject. In this instance, then, the reader is

called upon to compare written sources of information with an eye toward their agreements or disagreements, their completeness or incompleteness, and their thoroughness or superficiality in dealing with a subject.

Not included in our scheme.

3.4 *Judgments of Appropriateness.* Evaluation tasks of this type require the student to determine whether certain selections or parts of selections are relevant and can contribute to resolving an issue or a problem. For example, a student may be requested to judge the part of a selection which most apropriately describes a character. Or he may be called upon to determine which references will make significant contributions to a report he is preparing.

Not included in our scheme.

3.5 *Judgments of Worth, Desirability, or Acceptability.* In this instance, the student may be requested to pass judgments on the suitability of a character's action in a particular incident or episode. Was the character right or wrong, good or bad, or somewhere in between? Tasks of this nature call for opinions based on the values the reader has acquired through his personal experiences.

We do not see this task as different from Barrett's own 2.6, *Inferring Character Traits and Outcomes.* See 1.6.

4.0 *Appreciation.* Appreciation has to do with students' awareness of the literary techniques, forms, styles, and structures employed by authors to stimulate emotional responses in their readers. Obviously, tasks which fall into this category will require varying degrees of inference and evaluation, but their primary focus must be on heightening students' sensitivity to the ways authors achieve an emotional as well as an intellectual impact on their readers. More specifically, appreciation involves cognizance of and visceral response to: (a) the artistry involved in developing stimulating plots, themes, settings, incidents, and characters, and (b) the artistry involved in selecting and using stimulating language, in general. Examples of tasks that involve appreciation are:

Frankly, we have not dealt with this whole area in any substantive way. Our reluctance to do so should not be interpreted to mean that we regard such tasks as unimportant; rather it reflects our lack of skill in approaching such issues rigorously and systematically.

4.1 *Emotional Response to Plot or Theme.* Tasks of this type are based on the assumption that the plot or the theme of a given selection has stimulated and sustained a feeling of fascination, excitement, curiosity, boredom, sentimentality, tenderness, love, fear, hate, happiness, cheerfulness or sadness. Provided this assumption is met, the students may be requested to determine what the author did in the process of developing the plot or theme that elicited a given emotional response.

Not included in our scheme.

4.2 *Identification with Characters and Incidents.* Some appreciation tasks should require students to become aware of the literary techniques and devices which prompt them to sympathize or emphathize with a particular character, or to reject him, for that matter. Other tasks should require students to consider the placement, nature, and structure of events or incidents which cause them to project themselves into the action.

Not included in our scheme.

4.3 *Reactions to the Author's Use of Language.* In this instance, the student is required to recognize and respond to the author's craftsmanship as reflected in his selection of and use of words. Such tasks may deal with the connotations and denotations of selected words and the influence they have on reader's feelings. In addition, students should at times note figures of speech, e.g., similes and metaphors, and the effect their use has on the reader.

We deal with this topic directly in Chapter 4, denotation and connotation, and in Chapter 7, detecting bias and point of view.

4.4 *Imagery.* Tasks of this nature require the reader to recognize and react to the author's artistic ability to "paint word pictures." In other words, students should become sensitive to the techniques an author uses in order to enable them to see, smell, taste, hear, or feel things through reading.

Not included in our scheme.

That our scheme has so many tasks in common with Barrett's taxonomy underscores a point made in Chapter 1. These tasks can be found in many disguises, under many names. We suspect that this fact has caused undue confusion to teachers. But we hope that it has been instructive for you to engage in this comparison now that you have read Chapters 4 to 8. We hope that the detail we have provided you has given you an *independent* grasp of comprehension—its components, its intricacies, and its interrelations. Hopefully, armed with this knowledge, you can understand any taxonomy you encounter—be it in a college text, or in a basal reader, or in a skills management system in your school—and recognize these tasks for what they are regardless of how they are labeled. Another useful outcome of this comparison has been to point out some of the shortcomings of this volume. We have omitted some important issues in comprehension but for lack of knowledge rather than lack of intent.

A FINAL WORD

While examining a number of different aspects of comprehension in this chapter, we have attempted to focus on questions. As should be apparent, it is difficult to discuss questions without getting involved in a number of related issues. Such is the nature of this thing we call comprehension. From this study these conclusions seem warranted.

1. When we focus on questions, we do not introduce a totally new topic related to comprehension. Instead, we examine the same phenomenon from yet another perspective.

2. While linguists distinguish among several kinds of grammatically generated questions, only two are of substantial concern for reading comprehension, wh-questions and yes-no questions. The others are used, primarily in oral discussions, but no question type, including yes-no, is used with anywhere near the frequency of wh-questions.

3. There are many comprehension probes, notably direct commands to perform a task (Name the person who did X) and completion items (_____ did X), that ought to be regarded as pseudoquestions; that is, even though they do not meet the grammatical requirements for a question, they serve the same function. They direct the student to complete the same task as would be required by a wh-question.

4. Rather than classify questions, we choose to classify the relation between a question and an answer. Specifically, we distinguish three types of relations: textually explicit comprehension (reading the lines), textually implicit comprehension (reading between the lines) and scriptally implicit comprehension (reading beyond the lines).

5. This three-level taxonomy can be applied to the tasks introduced in Chapters 5 and 6 (for example, main idea–detail or causal relations); the benefit derived from this application is twofold: (1) it clarifies the

trade off between explicitness and complexity, and (2) it highlights the logical hierarchy among the three types of comprehension discussed in number 4 above.

6. In comparing our scheme, as it has unfolded in Chapters 4 to 8, with the widely used Barrett taxonomy, two conclusions arise: (1) the comparison verifies a point made in Chapter 1, that comprehension tasks which share common requirements often appear with different labels, and (2) our treatment of reading comprehension, as extensive as it may appear, has not addressed certain important issues, in particular, issues related to the affective aspects of comprehension.

REFERENCES

Barrett, T. Taxonomy of Reading Comprehension. In Smith, R. & Barrett, T. C. *Teaching Reading in the Middle Grades*. Reading, Mass.: Addison-Wesley, 1976.

Bormuth, J. *On the Theory of Acheivement Test Items*. Chicago: The University of Chicago Press, 1970.

Bormuth, J., Carr, J., Manning, J., and Pearson, P. D. Children's Comprehension of Between- and Within-Sentence Syntactic Structures. *Journal of Educational Psychology*, 1970, *61*, 349–357.

Coleman, E. B., The Comprehensibility of Several Grammatical Transformation. *Journal of Applied Psychology*, 1964, *48*, 186–190.

Flesch, R. F. *The Art of Plain Talk*. New York: Harper and Brothers, 1946.

Guszak, F. J. Teacher Questioning and Reading. *Reading Teacher*, 1967, *21*, 227–34.

Menzel, P. *Anaphora*. Unpublished paper. University of California at Los Angeles, 1967.

Pearson, P. D. The Effects of Grammatical Complexity on Children's Comprehension, Recall and Conception of Certain Sematic Relations. *Reading Research Quarterly*, 1974–75, *10*, 155–192.

Pearson, P. D., and Nicholson, T. *Scripts, Texts, and Questions*. Paper presented at the National Reading Conference, Atlanta, December, 1976.

Standal, T. C. *The Effects of Syntactic, Semantic and Contextual Variations on Children's Comprehension and Recall of Causal Relations*. Unpublished Ph.D. dissertation. University of Minnesota, 1976.

Taylor, W. L. *The Cloze Procedure: How It Predicts Comprehension and Intelligence of Military Personnel,* (Technical memorandum No. 13 to the United States Air Force). Urbana, Ill.: University of Illinois,

Human Resources Research Institute, Division of Communications, 1953, 1–22.

Thorndike, E. L. *Reading as Reasoning: A Study of Mistakes in Paragraph Reading*. The Journal of Educational Psychology, 1917, 8, 323–332.

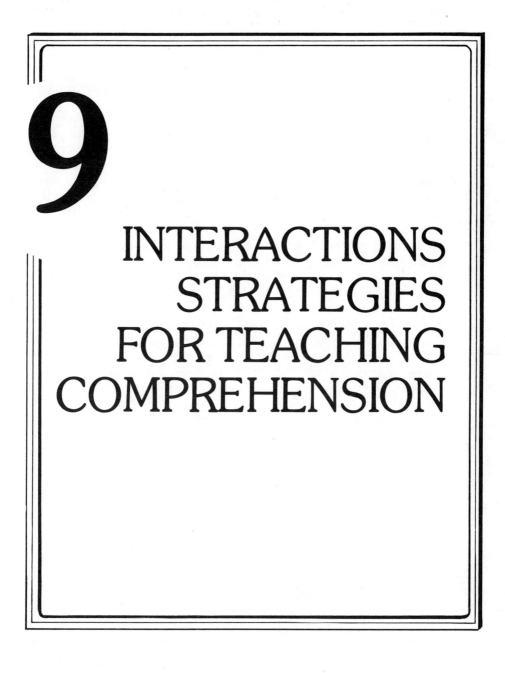

9

INTERACTIONS STRATEGIES FOR TEACHING COMPREHENSION

W‍E INDICATED that we would deal with discussion or interaction strategies that you can use in your classroom to promote the development of reading comprehension. Such a commitment is consistent with our belief that comprehension can, indeed, be taught. In fact, we would argue that much of the best instruction for developing comprehension of the *written* word is likely to emanate from activities that occur in the *oral* mode. In adopting this stance, we commit ourselves to a point of view that emphasizes the interrelatedness of all language activities.

There have been several points in previous chapters where we have already revealed this commitment to an interrelated view of language functions. For example, in Chapter 3, we suggested that our semantic map experimental procedure could be used with students to introduce the vocabulary in a new reading selection. In Chapters 4 to 7 we often suggested oral discussions for many of the activities and guidelines accompanying the specific tasks outlined at the concept and propositional levels of comprehension. And, also in Chapters 4 to 7 we suggested writing activities to accompany or to substitute for *reading* comprehension activities. But, heretofore, our commitment to an interrelated view of language functions has been incidental and implicit. We now propose to make it direct and explicit.

We illustrate four specific discussion techniques that you can use in your classroom to promote reading comprehension. In addition, we will refer you back to an earlier portion of this book in which we introduced a couple of discussion strategies in another context. These techniques are not meant to supplant skills or activities we introduced earlier; rather, they are meant to supplement those activities. The four specific strategies we will be dealing with in this chapter are concept stretching, slicing, previewing, and feedback and modeling.

CONCEPT STRETCHING

The principle of concept stretching is really an argument for more efficient instruction. We take the point of view that numerous opportunities arise in the course of instruction for you to develop and refine students' concepts. Suppose you are a first-grade teacher, and your students have completed a worksheet like the one in Figure 9.1. It is nothing but a simple, straightforward phonics workbook activity. Students see pictures of a top, a log, a pot, a cot, a mop, and a dog. For each

_op

l_g

do_

_ot

m_p

d_ _

Fig. 9.1.

picture they are required to fill in some missing letters in the words that are partially completed under each picture. A typical strategy would be to ask the students to complete the assignment on their own, and then correct the page with the whole group, while reinforcing correct letter-sound correspondences. Instruction usually stops there; after all, the objective of the activity has been met. Yet with a little imagination this activity provides an excellent opportunity to refine students concepts—for concept stretching. Let us illustrate by way of a classroom discussion.

Teacher: All right, students, let's take another look at this workbook page and see what else we can learn from it. I'm going to give you some directions, and I want you to follow and afterward we're going to discuss it. Ready? Okay, here we go. Would you put an S to the right of a picture that shows something that you can sleep on? Would you circle the pictures of anything that you could burn in a fireplace if you were really cold? Would you put an F over something that you could put flowers in? Would you put the letter T beside something that's a toy? Would you put the letter P above anything that shows something that you could play with? Would you put the letter C to the left of any pictures that show something that you could clean with? Would you put an H underneath a picture that shows something you'd be likely to find in a house. Put an L beside anything you'd expect to find in a closet. Now let's discuss your choices. What did you mark for something you could sleep on?
Student 1: Cot—you could sleep on a cot. We slept on a cot last year when we went camping.
Student 2: Yes, that's what I put down, cot.
Teacher: That seems reasonable. Anything else you could sleep on?
Student 3: Well, if the log was big enough, and you didn't have anything else to sleep on you could sleep on a log, but it probably wouldn't be very comfortable.
Student 4: Well, you could sleep on a dog, too, but then the dog might want to get up and move.
Teacher: Could you sleep on a mop or a pot?
Student 4: You could but you'd be sore when you woke up. But a bug could sleep on a mop, or a pot.
Student 3: Bugs don't sleep!
Student 4: They sure do. Everything that's alive has to sleep.
Student 2: Even plants? Plants don't sleep and they're alive.
Teacher: I don't think plants sleep. But, I don't know about insects, like bugs. But I do know that horses, cows, cats, dogs, squirrels—all animals like that—sleep. We'll have to find out. How about things you could burn in a fireplace if you were really cold?
Student 2: Log. You burn logs in fireplaces.
Student 1: Well, if you were really cold, you could put that cot in the fireplace too, and it would keep you warm for awhile.
Student 3: And you could burn a mop, too, but it wouldn't last very long either.

Student 4: You could burn a top if it was a wooden top, but not if it was made out of metal, because it wouldn't burn.

Teacher: How about a pot? Could you burn a pot?

Student 2: No, most pots are made out of clay or metal, and they won't burn too well.

Teacher: Okay, now how about our third question. It was to find something that you could put flowers in. What could you grow flowers in?

Student 4: A pot, of course. People grow flowers in pots all the time. We have lots of pots in our house, and we have some outdoors in the summer time.

Student 2: You could grow flowers in a log. In our backyard we have a couple old logs that are sort of cut out, and my Dad puts dirt in the hole and we grow flowers in it.

Teacher: Well, you could do that, but do we usually grow flowers in a log?

Student 2: No, but you could. We do.

Teacher: Which things are toys?

Student 2: Top. A top is a toy.

Student 4: Yes, but a mop could be a toy. You could play like you were cleaning up, and then the mop could be a toy.

Student 2: In the nurses room, they have cots, but they're not really toys. But it could be a toy if I were playing house.

Teacher: I think you're right. I think lots of things can be toys if we're playing games with them. But, when we think of something that is always a toy what would we think of that's on this page.

Student 3: A top.

Teacher: What's next?

Student 3: Things to play with.

Student 1: You could play with any of those things there. You can play with a top; you can play with a dog. If you had a bunch of pots, you could play with those. You can play with anything.

Student 2: Yes, but when you use a mop that's usually work except that it could be a toy. It could be something you could play with.

Student 3: How about a log? Can you really play with a log?

Student 1: Sure. You can play with logs. You can build things with them, I have some logs that you could build houses out of. You can use sticks as logs. Sticks are like little logs.

Teacher: Okay, how about the next one? The next one was, what could you clean with? What kinds of things could you clean with?

Student 2: A mop. You could clean with a mop.

Student 1: I don't see anything else you can clean with. Nope.

Teacher: I think you're right. I think a mop is the only thing on that page which you could clean with. Okay, how about things you could find in a house? Which of those things could you find in a house? Could you find a top in a house?

Student 1: Yes, you could find a top in a house.

Student 2: You could find a dog in a house. You could find pots in a house. You could find all those things in a house.

Student 3: How about logs? Logs are usually outside.

Student 2: Yeah, but you could find a log in a house if you were going to put it in your fireplace.

Teacher: I think you're right. I think you could find most of those things in a house. How about in a closet? Which of those things would you expect to find in a closet?

Student 1: Mop. People keep mops in closets.

Student 2: And, if you stored your camping equipment in a closet, then you could find a cot in a closet. You could keep a top in a closet.

Teacher: Could you keep a dog in a closet?

Student 2: You could, but it probably wouldn't like it very much. How about a pot?

Student 4: You could put a pot in a closet, but people usually don't put pots in closets.

Teacher: Well, I think you've done very well on this assignment.

If you think back to the concept model we presented in Chapter 3, you will recognize that much of this discussion centered on indicating the attributes of concepts, putting concepts into classes, and relating one concept to another. And all this from a mundane phonics workbook page. Perhaps the most significant part of the discussion were the alternatives suggested by the children. The kind of reasoning they went through when they speculated about things you could burn, things you could find in a closet, or the kinds of things that sleep. By the way, this discussion has yielded a classic "teachable moment." If that teacher does not have the students do some research about what kinds of animals do and do not sleep, he has lost an ideal opportunity for some worthwhile incidental learning. He will have failed to take advantage of the serendipity of the situation.

We offer this example because it demonstrates that teachers can accomplish worthwhile comprehension goals with the most unlikely materials and a little imagination. Almost any workbook page that has a few pictures on it, almost any set of objects sitting on a table, almost any stimuli in a classroom or on a playground could be used to generate a similar discussion. Again, the value of such a discussion lies in helping children to organize their world, helping them to see how things are related to one another. In short, the value of the activity lies in helping children to refine their semantic maps—to "stretch" their concept base.

SLICING AND OTHER QUESTIONING TECHNIQUES

While holding a discussion with a group of students most of us have probably had the unnerving experience of asking a question which was followed by what seemed like interminable silence. While many of us would sometimes pray for silence in a classroom, it is painful when it is not supposed to occur. What you have to ask yourself is why the silence has occurred. Quite often it should be taken as evidence that your students do not understand the question (or perhaps that they are afraid to answer). One way out in such an uncomfortable situation is to go right on to the next question. But then you have lost what might have seemed to be an important instructional goal. The students did not deal with the question you asked. An alternative to skipping the question is to engage in what we call *slicing*.

Essentially, there are two ways to "slice" a question. First, you can recast the question, asking for a smaller part of what was a larger issue. Second, you can change the task from a recall to a recognition mode by offering students alternatives from which to select. In short, you can make it a multiple-choice task. A variation of this second approach to slicing is to rephrase the question so that it requires a yes-no response.

Suppose question (1) was followed by silence; questions (2), (3), and (4) represent different ways of slicing (1) so that students might be able to handle it. Question (1) is very encompassing and rather imposing.

(1) What were the causes of the Civil War?
(2) Who can think of one cause of the Civil War?
(3) Let me give you some possibilities. Do you think it was railroad routes, states' rights, or slavery? Of those three, which helped to cause the Civil War?
(4) Was slavery one of the causes? Why? Who had the slaves—North or South? Who did not? Who thought slavery was immoral?

Students might balk at it, because they do not know *all* the causes. But they might know one cause. Or they might recognize one of the causes when they hear it. Then, once they get onto the right track, they may be able to expand their response. Sequence (4) illustrates an attempt to get students on the right track and then probe for expansion of knowledge.

Changing the Focus

It is difficult to overestimate the importance of slicing techniques. For students, slicing can be a subtle change of focus in the problem. Slicing can make students feel like they are fighting a battle, not a war. Let us illustrate a modification of slicing that foreshadows an activity called previewing, dealt with later in this chapter. Suppose you have asked question (5) and received no response.

(5) In 1865 how did they get rails from Pittsburgh to California?
(6) How do you think they might have moved rails from Pittsburgh to California in 1865?

Consider changing the question to (6). Notice that (5) requires the students to deal with real historical facts. There *is* a correct answer. For fear of being *wrong*, students may balk at (5). But (6) does not ask for historical accuracy. Instead it asks for speculation, a personal opinion about what might have happened. As such there is *no wrong* answer to (6). You have asked for an opinion, and whatever opinion a student suggests meets the requirements of the task. As with slicing techniques, changing the focus of a question so that speculation rather than factual accuracy is called for can make the task less imposing, less fraught with anxiety. There is nothing wrong with subsequently researching the question so that you arrive at a factually accurate answer to the question. But, at that point where personal opinion is asked for, then personal opinion, however bizarre, is acceptable.

A Teacher's Own Questioning Technique

Slicing techniques will work only if you, as a teacher, are honest and accepting in your questioning techniques. All too often, we believe, teachers ask open-ended speculation or opinion questions when what they really want is a very specific, factually correct response. Most often it is the response that they happen to be thinking of at the moment. They are playing a game that we call, "Guess what's in my head." The question is often phrased as a speculative-type question, such as (7). (We use question (7) to underscore the point that college professors are often the worst perpetrators of this practice.)

(7) How do you think we should teach phonics to children?

But the teacher has a specific response in mind. And each time a student fails to give the desired response, the teacher says, "Uh huh," or, "okay?" and calls on another volunteer until, finally, someone has accurately guessed what is in the teacher's head. And the usual feedback from the teacher is, "Right!" or, "Good," rather than "Uh huh," or "okay?"

Students learn rapidly not to trust the superficial sincerity of such a teacher. They learn that what appears to be a call for *their* opinion is really a probe for *the teacher's* opinion or for a specific fact. The negative reinforcement provided by the teacher helps them to learn to adopt a skeptical attitude. And rather than risk the inevitable, "Uh huh, next," reinforcement, they simply remain silent.

There are two rules of thumb you can use to avoid this self-defeating practice. First, *when you ask for an opinion or speculation, reward those who offer it*. They have, after all, satisfied the requirements of the task. You may want to list all the opinions offered on the blackboard, reserving judgment about their relative quality or accuracy until some later point. In other words remain neutral during the period when various opinions are being offered, treating them all equally. (We have found feedback such as, "I hadn't thought of that," to be an effective verbal reinforcement. It seems to tell the student that his or her point of view is unique.) When all the opinions are collected, offer the students some new data that they can use to evaluate their own opinion as well as the other opinions given—something to read or something you present orally. In a sense, this new information takes them "off the hook." Since it was not available to them before, there is no reason for them to feel badly about inaccurate speculation on their part.

The second rule of thumb: *When you have a specific fact or point of view that you want students to converge on, admit it*. In short, if you are playing, "Guess what's in my head," let the students know that you are. Do not disguise it. There is nothing wrong with guessing games. As evidenced by the popularity of daytime quiz shows, we seem to enjoy them. In fact, you are probably well-advised to make a guessing game out of such an activity, offering cues along the way:

> *Teacher:* I'm thinking of an animal that lives in the jungle.
> *Student 1:* Is it big?
> *Teacher:* Pretty big, but not so big as an elephant. And it can walk on two legs.
> *Student 2:* Would you find one in a zoo.?
> *Teacher:* Sure, but it would probably be in a cage.
> *Student 3:* A gorilla!
> *Teacher:* It's like a gorilla. But it lives in Borneo, not Africa. And, it starts with the letter, O.
> *Student 2:* An orangutan.
> *Teacher:* That's right! Now you try one.

A Conducive Environment

The success of slicing, changing the focus, and almost all discussion techniques depends upon the type of environment you, as a teacher, have established. Essentially, what you have to do is to create an atmosphere in which students know that it is not a sin to be wrong. In their preschool environment, children are not afraid to be wrong. In fact it is doubtful that a child can learn a concept like *dog* without calling a few cats, horses, and squirrels *dogs*. And parents, peers, or siblings usually respond, "No. That's not a dog; that's a cat." This whole process is more-or-less matter of fact, and children usually suffer no great psychic damage when they learn that a horse is not a dog. But something happens on the way to school. Suddenly, it is not only important to be *right;* being *wrong* becomes a sin only slightly more acceptable than misbehaving.

John Holt (1964) speaks eloquently on this issue, explaining several defense mechanisms children develop to avoid the stigma attached to being wrong. Most of them involve the avoidance of or the escape from risk-taking behaviors. For example, a simple *"I don't know"* response to a teacher's question allows the student to escape from the risk-taking situation. The student accepts a little anxiety—that associated with admitting ignorance—so that he or she does not have to run the risk of answering incorrectly. Ignorance is preferable to error. Other students adopt a *hand-waving strategy,* under the assumption that teachers never call on those students who obviously know the answer (a fact indicated by enthusiastic hand waving). Still others engage in what Holt calls the *Mumble Strategy.* When asked a question, the student mumbles an inaudible or unintelligible response. What the student hopes is that the teacher will be pleased that he said anything at all and will repeat the correct answer for all to hear or go onto another question (and student).

Why should students who, prior to school, never regarded being wrong as a personal indictment now adopt such clever and elaborate schemes to avoid being wrong? Possibly there is too much of a premium on being right in schools. Witness the oral reading circle, wherein not only teachers, but other students sit waiting to pounce upon the incorrectly pronounced word. Possibly, there are too many activities—too many questions, for which there is one and only one correct answer.

What can teachers to do avoid such a negative environment? We doubt that we have definite answers. However, we have found the following techniques to be helpful.

1. Use activities or questions which have more than a single correct answer. While convergent thinking activities (students converge on a single correct solution) are important, divergent thinking activities (students must seek divergent solutions) are also important. Contrast (8), a convergent task, with (9), a divergent task.

(8) How much is $17 + 18$?
(9) Besides erasing a blackboard, what else could you use an eraser for?

2. Engage students in activities in which they can learn that *no* is as useful an answer as *yes.* This is essentially because, as we pointed out earlier, the process of learning a concept requires the students to be exposed to incorrect examples. Our favorite game (after Holt's [1964]

suggestion) is, "guess what number I'm thinking of." You tell the students that you are thinking of a number between 1 and 1000. They can ask any question that can be answered yes or no, and their job is to guess the number with as few questions as possible. Suppose a student asks, "Is it between 501 and 1000?" Notice that a *no* response is equally as informative as a *yes* response. Yet a student who is used to regarding *no* as an indication of an error may not realize that he or she has gained just as much information as if *yes* had been the response.

3. Create an atmosphere in which it is all right to be wrong. One way to accomplish this goal is to model being wrong yourself. When students ask you questions, sometimes admit that you do not know the answer. Sometimes make an incorrect guess, and let the students do some research in a reference book to verify your error. Give credit for things that are "half right." If a student is reading orally and says "house" for "home," let the student know that it was a good try. It was half right, and it made sense. If a student's answer on a multiple-choice workbook activity does not match the answer key, regard it as acceptable if the student can give a plausible reason for it.

In summary, if discussion techniques are to facilitate reading comprehension, they must occur in a supportive environment, one in which students feel comfortable taking risks. Only in such an environment can you, as a teacher, guide students in the kind of give-and-take that will help them to become better readers, better thinkers.

PREVIEWING TECHNIQUES

In this section we will demonstrate how you can use previewing techniques in discussions to enhance students' comprehension of written discourse. We remind you of our discussion of concepts and scripts in Chapter 3 and invoke the principle of comprehension as *relating the new to the known*. In essence, previewing techniques serve the function of establishing what is *known* in anticipation of learning what is *new* in the text. But let us illustrate by way of an hypothetical discussion, one intended to prepare students to read a selection about the construction of the first transcontinental railroad.[22]

> *Instructor:* Tell me what you know about the Union Pacific Railroad. (No response.) Well, when was it built? (No response.) Before the Civil War? After? During?
> *Student 1:* Before!
> *Student 2:* After!

[22] We are indebted to W. Dorsey Hammond, Oakland University, for the example. He, we believe, is in turn indebted to Russell Stauffer.

Instructor: Now, why do you say before?

Student 1: Just seems right to me. Maybe it had something to do with the Gold Rush?

Student 2: No, it was after!

Instructor: You're sure about that?

Student 2: Pretty sure. There's something about a Golden Spike out West in Utah, or Nevada, or Wyoming, and that country wasn't even settled by the time of the Civil War.

Instructor: Didn't they have railroads before the Civil War?

Student 3: Sure the railroads came as early as 1820 or 1830. Right after the steam engine.

Student 4: But they were mostly in the Eastern United States.

Instructor: So no one is sure when it was built. Anyone want to guess about a date (several are offered ranging from 1840 to 1910)? Okay, where did it start and where did it end? (No responses.) Let me draw a map (draws sketchy map of the U.S.). Did it start over here on the East Coast, say Pittsburgh? Did it start up here, say Minneapolis? Did it start here, say St. Louis? Where?

Student 4: I think it was St. Joseph. Something started there.

Student 5: Omaha sounds right to me.

Student 3: St. Louis rings a bell for me.

Instructor: (Who has been jotting down guesses all along.) Well, we have three candidates. I'm not sure either. But we'll find out. Where did it end? Here, in Los Angeles? Here, in San Francisco? Here, in Seattle? Here, in Utah? Where?

Student 6: San Francisco, because Los Angeles was just a small town then.

Student 7: I seem to remember that it was not one railroad but two that built the first transcontinental railroad.

Student 8: That's right. It was a contest.

Instructor: So, when the railroad across the country was built it wasn't built from East to West?

Student 8: No, it wasn't! One company started from the East and the other started from the West.

Instructor: I think you're right. The first transcontinental railroad was built from both ends toward the middle. What do you need to build a railroad?

Student 5: Rails.

Student 4: Railroad ties.

Student 1: Workers.

Instructor: Okay. For the company that went from East to West, I can see how they got their materials.

Student 3: Yeah, they just loaded them onto railroad cars and hauled them to the end of the line.

Instructor: But how did they get their materials on the West Coast?

Student 5: Same way.

Student 7: Not then. No iron ore out there. But they could get ties.

Instructor: I think you're right. I think Pittsburgh was the center of steel production then. It still is, I guess. Well, let's assume they had to transport the rails. How could they do it? Overland Stage?

Student 6: No! Rails would have been too heavy for the wagons. And if they only took one or two it would have taken forever to haul the rails.

Instructor: Pony Express?

Student 6: No! By boat.

Instructor: (Pointing to map.) You mean they went from Pittsburgh to New York then around through the Panama Canal and up to San Francisco? (lots of nos. Why not, that's about the shortest way.

Student 3: The Panama Canal wasn't built yet. They had to go around South America.

Instructor: How do you know that? We haven't even established when the railroad was built. Maybe the Panama Canal was already finished.

Student 4: No!

Instructor: Did they have to go from Pittsburgh to New York to get a ship? Could they have gone another way?

Student 5: Maybe they went by barge down the Ohio River to the Mississippi, then to New Orleans.

Instructor: Could they? Does the Ohio River go through Pittsburgh?

Student 6: I'm not sure but I bet some river did that eventually went into the Mississippi.

Instructor: What about the ties? Do you think they just got those out in California and Nevada as they went along? Or do you think they hauled those from the Midwest or the East?

Student 7: There's lots of timber in California, in the mountains.

Instructor: But is it the right kind? Can you makes ties out of redwood or pine or fir?

Student 4: You could probably use fir, but not redwood or pine. They're too soft.

Instructor: I'm not sure myself. As a matter of fact, I'm not sure about much of this at all. Let's just review what we're not sure about at this point. (Instructor jots down the following points.) When was it built? Where did it start? Where did it end? Where and how did they get the rails and ties? Oh, one other thing—who were the workers?

Student 9: Coolies. Chinese coolies.

Student 7: On the West Coast. But from the East it was the Irish.

Instructor: Why the Irish and the Chinese?

Student 9: They brought in the Chinese just to work on the railroad because they were cheap.

Student 7: The Irish were new immigrants. They were cheap, too. It was the only kind of job they could get. They were discriminated against then.

Instructor: That's one more thing to look for—who built the railroad? And there's one other thing that's always puzzled me. Why did they build it from both ends toward the middle? It would seem to me to make more sense just to go from the East to the West. Then they wouldn't have had to worry about transporting materials by boat or whatever. Well, that's enough to look for. Here's an article about the railroad. Let's read it to see whether or not we were right about any of this.

Several points about this discussion deserve mention. First, the students already knew quite a bit about the topic they were going to read about. Admittedly, not all groups of students would have such good background knowledge. Yet most groups of students, collectively, will have some background for the topic. Much of that knowledge will be vague and imprecise. Notice the qualifiers that students use:

"It seems to me . . ."
"I seem to remember . . ."
"For some reason, that rings a bell."

But precision is not necessary. The goal of the previewing technique is to get the students into the right set—the appropriate script—for reading the selection.

Previewing can help students avoid what we call the Charlie Brown syndrome. Recall what Charlie Brown does whenever he gets a new book. Before he even looks at the book, he counts the pages (625 pages! I'll never learn all that!). He is defeated before he starts, before he has had a chance to realize that he does not have to learn *all* that. It is not *all* new. He already knows something about it. He has not given himself the chance to learn what he *already* knows about what he is *supposed* to know.

We fear that all too many students approach school subjects with the Charlie Brown syndrome. They start out believing, It's all Greek to me! That is not true! Chances are pretty good that they already know something about most topics they encounter in school. They just do not realize it. Indeed, one of the teacher's most important tasks is to help students make the connection between what they already know and what they need to know.

To cite another of our favorite literary figures, George Bernard Shaw allegedly said that every time he picked up a new book, the first thing he did was to construct a table of contents for it. Then he read the book to see what the author had left out. Not all of us are Shaws. But the point is clear: comprehension of any new material is facilitated when readers *know* they already *know* something about what they are supposed to *know*. Put another way, comprehension is facilitated when we approach what is new from what is already known.

The second point of the discussion relates to establishing motivation for reading a story. The teacher in our discussion could have saved a great deal of time and energy by handing out a worksheet with a set of questions similar to those asked in the discussion. But then the questions would have been the teacher's questions, not the students! By getting students to offer opinions, plausible explanations, and educated guesses, the teacher has "engaged" the students. They care. They want to know whether or not they are right—was it built in 1850, 1862, 1869, or 1910? They have something at stake.

We should point out that there is little that is unique in this recommendation. For example, Stauffer (1975) has advocated as much in his DRTA (Directed Reading-Thinking Activity), as have Thomas and Robinson (1972). A point of agreement among all these techniques is: if you can help students internalize pre-reading questions, it increases their motivation when they read the selection.

The third point of this discussion is somewhat negative, at least on the surface. Frase (1967) and others have demonstrated when questions are placed *before* text segments, students recall the information probed by those questions at the expense of other information they might otherwise have remembered. One possible implication of this finding is that students should not be given questions prior to reading. We disagree. The message we derive from Frase's finding is that you need to be very careful in selecting previewing questions. Make sure that your questions focus students' attention on important aspects of the text. Just as we believe that students rarely have to face text selections that are totally new to them, so we believe that students rarely *ought* to learn everything in a selection that is new to them.

Fourth, the distinction between so-called higher-level questions (calling for inferences and critical judgment) and rote recall questions (calling for specific factual information) is not always so clear as we might think. For example, question (10) is, on the surface, a rote recall question.

(10) For the Western half of the railroad, where did they get the rails?

Yet it introduces a set of complex issues related to transportation routes in the Mideastern United States as well as a set of issues related to the geographic distribution of natural resources such as iron ore, limestone, and so on. It may do as much to spur discussion as the seemingly higher-level question (11).

(11) Why did they have to get the rails from Pittsburgh?

The issue is not whether the question logically requires judgment or simple recall. The issue is: what purpose does the question serve? What is probably called for is some balanced sequence of higher- and lower-level questions, all serving the function of getting students to examine an important issue. Also, as we discussed earlier in this chapter (*cf.* section on Slicing), at times a simple recall question may seem less imposing to a student then a higher-level question.

A fifth and final point. Help given before a selection is read may elicit more and better reasoning from a wider range of students than help given after. Students approach a prereading task with a different attitude. After all, they have not yet read the selection. How can anyone expect them to know the "right" answers? It is a situation in which, because of ignorance, "your guess is as good as mine." In contrast, after they have read the selection they *are* supposed to know the right answers. And if they are not sure, they are reluctant to speculate.

In summary, we believe in previewing techniques. We think that the disadvantages that stem from these techniques are more than offset by the advantages that are derived from the motivational value of students setting their own goals, the linkages between the new and the known, and the relatively anxiety-free atmosphere. We recommend that you use previewing techniques, whenever possible, before content area reading assignments in social studies or science and occasionally before fiction reading assignments.

FEEDBACK AND MODELING STRATEGIES

We both recall—with some remorse—some of the practices we used while teaching elementary and junior high school reading. One seems particularly unfortunate in retrospect. Perhaps you will recognize the situation. Students have just completed a workbook page or a worksheet with several multiple-choice comprehension items. You ask the students to exchange papers. Then you say, "Here are the answers: 1A, 2C, 3B, 4A, 5A, 6B, 7D, 8D. Put the number wrong at the top of the page and pass it back to the person you got it from." Granted, the students will get *some* feedback about how they did, and they will get it right away. But it is questionable that such feedback is of any help, especially for a student who is having difficulty with the task.

There is an alternative. Assume that students have completed the following item, and now the teacher is ready to discuss their answers.

> With his new compass, his month's supply of food, and his stubborn *grubel*, the old prospector rode out once more to find the lost "Dutchmen" gold mine hidden deep in the Indian country.

A *grubel* is: (A) an old-fashioned type of back pack, (B) a new model pickup truck, (C) a secret map made of oil cloth, or (D) a packing animal like a mule or donkey.

> *Teacher:* Before we decide on the answer, I want you to reread the paragraph and underline the words that you think helped you decide on your answer. (After a pause.) All right. What do you think the correct answer is?

Theresa: D—a packing animal like a mule or donkey.
Teacher: What words helped you decide on a packing animal, Theresa?
Theresa: Stubborn. Mules are stubborn, like in "as stubborn as a mule."
John: Rode out. You could ride out on a donkey or a mule.
Teacher: Any others?
Matthew: Deep in Indian country. The ground would be rough, and it would be a long time ago, before they had pickups. And prospector. You always see pictures of prospectors with a mule to carry the gear.
Teacher: Why couldn't it be a pickup truck?
Theresa: Trucks aren't stubborn.
Teacher: But, don't people talk about a stubborn car? One that won't start.
Timothy: But it says, ride out. And . . . oh, yes, you *could* ride out on a truck.
Matthew: It would be too rough in Indian country.
Teacher: Come on, now. Haven't you ever seen those ads on television where the pickup trucks run through rocks and over hills.
Susan: That's right, Matthew. A truck could go almost anywhere, especially if it had four-wheel drive.
Teacher: But why couldn't it be a secret map made of oil cloth?
Kirk: Maps aren't stubborn.
Susan: My mom says a map is stubborn, when she's trying to open one while she's driving. But I don't think that's a good answer. Mule is the best answer.
Teacher: Why?
Susan: It makes sense. It can be stubborn. Prospectors usually have mules or donkeys.
Teacher: How could we change the paragraph so that the pickup truck would be the right answer?
John: If we said that he rode out *in* his grubel, then it would have to be a pickup truck. You couldn't ride out *in* a mule.

Three points about the discussion merit mention. First, the feedback was substantive. It had something to do with the item content. The student who may have missed the item has some idea of why mule is a better answer than pickup truck. Such feedback stands in sharp contrast to 1A, 2B, and so on.

Second, few items have one "right" answer. Some answers are better, more reasonable fits, than others. But the others are not wrong. They just do not fit as well. Furthermore, the student who can make a plausible case for an answer like a new model pickup truck should be given credit (even though you may want to try to convince him or her of the superiority of an answer like mule or donkey).

Third, a discussion like this provides models of reasoning and question-answering strategies for students who may have difficulty with the task. They are informed of the kinds of cues other students (and, perhaps, the teacher) attend to and the kinds of reasoning strategies they use.

We are reminded of the concept-stretching activity discussed earlier in this chapter. It does not take anything extraordinary in the way of materials to develop a good comprehension discussion. Even with something as mundane as a phonics worksheet or a multiple-choice vocabulary item, a teacher who is sensitive to students' needs, open to divergent points of view, and skilled in asking probing questions can do a great deal to promote reading comprehension and careful reasoning.

A FINAL WORD

An appropriate subtitle for this chapter might be, "Promoting Comprehension of *Written* Discourse through *Oral* Language Activities." In contrast to earlier chapters, such as 4, 5, 6, and 7 the teacher, not written materials, is the focal point of our discussion. We have tried to demonstrate that teachers serve a role more central than simply arranging for students to practice reading comprehension tasks.

Specifically, we have demonstrated four strategies for promoting comprehension: concept stretching, slicing, previewing, and feedback and modeling. These strategies share some common attributes. Each requires that a teacher choose questions judiciously, sometimes playing the devil's advocate and other times, a student's advocate; react flexibly, changing a line of questioning where necessary; and remain open to alternative student points of view, giving credit to good, but seemingly deviant reasoning.

We remind you of the interface between this chapter and the earlier chapters. First, everything we have discussed in Chapter 9 is consistent with our basic *new to known* principle introduced in Chapter 3. The whole point of previewing, concept stretching, and slicing is to find appropriate entries into a student's existing store of knowledge. Second, the feedback and modeling strategies should be systematically applied in student-teacher discussions of the tasks outlined in the two taxonomies in Chapters 4 and in Chapters 5 to 6. Third, there is a close relationship between concept stretching and the concept level tasks in Chapter 4.

At the end of each chapter on comprehension tasks, after we had outlined activities appropriate for each task, we offered the disclaimer that our activities were merely suggestions for you to try and revise according to your own circumstances or teaching style. In no way did we intend that our lists be regarded as exhaustive. We offer a similar disclaimer here. There are many other discussion strategies equally as appropriate as those we have outlined. We offer these as a starting point for you to develop and then to share other strategies which will accomplish our common goal of teaching students to read thoughtfully.

REFERENCES

Frase, L. Boundary Conditions for Mathemagenic Behaviors. *Review of Educational Research,* 1967, 58, 337–48.

Holt, J. *How Children Fail.* Pine Brook, N.J.: Dial Press, 1964.

Stauffer, R. *Directing the Reading-Thinking Process.* New York: Harper & Row, 1975.

Thomas, E. L., and Robinson, H. A. *Improving Reading in Every Class.* Boston: Allyn and Bacon, 1972.

10

THE ASSESSMENT OF READING COMPREHENSION

ASSESSMENT IS such an entrenched part of our educational system that we would be remiss in avoiding the issue, even if we did not believe in tests. Standardized, norm-referenced achievement tests have been used extensively since World War II. More recently, less formalized, criterion-referenced measures of specific objectives in a reading program (for example, *Wisconsin Design for Reading Skill Development,* 1972; *SMS-Skills Management System,* 1976) have gained popularity. An increasing number of states are creating their own tests (for example, *Minnesota State-wide Assessment,* 1973) and conducting their own statewide assessments. Basal-reading programs provide placement tests, end-of-unit tests, mastery tests (complete with criteria for determining when a child has mastered a skill), and progress tests. Elementary and secondary teachers continue to build their own tests for measuring reading skill mastery or knowledge of the content in a textbook chapter. Indeed, tests—or really, assessment procedures as a broader category—are widely used to help schools and teachers make educational decisions about individual students, groups of students, and instructional programs. In this chapter, we shall first review the kinds of comprehension assessment options that are available to you as a teacher. Then we shall address the general question of how one should use assessment data.

THREE PURPOSES OF TESTS

Before we begin to look directly at comprehension assessment it is necessary to address a prior question: "Why do we test reading comprehension?" Presumably we give tests in reading (or in anything else) because they help us make decisions. In fact, if testing does not lead to decision making, it has served no purpose. Let us examine some purposes for testing as shown in this outline.

I. Comparative Assessment
   A. Standardized Achievement Tests
   B. Most Useful to Administrators
II. Program Evaluation
   A. Published Tests (Basals)
   B. Teacher-made Tests
   C. Of Interest to Teachers and Administrators

III. Pupil Diagnosis
   A. Informal Reading Inventories
   B. Miscue Analysis
   C. Formal Diagnostic Tests
   D. Skills Management Systems (Criterion)
   E. Informal Diagnostic Tests
   F. Most Useful to Teachers

It seems there are three broad purposes for testing reading comprehension—purposes that can lead to instructional decisions: comparative assessment, program evaluation, and pupil diagnosis.

Comparative assessment might be more appropriately entitled comparative assessment and accountability. This is the type of testing typically done annually, in the spring or in the fall, in most school districts. Usually some respectable standardized achievement test like the Iowa, the California, the Stanford, the Metropolitan, the Step, the Gates-McGinitie, or any of the others are given to all children. Scores typically yielded by such tests are in the form of grade level equivalents or percentiles—and we will talk more about norm-referenced and criterion-referenced tests later in this chapter. Separate scores are usually reported for comprehension, vocabulary, and perhaps, rate of reading.

Such scores are of *virtually no use* to teachers. If a child scores poorly on comprehension, there is no indication of a cause—poor word knowledge, poor phonics, poor comprehension, or something else. Such tests are not intended to be diagnostic.

But if they do not help teachers make decisions (other than very gross ones like initial assignment to groups) who do they help? Presumably they help administrators. Administrators, by comparing the results at School A and School B could decide to allocate more recources to School A whose reading scores are consistently lower. Resources could be in the form of additional personnel, materials, or increased in-service training. Presumably administrators could fire (or retrain) teacher X whose first graders never score anywhere near so high as the first graders of teachers Y and Z, though all children in the school come from the same neighborhood and are grouped heterogeneously. Presumably, administrators use such test results to report to parents, the school board, and the community how well this year's crop compares with last year's or how well their district compares with others in the region, state, and nation. This is what we call accountability. Once we have these comparisons we are not sure what we do with them—what decisions they lead to. In fact, what we *really* believe is that such test results do not lead to very many decisions by anyone. They are typically given for three reasons:

1. Out of precedence—we have always done it.
1. Because of accountability—we are expected or required to report.
3. Because we must give them if we want to qualify for Title 1 money!

We would invite you to do some self-examination. Do you give such tests? If so, why? What decisions do they lead to?

A few words about program evaluation and pupil diagnosis. These purposes lead to tests of potential usefulness to teachers and to administrators as well. With program evaluation, our interest is not so much in the children as it is in the program. Is the program working? Is the new basal series, or the new phonics approach using games, or the new informal, free reading time working? Pre- and posttests such as the level-end tests of most basal series or the teacher-made tests of phonics or reading attitude, for example, can help teachers and administrators evaluate old and new, tried and true, innovative, enervative or any other kind of program. The decision? Let us keep it, or modify it, or reject it.

Pupil diagnosis is the type of testing of greatest usefulness to teachers. Who needs instruction in what? We know that all individuals are different, so why teach everything to everyone at the same time? Why not spare children the drudgery of instruction in things they already know? Earlier, we listed several types of diagnostic devices. Nearly all are individual tests rather than group tests. The exception is the criterion-referenced tests utilized by skills management systems. Thus, diagnostic tests permit teachers to analyze problems and strengths and prescribe appropriate instruction. If well constructed, they are highly useful to teachers.

To summarize this brief discussion of the purposes of testing we find Klein and Kosecoff's (1973) comments appropriate:

> A visitor to our planet Earth surveying the current state of educational testing would very likely be confused by what he found. He would observe, for example, the increasing use of tests in all phases and facets of the educational process including the evaluation of instructional personnel. He would learn, too, about the great technological improvements that have been made in tests and in their administration, scoring, and reporting procedures. All of these factors would tend to support the notion that tests are fulfilling an important and vital role. On the other hand, this same observer might also hear the valid complaints of the growing cadre of test critics. These critics complain that present tests are inappropriate for most educational decision making and, if a test is not going to be used for decision making, why bother giving it in the first place?

TYPES OF TESTS

Differences between Norm-referenced and Criterion-referenced Tests

Two major types of tests are used in reading: norm-referenced tests and criterion-referenced tests. The essential difference has to do with what the scores mean and what uses can be made of them. The score on a norm-referenced test tells how well the test taker did in relation to a national sample of test takers. The pupil's raw score is converted to some type of comparative score, such as a percentile rank or a grade level equivalence score. The score on a criterion-referenced test relates to a specific predetermined objective (criterion) or set of objectives. The criterion score does not compare the test taker with anyone else. Instead, it indicates whether or not a child has achieved a certain level of proficiency. When test givers are most interested in comparing children, they use norm-referenced tests. Criterion-referenced tests are more frequently used for diagnostic purposes, when the teacher is interested in discerning how well a child has learned a particular thing

While the notion of competency-based instruction and criterion-referenced testing could possibly be traced back to a Greek master and his pupil, Glaser's (1963) paper was probably the most seriously considered proposal; and this initiated the current movement. Previously, mastery of a skill was considered more a philosophical point of view than a measurement matter.

It is difficult to understand criterion-referenced testing without understanding the concept "minimum competencies," and the reverse is true as well. Simply, a *competency* is a behaviorally stated objective that specifies something a student should be able to do. In reading, a competency might include the ability to read common road signs, demonstrate certain kinds of phonics knowledge, or follow written directions. Since competencies are behaviorally stated, they must deal with measurable, observable skills and by their nature cannot be concerned with unmeasurable learnings, such as appreciation and feelings. Competencies are minimum measures in that they designate the least that a student is expected to perform, rather than the most, best, or ideal.

In the past decade mathematically based techniques for determining item numbers, score cutoffs, and other criteria have been developed; these have legitimized criterion-referenced test construction in the eyes of testing theorists. Later, though, we will want to look at two of the fundamental foundations of criterion-referenced testing—test validity and competency mastery.

So, with the criterion-referenced test a child's score is based on some predetermined criterion of excellence—a mastery level. On a norm-referenced test a score is based on its relation to the scores of the sample of children to whom the test has been given. A norming sample should be cross-sectional and representative of all types of schools and children, if it is to be used with cross sections of children. A revision of a popular high school–college reading achievement test presents percentile norms for college students based on a norm group of only sixty-seven college students in a university extension class! Such data are meaningless.

The content of criterion-referenced and norm-referenced tests can be and often is quite similar, and test item formats are often identical. While a criterion-referenced test generally offers more specificity in, for example, tests of reading comprehension (that is, main idea, sequence, cause-effect) than a norm-referenced test of comprehension, both tests typically involve reading a passage and answering the questions that follow. Thus the major *differences* between the two types of tests are the scores—what they mean and what can be done with them.

If, for example, one of your fifth-grade students correctly answered thirty-two questions on a fifty-item test, the grade norm conversion table might tell you to assign that child a grade norm of 4.3. The score means that the child answered correctly *as many* questions (not which ones) as the average for students in the sample who were in the third month of the fourth grade. The norm then represents a *standard* against which you can compare the performance of an individual, a classroom, a school, or a district. In contrast, a criterion-referenced test sets an absolute standard for achievement—in reading it is typically 75 or 80 or 90 percent correct. If you answer eight out of ten questions on a subtest of hard and soft C, for example, you go on to the next unit. If not, you need additional instruction.

Thus the expected or desired *spread* of scores is very different. With a norm-referenced test the distribution of scores should represent a bell-shaped curve as in Figure 10.2. You can then see if your pupils are at, above, or below the *bump*, the norm. On a criterion-referenced

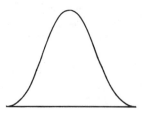

Fig. 10.2.

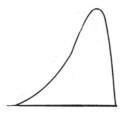

Fig. 10.3.

test you expect the curve to be skewed to the left as in Figure 10.3. That is, you would like your pupils to "top out," that is, to show mastery.

A final difference is that norm-referenced tests tend to provide scores that are more global (comprehension, rate, vocabulary) while criterion-referenced tests measure skills that are much more specific (short vowels, main ideas, root words with prefixes). The latter are of more use for diagnostic purposes, while the former are useful for comparisons. Now let us look at both types of test in greater depth.

Standardized Norm-referenced Tests

CHARACTERISTICS.   The terms *standardized* and *norm referenced* are critical, if somewhat overlapping. Both terms imply that the test has been administered to a large number of students, usually at a variety of grade levels. Subsequently, average scores have been computed for students at various grade levels. For example, it might have been determined for comprehension items one through fifty, that the average score for a nationwide random sample of students in the fourth grade, third month (4.3) was thirty-two items correct. Students in the third grade, first month (3.1) may have averaged twenty-two items correct. And so on for various groups of students. Enough samples are tested so that the test publisher is able to provide you with a table of norms. The norms allow you to translate a raw score into a grade norm score. For example, if you are a fifth-grade teacher, and one of your students got twenty-two items right on a fifty-item test, he would be assigned a grade level score of 3.1. He got as many answers correct as the average for pupils at the beginning of the third grade. (Most tests also include percentile conversion charts, which are similarly determined.) Note that the grade norm score says nothing about *which* items a student answered correctly; only the total number of correct answers is considered. The norm, then, represents a *standard* against which (hopefully) you can compare the performance of an individual, a classroom, a school, or a district. For example, if the average score in your fifth-grade classroom was thirty-three items correct, you could state that your classroom achieved an average grade norm score of 4.3. And you could infer that compared to the norm group, your class was below average.

It is typical for a norm-referenced test to include two, perhaps four, subtest scores for comprehension. For example, the widely used *Iowa Test of Basic Skills* (1973) includes a reading comprehension score and a vocabulary (word-meaning) score. *The Metropolitan Achievement Tests* (Durost *et al.* 1970) have traditionally included a reading sentences and a reading paragraphs subtest at the primary level and allow a teacher to examine performance separately on four subskills (main thought, inferential, literal, and word knowledge in context) in the batteries for upper grades, although norms are given only for the sum of these four subtests. The older forms of the *Stanford Achievement Test* (Madden *et al.*, 1972) have a word-meaning and a paragraph-meaning subtest; norms are provided for each.

Since comprehension, even as we have dealt with it, obviously consists of many components, why are there so few subtests? There are several reasons. It is only recently that the publishers of standard tests have felt the need to tailor their tests so that they could be used diagnostically by teachers. In the past, they were regarded as survey tests helping to answer questions like, "Where does Johnny Smith stand in relation to his peers nationally?" or, "How does my class (or school) stand up against other fifth-grade classrooms nationally?" If this is all the information you want, then a broadly based norm-referenced, standardized survey test serves as well as any other kind of test, perhaps better. If, however, you want to know which comprehension tasks Johnny Smith needs to practice, such tests were, until recently, useless. Partly, we suspect, in response to the increased spread of diagnostic-prescriptive (find the flaw and correct it) approaches to teaching, the makers of standardized tests have broken down items by subskill (main idea, details, inferences, and so on) making it possible for teachers to get some subtest scores for individuals.

Second, standardized tests have traditionally been subjected to measurement standards like reliability and validity. Reliability refers to the *consistency* of the distribution of scores on a test; that is, if you scored better than Henry Jones on one administration of a test, on a reliable test, you would score better than him on a second administration, whereas on an unreliable test you might not. A test is valid to the degree that it measures whatever it is designed to measure; *relevance* is a rough synonym for validity. As any test maker will tell you, it is difficult to create a test that can meet these standards of reliability and validity with fewer than fifteen or twenty items. Hence, when someone tells you that they can measure a student's grasp of a main idea with four test items, the person speaks out of ignorance (he does not know about these standards), faith (he hopes that the test just might work), or deceit (he does not think you know anything about measurement standards). So you can understand the reluctance of test publishers to break down their tests to too specific a level. They can do so only by increasing the number of items, a practice that will make the test less attractive from a convenience point of view, or by basing subtest scores on a few (five to 10) items, a practice they know is risky according to reliability standards. Incidentally, we will readdress reliability and the size of the subtest item pool when we discuss criterion-referenced tests, especially those that claim one can draw inferences about performance on the basis of three or four items per subtest.

Third, publishers of achievement tests tend to regard reading performance as only one of many areas of the total school curriculum, giving mathematics and language arts equal billing. With such a broad set of skills to be measured, some compromises have to be made. Refined diagnostic information about individuals has usually been sacrificed in favor of general survey information that would be more appropriate for evaluating a school- or district-wide program.

TEST FORMATS.   In general there are two popular formats for testing reading comprehension. Often one finds a paragraph or passage followed by a set of multiple-choice comprehension items testing a variety of relationships (main idea, details, cause-effect relations, inferences, and so on). The *Iowa Test of Basic Skills* (ITBS) has been using such a format for decades. Figure 10.4 is reprinted from the ITBS, Form 3, p. 8 (Lindquist and Hieronymus, 1964).

An increasingly popular format is what we might call a modified cloze technique. It is illustrated in Figure 10.5, from the *Stanford Achievement Test*, Advanced Form W, p. 2. (Kelley *et al.*, 1964). We call it a modified cloze technique because in a traditional cloze technique choices are not provided. It is more difficult to specify what relations are being assessed when one uses a cloze (or modified cloze) technique. Frankly, we would be hard pressed to label it literal comprehension because we believe that a student *has to* use scripts and schemata in order to decide which word makes sense in the context of the paragraph. However, we should point out that scores on a cloze test and scores on a question-answering test based on the same passage are highly correlated (Bormuth, 1966); that is, students tend to do about as well, compared to their peers, on one as they do on the other.

The two most popular formats for assessing vocabulary (word meaning) knowledge are probably familiar to you. In one a key word is presented in isolation or in a very meager context, as in (1), and the student is required to pick a synonym or a meaning for the key word.

4 ▸ GRADE 4
BEGIN HERE

One day last summer Mother took my cousin Tom and me to the zoo. The keeper told us about the animals. The one we liked the best was the giraffe, the tallest animal in the zoo. He was 13 feet, 6 inches high from the ground to the top of his head. His front legs were about 5 feet long, and his back legs were about 4 feet long. The door to his shed was 10 feet high. His feed box was 6 feet above the floor.

Recently I saw an unusual snowman. He was not made of snow at all. He was made of tumbleweeds! In some parts of our country one kind of large tumbleweed grows many hundreds of tiny branches. In the fall these weeds dry up and can be easily blown away by a gust of wind. The weeds become round as they are rolled and bounced about. You can understand why tumbleweed is such a good name for them. The tumbleweed snowman which I saw was made of three tumbleweeds stacked in order of size. The dull brown of the weeds had been covered with white paint. A long carrot nose, a black stovepipe hat, and cloth eyes and mouth had been added. And, presto, there was a "snowman."

12. Who is the writer of this story?
1) Tom
2) Tom's cousin
3) Tom's mother
4) The zoo keeper

13. What does the word "one" stand for in the third line?
1) Animal
2) Giraffe
3) Keeper
4) Story

14. How did the children learn about the giraffe?
1) They read a story about a giraffe.
2) They studied giraffes in science class.
3) The keeper let them measure the giraffe.
4) The keeper told them about the giraffe.

15. The giraffe's front legs are how much longer than his back legs?
1) 9 feet
2) 5 feet
3) 4 feet
4) 1 foot

16. Why is the feed box high above the floor?
1) So other animals cannot steal the food
2) To help keep the floor clean
3) So the giraffe can stand while eating
4) To make it easier to fill from the top

17. How tall was the giraffe?
1) 6 feet
2) 10 feet
3) 13 feet
4) More than 13 feet

18. When did the writer see the snowman?
1) Not long ago
2) Several years ago
3) At Christmas time
4) When the writer was a child

19. What part was missing from this snowman?
1) Arms   3) Body
2) Head   4) Face

20. Which of these was not used to make the snowman?
1) Carrot   3) Hat
2) Coal   4) Paint

21. Why was the tumbleweed man called a snowman?
1) He was made in the winter.
2) He had the right shape and color.
3) He had a jolly face.
4) He wore a snowman's hat.

22. Why is tumbleweed a good name for the plant?
1) It is prickly.
2) People tumble over it.
3) It tumbles over and over.
4) It is hard to catch.

23. Where did the author probably see this snowman?
1) Where there is lots of snow
2) Along the eastern seacoast
3) In the Far North
4) In the Southwest

24. How does the writer feel about the snowman?
1) Disappointed   3) Doubtful
2) Delighted   4) Angry

Fig. 10.4.

TEST 1: **Paragraph Meaning**

DIRECTIONS: Read each paragraph below. Decide which of the numbered words or phrases below the paragraph is *best* for each blank. Look at the answer spaces at the right or on your answer sheet (if you have one). Fill in the space which has the same number as the word(s) you have chosen.

SAMPLES

We went up in an airplane. At first we flew near the __A__ where we could see people and animals. Later we could not see them. Our plane was too __B__.

| A | 1 houses | 3 town | | 1 2 3 4 |
| | 2 ground | 4 hills | A | ○ ● ○ ○ |

| B | 5 high | 7 far | | 5 6 7 8 |
| | 6 low | 8 fast | B | ○ ○ ○ ○ |

The amount of stress or tension needed to snap a rope or cable is what determines its breaking point. The more __1__ a rope can stand, the higher is its __2__. Surprisingly enough, ten men pulling on a cable which is tied to a tree exert the same amount of __3__ as is exerted on a rope which ten men are pulling from each end.

| 1 | 1 cable | 3 stress | | 1 2 3 4 |
| | 2 breaking point | 4 amount | 1 | ○ ○ ○ ○ |

| 2 | 5 breaking point | 7 tension | | 5 6 7 8 |
| | 6 stress | 8 cable | 2 | ○ ○ ○ ○ |

| 3 | 1 elasticity | 3 cable | | 1 2 3 4 |
| | 2 breaking point | 4 tension | 3 | ○ ○ ○ ○ |

In the 1830's in the United States, a new type of daily press was born. Led by Benjamin Day's New York *Sun* and James Gordon Bennett's New York *Herald*, __4__ began to publish police court and crime stories, human interest stories, and much other local news. The *Herald*, under __5__, was often accused of pure sensationalism by its enemies, for it, perhaps more than other papers, emphasized __6__ stories.

4	5 pamphlets		
	6 magazines		
	7 newspapers		5 6 7 8
	8 authors	4	○ ○ ○ ○

5	1 Day		
	2 Bennett		
	3 James Benjamin		1 2 3 4
	4 Benjamin Gordon	5	○ ○ ○ ○

6	5 lurid crime		
	6 human interest		
	7 foreign affairs		5 6 7 8
	8 local society	6	○ ○ ○ ○

Fig. 10.5.

(1) a short *foreword*
   (a) conclusion
   (b) introduction
   (c) story

In the second popular format, a richer context is provided and the student selects a meaning or synonym, as in (2).

(2) If you don't finish your work, your boss may *terminate* your employment.
   (a) begin
   (b) end
   (c) congratulate

In a companion book, Johnson and Pearson (1978) discuss these and a number of other vocabulary test formats at greater length.

CONCERNS ABOUT STANDARDIZED TESTS..   In recent years standardized tests have been subjected to a variety of criticisms ranging from diagnostic uselessness to cultural bias to passage independence (including items that can be answered without reading the test). Having already discussed diagnostic uselessness, we will consider the other two issues: cultural bias and items that assess prior knowledge.

   1. Prior Knowledge and Reading Comprehension. Tuinman (1973–1974) and Mitchell (1965) have demonstrated that many of the items on commercially available comprehension tests can be answered correctly by many students *without* their actually reading the passages from which the test item stems. Assume that a fourth-grade student reads a test passage about George Washington that includes sentence (3) and is asked to answer item (4).

(3) George Washington was the first President of the United States.
(4) Who was the first President of the United States?
   (a) Abraham Lincoln
   (b) John Adams
   (c) George Washington
   (d) John Kennedy

Obviously, many fourth-grade students will be able to answer such questions without reading the passage. There are some less obvious examples. Consider item (5), taken from the ITBS, Form 3 (Lindquist and Hieronymous, 1964, p. 9). Any child who has ever made a snowman knows that snowmen

(5) What part was missing from this snowman?
  (a) arms
  (b) head
  (c) body
  (d) face

do not have arms (even tumbleweeed snowmen, as discussed in Figure 10.4).

Tuinman (1973–1974) compared how students performed on tests with and without passages. In some instances, he found only marginal increases from the passage-absent to the passage-present condition (Farr and Smith [1970] found items for which performance was better *without* the passage.) Tuinman concludes by recommending that test consumers will want to purchase the most passage-dependent (passage dependency increases when items cannot be answered without reading the passages) tests, other things being equal. We *think* we agree with Tuinman; however, we would never want to see tests where the items were not dependent to some degree on prior experience. In fact, our view of comprehension as a process of building bridges between the new and known commits us to value test items that require such integration. In short, for us, literal comprehension of the passage is not enough.

However, just because an item requires that the reader integrate textual information with prior knowledge (what we would call scriptally implicit comprehension: see Chapter 8) does not mean that it is not dependent. Remember our example from Chapter 8, in which the passage stated that *South Carolina was the land of Will Goodlad's birth,* and one question probe was, for *what side did Will fight during the Civil War?* While a response such as, *The Confederacy,* requires that the reader have prior knowledge, it is unlikely, beyond a chance level, that a group of readers would answer the question (50 percent assuming they all know that the North and South were the sides) unless they had been exposed to the sentence about *South Carolina* in the text. In fact, Weaver, Bickley, and Ford (1969) demonstrated that inference items were more passage dependent than literal, factual items. This is not surprising. If our example about George Washington, (4), is at all representative of items which are not passage dependent, then passage independence may be more a function of prior *factual knowledge* than of our ability to generate *inferences* from the text to our prior knowledge base (our schemata and scripts). Hence, we say we *think* we agree with Tuinman. We advise you, as a test consumer, to require information from test publishers about the passage dependency of their tests.

2. Cultural bias. The issue of cultural bias is not unrelated to passage dependency. Recall item (5). Children who have built snowmen

will surely have the advantage on such an item. We are reminded of a standardized test passage about ice fishing which was followed by an item asking how ice fishermen drilled their holes. In the Upper Midwest, most children above the age of three already know that you use an auger to drill the hole. Hence, on such an item, they have an advantage over those who dwell in warmer climates.

Many of the modified cloze items are subject to cultural bias. In Figure 10.6 there is a set of items from the *Stanford Diagnostic Reading Test,* green level Form B (p. 9). We suspect that the ability to answer such items would be improved with appropriate real-life experiences. For example, children who grow up seeing few trees or who live in a climate where leaves do not change markedly with the seasons might be disadvantaged on item 23.

What to do about cultural bias is another matter. One unsatisfactory option would be to use content that does not favor one regional or ethnic group over another. Test writers will tell you how difficult a task that is. If you opt for an imaginary situation (life on a desert island), then you may rule out the possibility of being able to use items that require inferences. Another, perhaps more reasonable, option is to balance potential bias so that each regional or ethnic group gets "an equal shake." We suspect that some test writers have tried to do just that. For example, in the latest edition of the *Stanford Diagnostic Test* (Karlsen *et al.*, 1976) we found an item in which a boy was helping his mother with dinner. We found another that related to television viewing and monster movies (presumably favoring children who watch a lot of television). A third option is to try to find content that is common to all ethnic or regional groups. We have found some of these also: incidents in the school yard, the answering of a telephone, events during a rainstorm.

In comparing older and newer versions of standardized tests, we conclude that test publishers are attempting to remove as much cultural

```
Just outside of Mary's window grew a tall
21        tree          man          building.
          O             O             O
Mary thought of it as her friend, even though
it wasn't a
22        plant         rock          person.
          O             O             O
She liked to watch the leaves change with the
23        seasons       hours         tides.
          O             O             O
One day some men came and cut it down.
Mary felt sad because she had lost her
24        dog           toy           friend.
          O             O             O
```

Fig. 10.6

bias (or trying to balance it) from their tests as they can while avoiding the undesirable situation of not requiring students to relate textual information to prior experience in order to answer test items.

ACCOUNTABILITY AND STANDARDIZED TESTS.   In May 1977 a principal in the Midwest created a furor by announcing that no student in his school would be sent on to ninth grade unless he or she achieved a 6.8 grade norm score on a standardized reading test. While we might sympathize with his intentions (he wants to maintain some standards), we do not understand his choice of 6.8 as a criterion. And we see some real dangers in this practice. First, why 6.8? Why not 9.2 or 4.9? What is magical about 6.8? The purpose of the standard was to guarantee that the students would be able to handle ninth-grade work. We know of no evidence to suggest that achieving a grade norm score of 6.8 means that you will be able to read ninth-grade textbooks. Remember what that score means: a student with a score of 6.8 scored at the mean of those students who were in the eighth month of grade six when they took the test. It does not mean that the student can handle material written at a particular readability level, even sixth-grade material. We know of only one attempt to put textual readability levels and students' comprehension test scores on the same scale (Carver, 1977–1978), and that effort is still in the developmental stages. We are not arguing that it would be inappropriate to be able to make such decisions. However, our psychometric technology has not reached a stage of precision that allows us to make such decisions with any satisfactory degree of accuracy or confidence.

More important, standardized tests were not designed for such a purpose. Hence, using them to make promotional decisions represents gross misuse. We suspect, also, that such a practice will encourage *teaching* that is specifically directed to the test and out-and-out cheating. We are both reminded of our senior English classes in high school. We spent the entire year practicing writing essays so that we would not flunk the college English entrance test and, accordingly, have to take "bonehead" English in our freshman year.

Finally, being able to "read" ninth-grade material is not, as we hope we have pointed out (see Chapters 2, 3, and 9), simply a matter of how well you can answer questions on a standardized test. It involves student motivation, interests, and teacher intervention as well as some level of reading skill.

Criterion-referenced Tests

CHARACTERISTICS.   By definition, the difference between a norm-referenced test and a criterion-referenced test rests on the standard against which a group or an individual is compared. The standard for norm-referenced test is the *mean* of an individual's peers in the norm group. So, if you get a percentile score of 40, it means that you did better than 40 percent of all the students who took the test when they were in the same month of the same grade as you. The standard is relative. It depends on how well the norm group does on the test. In such tests, a spread of scores is desired, even essential. In contrast, a criterion-referenced test sets an absolute standard for achievement, and we desire as skewed curve (all children scoring near mastery). For example, a criterion of 80 percent correct might be set for a reading test following a unit in a basal reader. If you correctly answer eight or more on all the ten-item tests, you get to go on to the next unit; if you do not, then you might have to go through the unit again or you might receive some special remedial help, after which you get to try again.

In practice, there is another difference between norm-referenced and criterion-referenced tests: most tests that are called criterion-referenced tests also measure reading skills at a more atomistic level. They tend to be tied to specific *objectives*. Indeed they are sometimes called objectives-referenced tests. Recall that norm-referenced tests usually yield two or three subtest scores for comprehension, for example, vocabulary and paragraph meaning. Criterion-referenced tests are likely to provide anywhere from five to ten to thirty subtest scores for comprehension (and even more for decoding skills). Now, the norm-referenced test may include items which would logically fit into each of the objectives corresponding to a subtest in the criterion-referenced test; but the norm-referenced test sums across all those items to yield aggregate scores for only a few areas. Put another way, a norm-referenced test and a criterion-referenced test might consist of exactly the same fifty items. But the criterion-referenced test might have ten subtests of five items each, whereas the norm-referenced test would have two subtests of twenty-five items each.

The claim commonly made by publishers of criterion-referenced tests is that they are diagnostically more useful than norm-referenced tests because they can pinpoint specific areas of weakness instead of simply informing you that the student does not comprehend very well. Since the standards that a student should achieve are absolute rather than relative, judgments of mastery are possible. Hence, a student might surpass the 80 percent criterion for mastery on seven of the ten subtests. As a teacher, you now have a clear direction for prescribing instruction; you can ignore or place less emphasis on the seven areas of strength and concentrate on the three areas of weakness. The logic is certainly attractive, almost compelling. But several assumptions must be satisfied before we are willing to accept decisions made about students based upon criterion-referenced tests (CRTs).

RELIABILITY AND VALIDITY.   First, we would require that the tests meet traditional standards of reliability and validity. If a test is unreliable, it implies that a second or third administration would yield a different score for a given student. Hence, our hypothetical student who achieved mastery on seven of the ten subskills might master four of ten, or ten of ten, or a different set of seven if we readministered unreliable tests.[23]

This is a must: if we are going to use CRTs to make important decisions about a student's instructional program, then we whould demand tests that will allow us to make those decisions confidently. Some of the commercially available CRTs offer no information at all about test or subtest reliability. Furthermore, many use only three or four items for a given objective. It is difficult, if not impossible, to obtain decent reliability scores with so few items. We feel very strongly about the importance of making accurate instructional decisions about what a student will or will not be taught.

CRTs tend to fare much better on judgments of validity. In fact, because they test at an atomistic level, it is even more possible (than is the case with a more general survey test, that is, a standardized test) to tie the testing to your instruction. In fact, many of the commercially available CRTs (for example *Wisconsin Design for Reading Skill Development,* 1972) were originally developed by surveying several widely used basal-reading systems in order to find a set of objectives that were widely taught. *CRTs* tend to test skills that are taught in reading programs. Hence, they generally have good content validity; they are relevant to instruction. So, the major validity issues are whether or not the tests are consistent with what is being taught and whether they are in line with the sequence of instruction.

The whole notion of a sequence or hierarchy of skills is, at best, a pedagogical convenience. While the idea may appeal to our sense of logic (just as we think of driving a car or riding a bicycle as a complex of sequenced subskills); there is precious little evidence to support the existence of separate skills, let alone separate skills which can be placed into a sequence or hierarchy. But sequences are necessary. We cannot teach or learn everything at once.

Examine any three or four skill-monitoring systems or three or four basal reader scope and sequence charts, and you will realize that there is no agreement as to sequence. Some begin with the alphabet, proceed

---

[23] Recall that earlier we stated that about twelve to fifteen good items are usually necessary to obtain a decent reliability estimate (somewhere about 0.6 to 0.7 on a scale where 0 means total unreliability and 1.0 equals complete reliability [Downie, 1967]). It has been demonstrated that with items of mid-level difficulty (somewhere between 40 percent and 70 percent of the students answer each item correctly), it is possible to get decent reliabilities with eight or ten items (Aulls, 1975). However, many CRTs use only three or four items per subtest.

through the consonants' sounds alphabetically, and eventually teach some vowels; others begin with rhyming elements and graphic shapes and colors before looking at a few words and some letters.

It just seems sensible to test what is being taught and a gross waste of time to administer tests, many of which may not be related to what is being taught. Hence, it seems logically sensible to have a management system that is an integral part of the basic instructional components.

The clearest cases of high content validity are for the CRTs that are part of the internal skills management systems of many of the new basal programs published since 1970. Most basals have end-of-unit or end-of-book tests designed to help a teacher decide whether or not a student has mastered the skills (or sometimes content) of the unit or book. However, some CRTs accompanying basal readers suffer from the same concerns about reliability as do the commercially available CRTs.

A related concern is the validity of the testing instrument. Does the test measure what it says it does? One CRT, for example, purports to test decoding (attaching sounds to letters) through a multiple-choice encoding (spelling) test (choosing letters for spoken sounds in nonsense words). These two language *processes* are not the same nor are letter-sound correspondences bi-directional. If I ask you to spell the nonsense word *taff*, you have at least four choices for the spelling of the final *f* sound. If, on the other hand, you are asked to pronounce *taf*, there are only two sounds the *f* can represent. Users of CRTs (or any tests for that matter) are strongly urged to study the items carefully to see if they really measure what they say they do and in a way that is compatible with the instructional materials in use.

MASTERY LEARNING. A more critical problem is the issue of what it means to master a skill. The mastery-learning approach is not new. As early as 1926, in the Laboratory School at the University of Chicago, Henry Morrison (1932, p. 81) was applying what he termed the "mastery formula."

> The learning units having been identified, the next problem is the technique of pedagogical attack. Here we apply what we shall call the "mastery formula": Pre-test, teach, test the result, adapt procedure, teach and test again to the point of actual learning.

Concurrently, Carleton Washburne (1932, p. 1) was employing a mastery-learning approach in the public schools in Winnetka, Illinois:

> To treat children whose abilities range through four or five grades as if they were alike, giving them all the same assignment and the same time to accomplish that assignment, and then to mark them all by a common standard, is so preposterous in the light of present-day knowledge that ev-

eryone is looking for a remedy for the situation. It seems to some of us that this remedy lies partly in substituting piecework for time-work in education, allowing every child to master—temporarily, at least—each unit of his work before he goes on to the next unit, without being held back by slower children or forced forward by faster ones too rapidly for mastery.

Assuming that the appropriate subskills of reading can be or have been identified, and assuming that test items can be or have been properly constructed and possess a high degree of validity, how do we know that mastery has been reached?

Mastery can be viewed in two different ways: mastery as a designated level on a continuum, and mastery as an absolute state. In other words, many will seek perfection, but few will find it. Some would say that partial mastery is as self-contradictory as partial pregnancy or partial death. Mastery, but this definition is complete knowledge or skill, an absolute state, and the only concern is whether or not the individual has achieved mastery. In criterion testing in reading, on the other hand, the process is necessarily an intuitive one, where the test maker chooses a level of performance along the continuum that seems right. Most systems say that 80 or 90 percent correct indicates mastery. But 80 percent *of what?* Are three items sufficient—even if properly constructed—or do we need five or ten or more. One skills management test of variant consonant sounds contains ten items. Two are initial $c \rightarrow /s/$, one is final $c \rightarrow /k/$, three test $g \rightarrow /j/$, one tests $g \rightarrow /g/$, and three test the $/z/$ sound of s.

What does mastery mean on such a test? One could score 80 percent, showing mastery, and not know hard or soft c, or hard g. Or, one could fail to show mastery of variant consonants while knowing soft g, or $s \rightarrow /z/$. Terwilliger (1972) pointed out that on a ten-item test with an 80 percent mastery level, there are fifty-six different combinations of correct items that will yield mastery. On a twenty-item test there are 6196 such combinations. While the concept of mastering a word identification skill makes sense to us intuitively, the corollary concept of mastering a comprehension task makes no sense whatever. We can visualize a situation in which a teacher might decide to stop instructing Johnny or Susie in the final consonants skills (although one must be careful about an allegedly mastered skill), but we cannot imagine why a teacher would stop all main idea or multiple meanings activities simply because a child answered eight of ten such items correctly. If you show us a child who has mastered the level X main idea test, we can demonstrate his or her lack of mastery simply by increasing the conceptual difficulty of the words or context relationships. Comprehension is, by its nature, an ongoing, never-ending process. It can have no precise starting or stopping point. It is pervasive in all reading and in all verbal discourse.

We do not want to imply that CRTs are totally useless, only that we do not agree with some of the uses to which they have been put without the necessary technical refinement.

Informal Classroom Assessment

Teachers make tests for use in their classrooms: reading tests, science tests, history tests, geography tests. What about applying standards of reliability and validity to teacher-made tests? We seriously doubt that many teachers have the time or energy left over from hectic schedules to do reliability estimates for the test given, for example, for Chapters 1–12 in the biology text. Yet we would caution you that hard-and-fast decisions about a student's future instruction based on an unreliable teacher-made test will be no better than decisions based on an unreliable CRT from a basal reader or purchased from a CRT publisher.

Fortunately, as a teacher, you are in a position to collect many samples of student performance over a long period of time. Hence, you need not rely on one particular test or one particular assessment procedure. Because you are in a position to collect many samples of behavior on a particular student, you are likely to get a reliable estimate of how that student is performing on a particular task—main ideas, for example (remember that the more items used to make an assessment, the more likely it is to be reliable).

INSTRUCTION AS ASSESSMENT.   Let us illustrate. If you are a fifth-grade teacher who uses a basal reader, you need not rely solely on the end-of-unit test on main ideas to determine how students handle main ideas. Chances are that students will be doing main idea activities throughout the unit. There may be some workbook pages that deal with it. You may engage the students in a discussion about the main ideas of paragraphs in the selections they read in the unit. In addition, the students may be using some supplementary materials that require them to answer main idea questions. Occasionally, you may ask a student to summarize a story for you, in which case you can judge whether or not the student offers you a random mix of details or a nicely ordered set of main ideas and details. In other words, instruction itself allows you opportunities to assess student performance and progress on various comprehension tasks. Granted, such assessment is likely to be informal and imprecise (you would be hard pressed to assign a score to any students); but because it is continuous and based upon many samples of behavior, chances are it will be useful in making decisions about students. At the very least, it ought to be used to temper judgments you might make on the basis of test data alone.

Informal Tests for Comprehension Tasks

In case it has not already occurred to you, we have yet to suggest any means for assessing the host of comprehension tasks outlined in Chapters 4–7. There are two reasons for our procrastination. First, we are not altogether sure that we want you to develop a whole host of specific mastery tests to assess each and every task at every grade level. Second, if you are going to develop such tests anyway, they should probably be very similar to the instructional practice materials you would develop by following the guidelines suggested for teaching each of those tasks. We invoke an old principle in learning theory, the *transfer of identical elements*. It suggests that task A will transfer to task B to the degree that they are similar. Hence, if you want to evaluate the specific effects of your instruction, then the tests ought to be similar to the instruction. Such tests would answer one and only one specific question: Did the students learn what I taught? They will not tell you whether or not what they learned transferred to any other reading behavior: Did my instruction in cause-effect relations help students to become better at predicting outcomes or answering main idea questions? Nor will they tell you whether or not the instruction has transferred to reading behavior generally.

Another important point in creating informal tests for comprehension tasks: The kind of test you develop will depend upon what you believe students *learn* when they practice these tasks and participate in discussions about them with you (see Feedback and Modeling section in Chapter 9). When students learn that *big* is a synonym for *enormous*, have they learned that specific relationship, or have they learned something about the nature of synonyms? When they learn the analogy, *tiger:cub = cow:calf,* do they also learn something about the nature of analogous relations in general? When they have successfully identified the main idea of paragraph 2 on page 27, do they learn the content of that paragraph or do they learn something about the nature of main ideas?

Frankly, we are not sure! Nonetheless, we will stand with the point of view that assumes that students learn transferable strategies for dealing with new content. Hence, if you want to evaluate the value of an assignment on analogies, you would be better advised to use a test that included similar analogies with different vocabulary than a test of the vocabulary included in the original assignment. We say this with some trepidation, because we believe that it probably easier to demonstrate progress by testing old content rather than transfer of a type of relation to new content. Yet we know that what really counts is helping students see relations between concepts and between propositions, and we hope that this assistance will help them in reading a variety of types of content.

Earlier in this section we suggested that we were not sure that we wanted you to develop informal tests for each of the tasks we have outlined. We will close this discussion by elaborating on our uncertainty. It stems from two sources. First, we do not accept the notion of mastery as it applies to comprehension (*cf.* section on CRTs). We see no reason to place less emphasis on instruction on cause-effect relations just because a student has answered eight of ten items correctly. Therefore, if we thought you were going to use such tests for making mastery judgments, we would be disappointed. Now if you were going to use the test as a progress check without making any momentous decisions, we would concede your wisdom in using the test. Or, if you were going to use it to evaluate the quality of *your* instruction, we would say, yes. These seem to us to be legitimate uses of such tests. Second, we do not want to be accused of leading you down the path of test mania, a disease that seems to plague our schools increasingly these days. If, by giving so many tests, you have no time left for the kinds of activities suggested in Chapters 4–9 (particularly Chapter 9), then the tests have defeated their purpose (we know a few teachers who complain of having been promoted to high-class record clerks in the name of diagnostic-prescriptive instruction). Besides, as we pointed out earlier, instruction itself can serve assessment functions.

In the final analysis, our best advice about specific tests for specific tasks is (and this would hold for CRTs), if you use them, do not let them become a fetish. We are convinced that too much time is spent on testing activities.

THE USES OF ASSESSMENT DATA

Having reviewed three commonly used assessment tools, we close this chapter by addressing what we regard as the most important set of questions about assessment, a set of questions we raised at the outset of this chapter.

What is the purpose of the assessment? What use will be made of the data collected? What kinds of decisions will be made?

If your school or district wants to know, more or less generally, how its reading program is doing in comparison to similar schools or in comparison to an earlier program in the same school, then a straightforward survey, a norm-referenced test will serve well. Survey tests have an added virtue: Since they assess comprehension at a highly aggregative level, they require that students integrate several skills in order to perform the tasks required. This seems useful to us in a test designed to evaluate a total program. Incidentally, we should point out that a school, and especially a district, need not test every student in order to obtain reliable data. A representative sample from each school will do, thus saving some funds for other purposes.

Data from this type of assessment can be used to draw inferences about program effectiveness with an eye toward modification, to redirect personnel and material resources (from school A to school B for example), or, if it has been given to all students, to identify students who may need to be tested further for possible remedial help.

If you, as a teacher, want to evaluate the effectiveness of your own instruction with an eye toward changing emphases from some kinds of tasks to others, a CRT would serve you well. While we have been skeptical about decisions made about individuals from CRT data, we support decisions made about groups of students (in general, inferences about *groups* of students are more reliable than inferences about individuals; for one thing, there are more data available). *The Stanford Diagnostic Test* (Karlsen *et al.*, 1975) suggests exactly such a use for its subtests. The data obtained may give you clues about aspects of reading comprehension that you have been neglecting.

For making decisions about individuals—what tasks they will or will not be practicing—we, as you might suspect, recommend that you emphasize ongoing informal assessment. For reasons stated earlier, we ask you to exercise caution in exclusively using data from teacher-made tests or CRTs. Always temper the implications of such information with informal judgments based upon day-to-day observation from written assignments and classroom discussions.

A FINAL WORD

Perhaps the most important summary statement we can make about the assessment of reading comprehension is that the assessment procedure you use will depend upon the kinds of decisions you want to make. Standardized tests, criterion-referenced tests, and informal assessment procedures all have their place within a school.

We offer you one general caution about all types of assessment: tests should never become so paramount that they dictate or displace instruction. We remind you that you are members of the teaching profession, not the testing profession. Tests should serve instruction, assisting us in making more rational decisions. As long as we keep them in proper perspective, they can be an asset to an effective reading program.

REFERENCES

Aulls, M. *Technical Report: Minnesota Statewide Assessment in Reading*. Minnesota: State Department of Education, 1974.

Bormuth, J. R. Readability: A New Approach. *Reading Research Quarterly*, Spring, 1966, 1, 79–131.

Carver, R. Toward a Theory of Reading Comprehension and Rauding. *Reading Research Quarterly*. 1977–78, *12*, in press.

Downie, N. M. *Fundamentals of Measurement: Techniques and Practices* (2nd ed.). New York: Oxford University Press, 1967.

Durost, W. N., Bixler, H. H., Wrightstone, J. W., Prescott, G. A., and Balow, I. *The Metropolitan Achievement Tests*. New York: The Psychological Corporation, 1970.

Farr, R., and Smith, C. B. The Effects of Test Item Validity on Total Test Reliability and Validity. In G. Schick (ed.), Reading: Process and Pedagogy, *Nineteenth Yearbook of the National Reading Conference*. 1 Milwaukee, 1970, 122–134.

Glaser, G. R. Instructional Technology and Measurement of Learning. *American Psychologist, 18,* 1963, 519–521.

Hieronymus, et al. *Iowa Test of Basic Skills*. Boston: Houghton Mifflin, 1973.

Karsen, B., Madden, R., and Gardner, E. F. *Standford Diagnostic Reading Test*. New York: Harcourt Brace Jovanovich, 1976.

Kelley, et al. *Stanford Achievement Test*. New York: Harcourt Brace Jovanovich, 1964.

Klein, S. P., and Kosecoff, J. *Issues and Procedures in Development of Criterion Referenced Test,* Eric Document, TM, Report 26, September, 1973, 18.

Lindquist, E. F., and Hieronymus, A. N. *Iowa Test of Basic Skill*. Boston: Houghton Mifflin, 1964.

Madden, R., Gardner, E., Rudman, H., Karlsen, B., and Merwin, J. *Stanford Achievement Test*. New York: Harcourt Brace Jovanovich, 1972.

Mitchell, R. W. *A Comparison of Children's Responses to an Original and Experimental Form of Subtests GS and ND of the Gates Basic Reading Tests*. Unpublished Doctoral Dissertation, University of Minnesota, 1967.

Morrison, H. C. *The Practice of Teaching in the Secondary Schools*. Chicago: University of Chicago Press, 1932.

Otto, W., and Askov, E. *The Wisconsin Design for Reading Skill Development: Word Attack*. Minneapolis: National Computer Systems, 1972.

Ringler, L. *Skills Monitoring Systems—Reading*. New York: Harcourt Brace Jovanovich, 1974.

Terwilliger, J. *Some Problems Associated with the Concept of Mastery.* Unpublished manuscript, University of Minnesota, 1972.

Truman, J. J. Determining the Passage Dependency of Comprehension Questions in 5 Major Tests. *Reading Research Quarterly,* 1973–1974, *9,* 206–223.

Washburne, C. *Adjusting the School to the Child.* New York: World Book Co., 1932.

Weaver, W., Bickley, A. C., and Ford, F. A Cross-Validation Study of the Relationship of Reading Test Items to Their Relevant Paragraphs. *Perceptual and Motor Skills,* August, 1969, *29,* 11–14.

11
REFLECTIONS ON READING COMPREHENSION

In Chapter 1 we made a commitment to you. We repeat it here as an introduction to our conclusion:

> *In trying to convince you that our approach to comprehension is both reasonable and helpful, we plan to take you on a journey through your own mind into the minds of children, onto the printed page of textbooks and fiction, and over the surface of the notorious workbook and ditto master. We will not withhold theory (even though there is an apparent movement afoot to remove theory from the lives of teachers). Neither will we avoid specific matters of practice (including step-by-step procedures as well as games, worksheets, kits, and so on). What we really want to do is to integrate theory and practice as well as we can. We want to persuade you that nothing is more practical than a good theory. We plan to carry out this friendly persuasion by showing you how a theory generates instructional principles that can be accomplished through methods and materials that a classroom teacher can readily put to use.*

We leave it to you to decide whether or not we have succeeded in our "friendly persuasion," whether or not the journey was worth the effort. We close by retracing some of our steps, not so much as an effort to summarize but rather as an effort to draw some conclusions about the worth of the journey. Think of it as an invitation to view a few "slides" snapped inconspicuously along the way. If you are the type who cannot tolerate viewing the family slides, so be it. If you are, welcome. Just remember, a journey revisited is never quite the same as the journey itself. Some detail is lost. Some experiences cannot be recaptured. But others seem more glamorous than the events themselves (we often invoke our scripts of what *ought* to have happened and conveniently repress what *actually* occurred).

WHAT YOU MAY HAVE LEARNED

1. The title of Chapter 1 was, *The Confused World of Reading Comprehension*. We hope by now you find reading comprehension a little less confusing than you did when you started the book. We do *not* hope that you find it less *complex*. If you do, then we have misled you. Reading is, to echo Huey (1908), as complex as the mind itself. But

complexity, by itself, is no reason for discouragement. One should be discouraged only when complexity is confounded with enigma—a puzzle that defies analysis. We do not consider reading comprehension to be enigmatic, simply difficult to understand.

2. We hope that you have learned that reading comprehension is at once a unitary process and a set of discrete processes. It is unitary in three senses. First, all of the relations we have discussed share a common thread—comprehension is a process of building bridges between the *new* and the *known*. Second, the ability to deal with any one of those relations is likely to be highly related to the ability to deal with any of the other relations we have discussed. Third, even on a logical or grammatical basis, there is much overlap. Time relations are often causal relations in disguise. Single words contribute to the bias of a whole passage. Sometimes, we fear that by looking at the process as a set of discrete activities we have given you the impression that the separation is real rather than apparent. We examined them as separate entities only because we could not discuss more than one thing at a time, a lamentable limitation of our human condition.

Reading comprehension must also be regarded as a set of discrete processes. The simple fact is that you cannot deal with the universe of comprehension tasks at once. Even though we never go to the extreme of providing you with a tight scope and sequence of tasks across grade levels, we recognize that, for the sake of instructional convenience and sanity, you have to start somewhere and move toward something else. Furthermore, we admit (and have even recommended subsequences) that certain kinds of tasks do not merit instructional effort until a certain level of reading ability and developmental maturation has been achieved.

3. We hope that you have learned that theory and practice need not be antagonists. We have gone to great pains to demonstrate that they are intrinsically and undeniably related; this is evidenced by what may have seemed to you to be excessive cross-referencing among chapters. We think a good theory implies—even dictates—certain practices. We see few inconsistencies between our theory (model) of comprehension in Chapter 3 and the specific instructional practices outlined in Chapters 4–9. We hope you see as few.

4. We hope that you have learned some new instructional practices that you will consider worth trying out in your own classroom. We do not demand that you accept any or all of them, only that you consider them. To be consistent with our notions of schemata and scripts and our dogged adherence to the *new* to *known* principle, consideration, not blind acceptance, is all we ever could or would want to demand. To use the constructs in Chapter 3, we hope that you have assimilated some of these practices—said to yourself, "Sure! That fits with what I do when I.

. . ." We hope also that you have accommodated by changing some of your schemata—said to yourself, "You know! I never quite thought of it that way before. Maybe I'll try that."

5. We hope that our theory, guidelines, and activities have stimulated you to go "beyond the lines" of this text. We hope you have, at least on a few occasions, said, "You know! If that will work, then I bet . . . will work even better." If we have served such a purpose, then we have done as much as we think any teacher could or even ought to do.

6. We hope that you have acquired a grasp of the requirements of various conceptual and propositional relations that is sufficiently general to allow you to categorize and evaluate any comprehension activity you meet, no matter the label someone happens to have tied to it. In other words, we hope that the concepts are sufficiently well formed in your mind (that your semantic maps are sufficiently well developed) to overcome the possible confusion that might result when different writers use different terms to describe the same relations or when a given writer uses two different labels to describe the same relation.

7. We hope that you have learned that your role as a teacher in developing and implementing a comprehension program is active, not passive. You can and should create your own materials; you can and should create your own assessment techniques. But above all, you can, you should, and you must be an active participant in the interplay of minds (the interactions and discussions) that is necessary to guide students toward habits of clear thinking, to encourage them to take risks, and to demonstrate to them that they can deal successfully with what must sometimes seem impossible tasks. Again we highlight our advice in Chapter 9. There exists no relation in our scheme that is so obvious and so clear that it will naturally and optimally develop on its own; there is no relation that cannot be enhanced by thoughtful guidance on your part.

8. We hope you have learned to take seriously our often repeated disclaimer that our suggestions are starting points, not ending points. We would be surprised if, five years from now, we had not modified our own views on many issues in the present volume. We doubt that there will ever be a truly *definitive* point of view about comprehension. We had hoped—and still do—for a more modest proposal—a *helpful* point of view.

9. We hope that you encountered the word *relation* so often that you are near the point where you hope you never see it again. We have used it often, because that is what we think comprehension is about—seeing relations among concepts and propositions. Every time we invoked our *new* to *known* principle, we were saying as much. For what was *new* and what was *known* were concepts or propositions. And building bridges, another of our often used metaphors, was meant to capture the essence of the term, *relation*.

WHAT YOU MAY NOT HAVE LEARNED

Ours has been a book of the head not the heart. At times it may have seemed intolerably technical to you. But we have tried to be technical only when we thought it was necessary to do so—to convince you that certain practices were unwise or to provide you with the kinds of subtle distinctions among ideas necessary to understand a particular type of relation. Nonetheless, we have not faced issues of affect as squarely as we might have. We have not dealt with "response to literature," with emotions, with identification. Why? As we admitted in Chapter 8, partly because of a lack of rigorous knowledge and background on our part, but also partly because we thought our treatment sufficiently "fuzzy" without introducing even more. And partly because we had to stop somewhere, sometime.

1. We never dealt directly with the close procedure as a teaching or a testing device. First, we have dealt with it in our companion volume Teaching Reading Vocabulary (Johnson and Pearson, 1978). Second, we do not fully understand how it works, why it works, and what you know about a reader's performance when he or she has filled in (reached closure on) all those blank spaces representing deleted words.

2. We never covered the so-called reading-study-skills (dealing with maps, graphs and other visual displays). We wish we had, for we believe that a reader understands a graph, a chart, a table, or a map in the same way he or she understands a passage. The underlying content—the basic concepts and propositions—is identical. For example, if we wanted to get you from Madison to Minneapolis, we could write an essay describing the steps you would have to take, or we could put it into a chart with little boxes and circles to represent sequential steps, or we could draw a map for you indicating the desired route. But you would have to apply the same mental capacity, the same schemata and scripts, to all of the messages. What would differ would be the "syntax", if you will, of the various messages. But the propositions and concepts you derive from the message would have to be similar. We doubt very much that God or Mother Nature or the Great Force of Evolution (whoever is responsible for your mind and ours) created a special area of your brain to deal with maps and another for charts (and another for graphs?). Indeed, we would contend that many of the activities and questions we have suggested could be applied to "comprehension of visual displays."

3. We did not deal with comprehension and the remedial reader. We did not give you a set of step-by-step procedures for helping such students through difficult passages or difficult assignments. We could have, but we doubt that we would have said much that was different from what we said in Chapters 4–9. We would have added only this;

whatever we said in Chapter 9 goes double for the student who is experiencing difficulty.

A FINAL WORD

We close by restating a metaphor introduced in Chapter 8. We likened understanding comprehension to a doctor attempting to diagnose a respiratory ailment. The doctor collects several sets of data: (1) a blood test to determine relative white and red blood cell counts, (2) an x-ray to determine specific types of congestion or blocking, (3) a temperature reading, (4) stethoscopic examination, (5) blood pressure reading. Each new datum offers a different perspective on the same organism. The human body under study has not changed, only the perspective. Each technique offers something unique, but some of the information is redundant. The redundancy is important, however, because it helps the doctor to settle on a diagnosis (it must be pneumonia; both the blood count and the x-ray point that way).

We think we have tried to put you in the same situation as the doctor. Each chapter was a different perspective on the same phenomenon—reading comprehension. The phenomenon did not change; our perspective did. We hope you found yourself saying, this is just like what they said in Chapter 3 (or 4 or 5). If you did, then we have partially succeeded in our attempt to convince you that reading comprehension, while a complex and highly integrated process, lends itself to analysis—analysis that can help us to understand the process itself as well as the process of teaching it.

We close by letting Huey (1908) restate our goal.

> And so to completely analyze what we do when we read would almost be the acme of a psychologist's achievements, for it would be to describe very many of the most intricate workings of the human mind, as well as to unravel the tangled story of the most remarkable specific performance that civilization has learned in all its history.

REFERENCES

Huey, E. B. *Psychology and Pedagology of Reading.* New York: Macmillan, 1908.

Johnson, D., and Pearson, P. D. *Teaching Reading Vocabulary.* New York: Holt, Rinehart and Winston, 1978.

GLOSSARY

Abstractness—A property of words that lack concrete referents in the world. "Joy" and "disappointment" are abstract terms. "Dog" and "knife" are concrete.

Accommodation—A process in which the knowledge base (schemata) is changed so that new information can fit into the existing schemata.

Advance Organizer—A more general summary statement of a concept that helps students to know what to expect from their reading.

Anaphora—Words or groups of words used as a regular substitute for a preceding word or groups of words. Anaphora include personal and demonstrative pronouns.

Artificial Intelligence—Computer simulation of human behavior, such as answering questions, paraphrasing statements, and so on.

Assimilation—A process in which new knowledge is added to (and fits into) an already existing knowledge base during comprehension and learning.

Attribute—An inherent characteristic or property of something. Barking is an attribute of dogs.

Backward Inferencing—The process of drawing conclusions about the probable (and often unstated) causes of events.

Case Grammar—A grammar emphasizing relationships among sentence parts (that is, noun phrases, verbs).

Class Relation—The group or set to which a concept belongs.

Cloze Procedure—A technique in which every nth word of a passage is deleted. The reader's task is to correctly supply the missing words. Readability, comprehension, and use of context may be measured through the use of this technique.

Conditional Relations—A statement which indicates the general conditions under which A will cause B to happen. The statement, "If John finishes his work, he will get an allowance," demonstrates a conditional relation.

Criterion-referenced—Performance is referenced or compared to some specified behavioral criterion of proficiency, for example, 80 percent correct.

Example—A particular item that is representative of a concept. Fido is an example of dog.

Forward Inferencing—Predicting the outcome of events.

Frequency—An account of how often a particular word occurs in the language.

Juncture—The articulation of word boundaries such as saying "I Scream" and "Ice Cream".

Network—An interconnected or interrelated system. This term is used to describe how information is stored in human memory.

Norm-referenced—Performance is referenced or compared to a norm which is based upon the scores of other persons who are similar in some relevant way.

Paradigmatic Association—An association between two words of the same form class, for example, dog and cat.

Phonology—The study of the sound patterns of language.

Pitch—The rise or fall of the voice to convey meaning, demonstrated by asking questions or making statements.

Proposition—A clause or unitary statement about the world. It is considered to be a basic unit of thought in comprehension.

Related Concept—One concept related to another through common attributes or common class relations.

Schema—A conceptual framework for understanding and organizing the world around us. Schemata are considered to be primary units of meaning.

Script—All the mundane, taken for granted, information about an event.

Semantics—The study of the meanings, especially of concepts and relations among concepts.

Semantic Map—A graphic representation used to illustrate concepts and relationships between concepts such as classes, properties and examples.

Stress—The accent or emphasis on a word in a sentence. It is generally produced by higher pitch and greater intensity of the voice.

Syntagmatic Association—An association between two words based upon their probable co-occurence in sentences, for example, dog and bark.

Syntax—The orderly arrangement of words in sentences.

BIBLIOGRAPHY

Anderson, R. The Notion of Schemata and the Educational Enterprise. In R. Anderson, J. Spiro, and W. E. Montague (eds.), *Schooling and the Acquisition of Knowledge.* Hillsdale, N.J.: Lawrence Erlbaum, Associates, 1977.

Aulls, M. *Technical Report: Minnesota Statewide Assessment in Reading.* Minnesota: State Department of Education, 1974.

Ausubel, D. P. The Use of Advance Organizers in the Learning and Retention of Meaningful Verbal Material. *Journal of Educational Psychology,* 1960, *51,* 267–272.

Ausubel, D. P. In Defense of Verbal Learning. *Educational Theory,* 1961, 2, 15–25.

Ausubel, D. P. Cognitive Structure and the Facilitation of Meaningful Verbal Learning. *Journal of Teacher Education,* 1963, *14,* 217–222.

Barrett, T. Taxonomy of Reading Comprehension. In Smith, R. and Barrett, T. C. *Teaching Reading in the Middle Grades.* Reading, Mass.: Addison-Wesley, 1976.

Bormuth, J. *On the Theory of Achievement Test Items.* Chicago: The University of Chicago Press, 1970.

Bormuth, J. R. Readability: A New Approach. *Reading Research Quarterly,* Spring, 1966, *1,* 79–131.

Bormuth, J., Carr, J., Manning, J., and Pearson, P. D. Children's Comprehension of between-and within-Sentence Syntactic Structures. *Journal of Educational Psychology,* 1970, *61,* 349–357.

Bransford, J., and Johnson, M. K. Considerations of Some Problems of Comprehension. In W. G. Chase (ed.), *Visual Information Processing,* New York: Academic Press, 1973.

Capponecchi, W. P. *A Comparative Study of an Advance Organizer in Mathematics to Determine its Effectiveness on Knowledge Acquisition and Retention.* Unpublished doctoral dissertation, University of Oklahoma, 1973.

Carver, R. Toward a Theory of Reading Comprehension and Rauding. *Reading Research Quarterly.* 1977–78, *12,* in press.

Chomsky, C. *The Acquisition of Syntax in Children from 5 to 10.* Cambridge: MIT Press, 1968.

Clark, E. V. On the Acquisition of the Meaning of 'before' and 'after'. *Journal of Verbal Learning and Verbal Behavior,* 1971, *10,* 266–275.

Coleman, E. B. The Comprehensibility of Several Grammatical Transformations. *Journal of Applied Psychology,* 1964, *48,* 186–190.

Collins, A., and Quillian, R. Retrieval Time from Semantic Memory. *Journal of Verbal Learning and Verbal Behavior,* 1969, *8,* 240–247.

Davis, F. B. Fundamental Factors of Comprehension in Reading. *Psychometrika,* 1944, *9,* 185–197.

Dooling, D. J. and Mullett, R. L. Locus of Thematic Effects in Retention of Prose. *Journal of Experimental Psychology,* 1973, *97,* 404–406.

Downie, N. M. *Fundamentals of Measurement: Techniques and Practices* (2nd ed.). New York: Oxford University Press, 1967.

Durost, W. N., Bixler, H. H., Wrightstone, J. W., Prescott, G. A., and Balow, I. *The Metropolitan Achievement Tests.* New York: The Psychological Corporation, 1970.

Durrell, D. *Durrell Analysis of Reading Difficulty.* New York: Harcourt, 1955.

Estes, T., and Vaugh, J. Reading Interests and Comprehension: Implications. *The Reading Teacher,* 1973, 27, 149–153.

Farr, R., and Smith, C. B. The Effects of Test Item Validity on Total Test Reliability and Validity. In G. Schick (ed.), Reading: Process and Pedagogy. *Nineteenth Yearbook of the National Reading Conference,* Milwaukee, 1970, 122–134.

Fay, L., Ross, R. R., and LaPray, M. *The Young America Basic Reading Program Skillbook,* 6, Chicago: Rand McNally, 1972.

Feller, W. A. *The Effects of Two Types of Advance Organizers and Two Types of Spaced Questions on the Ability of a Selected Group of Tenth Grade Biology Students to Recall, Comprehend and Apply Facts from Written Science Material.* Unpublished doctoral dissertation, Temple University, 1973.

Fillmore, C. J. The Case for Case. In E. Back and R. G. Harms (eds.), *Universals in Linguistic Theory.* New York: Holt, Rinehart and Winston, 1968.

Flesch, R. F. *The Art of Plain Talk.* New York: Harper & Row, 1946.

Frase, L. Boundary Conditions for Mathemagenic Behaviors. *Review of Educational Research,* 1967, 58, 337–48.

Frederiksen, C. H. Effects of Context-Induced Processing Operations on Semantic Information Acquired from Discourse. *Cognitive Psychology,* 1975, 7, 139–166.

Glaser, G. R. Instructional Technology and Measurement of Learning. *American Psychologist, 18,* 1963, 519–521.

Goodman, Y., and Burke, C. L. *Reading Miscue Inventory: Procedure for Diagnosis and Evaluation.* New York: Macmillan, 1972.

Gorrell, R., and Lair, C. *Modern English Handbook.* Englewood Cliffs, N.J.: Prentice-Hall, 1953.

Gove, P. B., Editor, *Webster's New Dictionary of Synonyms,* Springfield, Mass.: Merriam, 1973.

Greiling, M. G. *Recognition and Comprehension of Lexical Words Used Alone or in Context as a Function of Spelling Pattern Predictability, Word Frequency and Word Abstractions.* Unpublished Master of Arts paper. University of Minnesota, 1974.

Guszak, F. J. Teacher Questioning and Reading, *Reading Teacher,* 1967, *21,* 227–34.

Hellman, G. Time Lumbers On. *The New Yorker,* April 16, 1955, 34–36.

Hieronymus, et al. *Iowa Test of Basic Skills,* Boston: Houghton Mifflin, 1973.

Holt, J. *How Children Fail.* Pine Brook, N.J.: Dial Press, 1964.

Hopkins, D. L., Schuttle, R. C., and Garten, K. L. The Effects of Access to a Playroom on the Rate and Quality of Printing and Writing of First and Second Grade Students. *Journal of Applied Behavior Analysis,* 1971, 4, 77–87.

Huey, E. B. *Psychology and Pedagology of Reading,* New York: Macmillan, 1908.

Johnson, D. D., and Pearson, P. D. *Teaching Reading Vocabulary,* New York: Holt, Rinehart and Winston, 1978.

Karlsen, B., Madden, R., and Gardner, E. F. *Stanford Diagnostic Reading Test.* New York: Harcourt, 1976.

Kelley, et al. *Stanford Achievement Test.* New York: Harcourt, 1964.

Kintsch, W. *The Representation of Meaning in Memory.* Hillsdale, N.J.: Erlbaum, 1974.

Klein, S. P., and Kosecoff, J. *Issues and Procedures in Development of Criterion Referenced Test,* Eric Document, TM, Report 26, September, 1973, 18.

LaBerge, D., and Samuels, S. J. Toward a Theory of Automatic Information Processing in Reading. In H. Singer and R. Ruddell (eds.), *Theoretical Models and Processes of Reading.* Newark: International Reading Association, 1976.

Lehnert, W. *Question Answering in a Story Understanding System.* Research report #57, Yale University Department of Computer Sciences, 1975.

Lesgold, A. M. Variability in Children's Comprehension of Syntactic Structure. *Journal of Educational Psychology.* June, 1974, 66, 333–338.

Lindquist, E. F., and Hieronymus, A. N. *Iowa Test of Basic Skills.* Boston: Houghton Mifflin, 1964.

Lindsay, P., and Norman, D. *Human Information Processing.* New York: Academic Press, 1972.

Madden, R., Gardner, E., Rudman, H., Karlsen, B., and Merwin, J. *Stanford Achievement Test.* New York: Harcourt, 1972.

McCanne, R. *Use of a Checklist of Reading Skills with Migratory Children.* Office of Instructional Services, Colorado State Department of Education, June, 1963.

Menzel. P. Anaphora. In Bormuth, J. R. *On the Theory of Achievement Test Items.* Chicago: University of Chicago Press, 1970.

Meyer, B. J. *Organization in Prose and Memory: Research with Application to Reading Comprehension,* a paper read at NRC Convention, Kansas City, 1969.

Minsky, M. A Framework for Representing Knowledge. In P. Winston (ed.), *The Psychology of Computer Vision.* New York: McGraw-Hill, 1975.

Mitchell, R. W. *Kindergarten Children's Responses to Selected Visual Discrimination Exercises in Readiness Materials.* Unpublished master of arts paper, University of Minnesota, 1965.

Morrison, H. C. *The Practice of Teaching in the Secondary Schools.* Chicago: University of Chicago Press, 1932.

National Institute of Education. *Request for Proposal for a National Center for the Study of Reading.* Washington, D.C.: Department of Health, Education and Welfare, 1976.

Olds, H. F. *An Experimental Study of Syntactical Factors Influencing Children's Comprehension of Certain Complex Relationships.* (Report No. 4), Cambridge, Mass.: Harvard University, Center for Research and Development on Educational Differences, 1968.

Otto, W., and Askov, E. *The Wisconsin Design for Reading Skill Development: Word Attack.* Minneapolis: National Computer Systems, 1972.

Pearson, P. D. *Children's Comprehension of Sequential Relations among Events.* Unpublished paper. University of Minnesota, 1977.

Pearson, P. D. The Effects of Grammatical Complexity on Children's Comprehension, Recall and Conception of Certain Semantic Relations. *Reading Research Quarterly,* 1974–75, *10,* 155–192.

Pearson, P. D., Boesen, M., and Carr, J. *A Rationale for Scoring Constructed-Response Items.* A paper read at IRA Convention, Kansas City, 1969.

Pearson, P. D., and Nicholson, T. *Scripts, Texts, and Questions.* Paper presented at the National Reading Conference, Atlanta, December, 1976.

Pearson, P. D., and Studt, A. Effects of Word Frequency and Contextual Richness on Children's Word Identification Abilities. *Journal of Educational Psychology,* 1975, *67,* 89–95.

Richek, M. A. Reading Comprehension of Anaphoric Forms in Varying Linguistic Contexts. *Reading Research Quarterly,* 1976–77, *12,* 145–165.

Ringler, L. *Skills Monitoring Systems–Reading.* New York: Harcourt, 1974.

Rumelhart, D. E. Notes on a Schema for Stories. In D. Bobrow and A. Collins (eds.), Representation and Understanding: *Studies in Cognitive Science.* New York: Academic Press, 1975.

Russell, D. H. *Children Learn To Read,* Boston: Ginn, 1961.

Schank, R. C. Identification of Conceptualizations Underlying Natural Language. In R. C. Schank & K. M. Colby (eds.), *Computer Models of Thought and Language.* San Francisco: Freeman, 1973.

Schultz, R. W. *The Role of Cognitive Organizers in the Facilitation of Concept Learning in Elementary School of Science.* Unpublished doctoral dissertation, Purdue University, 1966.

Smith, F. *Understanding Reading: Psychological Analysis of Reading and Learning to Read.* New York: Holt, Rinehart and Winston, 1971.

Spearritt, D. Identification of Subskills of Reading Comprehension by Maximum Likelihood Factor Analysis. *Reading Research Quarterly,* 1972, *8,* 92–111.

Standal, T. C. *The Effects of Syntactic, Semantic and Contextual Variations on Children's Comprehension and Recall of Causal Relations.* Unpublished Ph.D. dissertation. University of Minnesota, 1976.

Stauffer, R. *Directing the Reading-Thinking Process.* New York: Harper & Row, 1975.

Stein, N., and Glenn, C. An Analysis of Story Comprehension in Elementary School Children. In R. Freedle (ed.), *Discourse Processing: Multidisciplinary Perspectives,* Hillsdale, N.J. Lawrence Erlbaum Associates, in press.

Taylor, W. L. *The Cloze Procedure: How It Predicts Comprehension and Intelligence of Military Personnel* (Technical Memorandum No. 13 to the United States Air Force). Urbana, Ill.: University of Illinois, Human Resources Research Institute, Division of Communications, 1953, 1–22.

Terwilliger, J. *Some Problems Associated with the Concept of Mastery.* Unpublished manuscript, University of Minnesota, 1972.

Thomas, E. L., and Robinson, H. A. *Improving Reading in every Class.* Boston: Allyn and Bacon, 1972.

Thompson, M. *Trait, State and Academic/test Anxiety: Their Relationship to*

Reading Performance. Unpublished Ph.D. dissertation, University of Minnesota, 1976.

Thorndike, E. L. Reading as Reasoning. A Study of Mistakes in Paragraph Reading. *The Journal of Educational Psychology.* 1917, *8,* 323–332.

Thorndyke, P. Cognitive Structures in Comprehension and Memory of Narrative Discourse. *Cognitive Psychology,* 1977, *9,* 77–110.

Thurstone, T. G. The Red Book, *Readiness for the SRA Reading Program,* Chicago: Science Research Associates, 1967.

Tuiman, J. J. Determining the Passage Dependency of Comprehension Questions in 5 Major Tests. *Reading Research Quarterly.* 1973–1974, *9,* 206–223.

Tulving, E., and Gold, C. Stimulus Information and Contextual Information as Determinants of Tachistoscopic Recognition of Words. *Journal of Experimental Psychology,* 1963, *66,* 319–327.

Washburne, C. *Adjusting the School to the Child.* New York: World Book, 1932.

Weaver, W., Bickley, A. C., and Ford, F. A Cross-validation Study of the Relationship of Reading Test Items to their Relevant Paragraphs. *Perceptual and Motor Skills,* August, 1969, *29,* 11–14.

Whitford, H. C. *A Dictionary of American Homophones and Homographs.* New York: Teachers College Press, 1966.

Woolf, H. B., Editor. *Random House Dictionary of the English Language.* Springfield, Mass.: Merriam, 1973.

Index